THE
AFFIRMATIVE ACTION
DEBATE

THE
AFFIRMATIVE ACTION
DEBATE

EDITED BY

STEVEN M. CAHN

ROUTLEDGE
New York • London

Published in 1995 by

Routledge
29 West 35th Street
New York, NY 10001

Published in Great Britain by

Routledge
11 New Fetter Lane
London EC4P 4EE

Copyright © 1995 by Routledge, Inc.

Printed in the United States of America on acid-free paper

Library of Congress Cataloging-in-Publication Data

The affirmative action debate/edited by Steven M. Cahn.
    p.   cm.
  Includes bibliographical references.
  ISBN 0-415-91492-2 (cl). — ISBN 0-415-91493-0 (pb)
  1. Affirmative action programs—United States. I. Cahn, Steven M.
HF5549.5.A34A4632   1995
331.13'3'0973—dc20   95-38816

To Geoffrey Marshall

Contents

Acknowledgments

The impetus for this book came from a conversation with Adrian Driscoll of Routledge, and I am grateful for his encouragement. My editor, Maureen MacGrogan, has been most supportive. I also appreciate the help I received from Daniel Kaufman, my research assistant at the Graduate School of the City University of New York. Christine Cipriani was the able production editor, and Ian Gardiner provided skilled proofreading.

Introduction

Steven M. Cahn

In March 1961, less than two months after assuming office, President John F. Kennedy issued Executive Order 10925, which established the President's Committee on Equal Employment Opportunity. Its mission was to end discrimination in employment by the government and its contractors. The order required every federal contract to include the pledge that "The Contractor will not discriminate against any employee or applicant for employment because of race, creed, color, or national origin. The Contractor will take affirmative action, to ensure that applicants are employed, and that employees are treated during employment, without regard to their race, creed, color, or national origin."

Here for the first time in the context of civil rights the government called for "affirmative action." The term meant taking appropriate steps to eradicate the then widespread practices of racial, religious, and ethnic discrimination. The goal, as the President stated, was "equal opportunity in employment."

In other words, affirmative action was instituted to insure that applicants for positions would be judged without any consideration of their race, religion, or national origin. These criteria were declared irrelevant. Taking them into account was forbidden.

The Civil Rights Act of 1964 restated and broadened the application of this principle. Title VI declared that "No person in the United States shall, on the ground of race, color or national origin, be excluded from participation in, be denied the benefits of, or be subjected to discrimination under any program or activity receiving Federal financial assistance."

But within one year President Lyndon B. Johnson argued that fairness required more than a commitment to impartial treatment. In his 1965 commencement address at Howard University, he said:

> You do not take a person who for years has been hobbled by chains and liberate him, bring him up to the starting line of a race and then say, "you're free to compete with all the others," and still justly believe that you have been completely fair.
>
> Thus it is not enough just to open the gates of opportunity.
>
> All our citizens must have the ability to walk through those gates....
>
> We seek not...just equality as a right and a theory but equality as a fact and equality as a result.

And so several months later President Johnson issued Executive Order 11246, which stated that "It is the policy of the Government of the United States to provide equal opportunity in Federal employment for all qualified persons, to prohibit discrimination in employment because of race, creed, color or national origin, and to promote the full realization of equal employment opportunity through a positive, continuing program in each department and agency." Two years later the order was amended to prohibit discrimination on the basis of sex.

While the aim of President Johnson's order was stated in language similar to that of President Kennedy's, President Johnson's abolished the Committee on Equal Employment Opportunity, transferred its responsibilities to the Secretary of Labor, and authorized the Secretary to "adopt such rules and regulations and issue such orders as he deems necessary and appropriate to achieve the purposes thereof."

Acting on the basis of this mandate, the Department of Labor in December 1971, during the administration of President Richard M. Nixon, issued Revised Order No. 4, requiring all contractors to develop "an acceptable affirmative action program," including "an analysis of areas within which the contractor is deficient in the utilization of minority groups and women, and further, goals and timetables to which the contractor's good faith efforts must be directed to correct the deficiencies." Contractors were instructed to take the term "minority groups" to refer to "Negroes, American Indians, Orientals, and Spanish Surnamed Americans." The concept of "underutilization" meant "having fewer minorities or women in a particular job classification than would reasonably be expected by their availability." "Goals" were not to be "rigid and inflexible quotas" but "targets reasonably attainable by means of applying every good faith effort to make all aspects of the entire affirmative action program work."

Such preferential treatment required that attention be paid to the same criteria of race, sex, and ethnicity that had previously been deemed irrelevant. Could such use of these criteria be morally justified?

That is the key question in a debate that has continued for more than two decades. This collection of scholarly articles presents the major lines of argument within the controversy.

The authors agree that injustices have occurred, that their victims deserve compensation, and that strenuous efforts should be made to try to prevent any further wrongdoing while striving to achieve a more enlightened society. The disagreements arise in specifying who has suffered injustice, what is appropriate compensation to them, and which steps should be taken to promote justice and amity.

Affirmative action has been a divisive issue in the United States. And with recent attempts by referendum, legislation, and judicial action to change current policies, emotions have intensified.

What is most needed now is not increased passion but greater attention to recognizing and analyzing the subject's complexities. That is the aim of the essays that follow.

In his classic work *On Liberty*, John Stuart Mill wrote that "He who knows only his own side of the case, knows little of that." Readers may not change their minds about affirmative action after studying the materials collected here. They will, however, become more aware of challenging considerations that have been offered by opposing advocates. And that is a crucial step towards the deepened understanding sought through philosophical inquiry.

I. Individuals, Groups, and Discrimination

1

Discrimination and Morally Relevant Characteristics

James W. Nickel

Suppose that a characteristic which should be morally irrelevant (e.g., race, creed, or sex) has been treated as if it were morally relevant over a period of years, and that injustices have resulted from this. When such a mistake has been recognized and condemned, when the morally irrelevant characteristic has been seen to be irrelevant, can this characteristic *then* properly be used as a relevant consideration in the distribution of reparations to those who have suffered injustices? If we answer this question in the affirmative, we will have the strange consequence that a morally irrelevant characteristic can become morally relevant if its use results in injustices.

The context in which this difficulty is likely to arise is one in which a group has been discriminated against on the basis of morally irrelevant properties, but in which this discrimination has been recognized and at least partly come to an end; and the question at hand concerns how the members of this group should now be treated. Should they now be treated like everyone else, ignoring their history, or should they be given special advantages because of past discrimination and injustices? There are a variety of considerations which are pertinent in answering this question, and I will deal with only one of these, the "reverse discrimination argument." This argument claims that to extend special considerations to a formerly oppressed group will be to persist in the mistake of treating a morally irrelevant characteristic as if it were relevant. For if we take a morally irrel-

Reprinted from *Analysis* 32 (1972), by permission of the author.

evant characteristic (namely the characteristic which was the basis for the original discrimination) and use it as the basis for granting special considerations or reparations, we will be treating the morally irrelevant as if it were relevant and still engaging in discrimination, albeit reverse discrimination. And hence, it is argued, the only proper stance toward groups who have suffered discrimination is one of strict impartiality.

To state the argument in a slightly different way, one might say that if a group was discriminated against on the basis of a morally irrelevant characteristic of theirs, then to award extra benefits now to the members of this group because they have this characteristic is simply to continue to treat a morally irrelevant characteristic as if it were relevant. Instead of the original discrimination *against* these people, we now have discrimination *for* them, but in either case we have discrimination since it treats the irrelevant as relevant. Hence, to avoid discrimination we must now completely ignore this characteristic and extend no special considerations whatsoever.

The objection which I want to make to this argument pertains to its assumption that the characteristic which was the basis for the original discrimination is the same as the one which is used as the basis for extending extra considerations now. I want to suggest that this is only apparently so. For if compensation in the form of extra opportunities is extended to a black man on the basis of past discrimination[1] against blacks, the basis for this compensation is not that he is a black man, but that he was previously subject to unfair treatment because he was black. The former characteristic was and is morally irrelevant, but the latter characteristic is very relevant if it is assumed that it is desirable or obligatory to make compensation for past injustices. Hence, to extend special considerations to those who have suffered from discrimination need not involve continuing to treat a morally irrelevant characteristic as if it were relevant. In such a case the characteristic which was the basis for the original discrimination (e.g., being a black person) will be different from the characteristic which is the basis for the distribution of special considerations (e.g., being a person who was discriminated against because he was black).

My conclusion is that this version of the "reverse discrimination argument" has a false premise, since it assumes that the characteristic which was the basis for the original discrimination is the same as that which is the basis for the granting of special considerations. And since the argument has a false premise, it does not succeed in showing that to avoid reverse discrimination we must extend no special considerations whatsoever.

2

Inverse Discrimination

J. L. Cowan

The justice or injustice of "inverse discrimination" is a question of pressing social importance. On the one hand it is argued that when a morally irrelevant characteristic such as race, creed, or sex has been treated as morally relevant and injustices have resulted, it is then proper to treat that characteristic as morally relevant in order to make reparations. On the other hand it is argued that if the characteristic in question is morally irrelevant, its use even in this manner would still constitute discrimination, discrimination now in favor of those possessing the characteristic and against those not, but unjust discrimination still.

Public discussion of this issue all too rarely goes far beyond the level of the arguments as given. Yet the logic of these arguments is murky, to say the least. It is therefore to be hoped that the analytical skills supposedly characteristic of philosophers might here play a valuable social role, and we are indebted to J. W. Nickel for beginning such a clarification. I should like here to try to continue it.

Nickel maintains that the argument against inverse discrimination given above goes wide of the mark since the characteristic which is now operative is not actually the original morally irrelevant one. "For if compensation in the form of extra opportunities is extended to a black man on the basis of past discrimination against blacks, the basis for this compensation is not that he is a black man, but that he was previously subject to unfair

Reprinted from *Analysis* 32 (1972), by permission of the author.

treatment because he was black... in such a case the characteristic which was the basis for the original discrimination (e.g., being a black person) will be different from the characteristic which is the basis for the distribution of special considerations (e.g., being a person who was discriminated against because he was black)" (p. 114 [p. 4, this volume]).

The problem is that Nickel does not make it entirely clear just what he is about here. He may simply be pointing out that if a person has suffered injustice through morally unjustified discrimination, then reparation to that person will be appropriate. But surely it was not against this relatively uncontroversial point that the original argument was directed. And Nickel's formulation leaves open the possibility that he is actually trying to support the far more questionable claim which was the original target of that argument.

"Being discriminated against because he was black" is clearly a complex predicate. What I would like to suggest is that the portion of it which was morally irrelevant in independence remains so within the complex and is thus mere excess baggage. The reason why he was discriminated against is not what should now ground reparation, but rather simply the fact that, and extent to which, he was unjustly discriminated against for whatever reason. Thus, assuming that the discrimination is otherwise the same, we would presumably not wish to say that Jones, who has been discriminated against as a black, should now be favored over Smith, who has been equally discriminated against as a woman or a Jew or whatever. We are therefore left without a moral relevance for blackness, and thus without a moral basis for inverse discrimination based on blackness as opposed to discriminatory injustice per se.

Nickel's reasoning thus does not really, as it might be taken to do, provide any support at all for the kind of self-contradictory thinking the original argument was surely intended to rebut. This is the reasoning that since blacks, to retain this example, have suffered unjust discrimination we should now give them special treatment to make it up to them. Once again there is no problem insofar as this simply means that where individual blacks have suffered injustice it should, as with anyone else, insofar as possible be made up to those individuals who have so suffered. The fallacy arises when rather than individuals it is the group which is intended, and individuals are regarded merely as members of that group rather than in their individuality. This creates a contradiction, since the original premise of the moral irrelevance of blackness on the basis of which the original attribution of unjust discrimination rests implies that there is and can be no morally relevant group which could have suffered or to which retribution could now be made. Thus those who would argue that since "we" brutally kidnapped "the" blacks out of Africa and subjected "them" to the abominations of slavery, or that since "we" have exploited and degraded "women" since Eve, "we" therefore now owe retribution to our neighbor who happens to be black or a woman, are involved in inextricable self-contradiction. Except to the extent that he or she as an individual has unjustly suffered or will unjustly suffer from this history while we as individuals have unjustly profited or will unjustly profit, there can be no such obligation.

Nickel's original formulation is thus ambiguous. "The context in which this difficulty is likely to arise is one in which a group has been discriminated against on the basis of morally irrelevant properties, but in which this discrimination has been recognized and at least partly come to an end; and the question at hand concerns how the members of this group should now be treated. Should they now be treated like everyone else, ignoring their history, or should they be given special advantages because of past discrimination and injustices?" (p. 113 [3]) Once the question is disambiguated the answer is clear. They should most certainly be treated like everyone else. But this does not mean "their" individual histories should be ignored. As with anyone else, injustices done "them" as individuals should be prevented or rectified insofar as possible. But past or future discrimination and injustice done "them" as a group and special advantages to them as a group are both out of the question, since in the moral context there is no such group.

3

Reverse Discrimination and Compensatory Justice

Paul W. Taylor

Two articles have recently appeared in *Analysis* concerning the apparent contradiction between

>   (1) At time t_1 members of group G have been discriminated against on the basis of a *morally irrelevant* characteristic C

and

>   (2) At time t_2 characteristic C is a *morally relevant* ground for making reparation to members of group G.

In the first article ("Discrimination and Morally Relevant Characteristics"), J. W. Nickel presents what he calls the "reverse discrimination argument" and offers a counter-argument to it. The "reverse discrimination argument" is that, if we grant as a matter of compensatory justice special advantages or benefits to persons who have been unjustly treated on the basis of a morally irrelevant characteristic (such as being a woman, being black, being a Jew, etc.), we are in effect using a morally irrelevant characteristic as if it were morally relevant and thus still engaging in an unjust treatment of persons. Hence if we are to be just we must avoid reverse discrimination. Nickel's counter-argument is that the special treatment given

Reprinted from *Analysis* 33 (1973), by permission of the author.

to persons having characteristic C at time t_2 is not grounded on the (morally irrelevant) characteristic C, but on the (morally relevant) characteristic C', namely, being a person who has been discriminated against because he was C.

In an article by J. L. Cowan ("Inverse Discrimination"), Nickel is criticized for failing to realize that characteristic C' is actually a complex predicate made up of a conjunction of two characteristics—C", namely: having been discriminated against (for whatever reason), and the characteristic C itself. Cowan's point is that C" is a morally relevant characteristic in matters of compensatory justice but that C remains morally irrelevant. He holds that reverse discrimination is wrong, since it involves giving people favorable treatment *because they are C* and hence using a morally irrelevant characteristic as a justifying ground for special treatment. Nevertheless, he concludes, special treatment should be extended to any *individual* who has been discriminated against (for whatever reason) in the past, that is, anyone who has characteristic C". For it is a requirement of compensatory justice that reparation be made to those who have been dealt with unjustly (for whatever reason).

In this paper I want to defend three views, all of which are inconsistent with the claims made by Nickel and Cowan. (I) With respect to the principle of compensatory justice, characteristic C has been *made* a morally relevant characteristic by those who engaged in a social practice which discriminated against persons because they were C. (II) Since C is a morally relevant characteristic at time t_2 with respect to the principle of compensatory justice, that principle requires reverse discrimination. (III) The reverse discrimination in question is aimed at correcting an injustice perpetrated at time t_1 by a social practice of discriminating against C-persons because they were C. Given this aim, the reverse discrimination must be directed toward the class of C-persons as such. Furthermore, the obligation to compensate for the past injustice does not fall upon any particular individual but upon the society as a whole. The society is obligated to establish a social practice of reverse discrimination in favor of C-persons. (It is assumed, of course, that this practice will be consistent with all other principles of justice that may apply to the action-types which are involved in carrying it out.) I offer the following considerations in support of these views.

I

Suppose there is a socially established practice at time t_1 of unjustly treating any person who has characteristic C, such treatment being either permitted or required on the ground that the person is C. For the purposes of this account I hold that the treatment in question is unjust because characteristic C would not be mutually acknowledged as a proper ground for such treatment by all who understood the practice and took an impartial view of it (in accordance with John Rawls' *A Theory of Justice*, Harvard University Press, 1971).

When a social practice of this kind is engaged in, the members of the class of C-persons are being discriminated against because they are C. By reference to the rules of this practice, having C is a relevant reason or ground for performing a certain kind of action which is in fact unjust (though not recognized to be so by the practice itself). In this context the characteristic C is not accidentally or contingently associated with the unjust treatment, but is essentially tied to it. For the injustices done to a person are based on the fact that he has characteristic C. His being C is, other things being equal, a sufficient condition for the permissibility of treating him in the given manner. Within the framework of the social practice at t_1, that someone is C is a ground for acting in a certain way toward him. Therefore C is a relevant characteristic of a person.

But is it *morally* relevant? The answer to this question, it seems to me, is that at time t_1 characteristic C is not morally relevant, but, if we accept the principle of compensatory justice, at time t_2 it is. The principle of compensatory justice is that, in order to restore the balance of justice when an injustice has been committed to a group of persons, some form of compensation or reparation must be made to that group. Thus if there has been an established social practice (as distinct from an individual's action) of treating any member of a certain class of persons in a certain way on the ground that they have characteristic C and if this practice has involved the doing of an injustice to C-persons, then the principle of compensatory justice requires that C-persons as such be compensated in some way. Characteristic C, in other words, has become at time t_2 a characteristic whose *moral* relevance is entailed by the principle of compensatory justice. In this kind of situation, to ignore the fact that a person is C would be to ignore the fact that there had been a social practice in which unjust actions were directed toward C-persons as such.

II

Given that characteristic C is morally relevant to how C-persons are to be treated if compensatory justice is to be done to them, it follows that reverse discrimination is justified. For this is simply the policy of extending special benefits, opportunities, or advantages to the class of C-persons as such. Contrary to what Nickel affirms, this is not selecting C-persons for

11

special treatment on the basis of the complex characteristic C', namely: being a person who was discriminated against because he was C. For even if the individual C-person who now enjoys the favorable compensatory treatment was not himself one of those who suffered injustice as a result of the past social practice, he nevertheless has a right (based on his being a member of the class of C-persons) to receive the benefits extended to all C-persons as such. This follows from our premise that the policy of reverse discrimination, directed toward anyone who is C because he is C, is justified by the principle of compensatory justice.

Cowan claims that compensatory justice does not require a policy of treating all C-persons favorably (other things being equal) because they are C. His argument is that, if the original unjust treatment of C-persons was unjust precisely because their being C was morally irrelevant, then "there is and can be no morally relevant group which could have suffered or to which retribution could now be made" (p. 11 [6]). My reply to this argument is that the moral relevance or irrelevance of a characteristic is not something that can be determined outside the framework of a set of moral principles. It is true that the principles of *distributive* justice were transgressed by the past treatment of C-persons precisely because, according to those principles, characteristic C is morally irrelevant as a ground for treating persons in a certain way. Nevertheless, according to the principle of *compensatory* justice (which applies only where a violation of other forms of justice has taken place), the fact that systematic injustice was directed toward a class of persons as being C-persons establishes characteristic C as morally relevant, as far as making restitution is concerned. For the same reason, it may be noted, characteristic C will become again morally irrelevant the moment all the requirements of compensatory justice with respect to the treatment of C-persons have been fulfilled. Thus justified reverse discrimination is limited in its scope, being restricted to the righting of specific wrongs within a given range of application. Once the balance of justice with regard to C-persons has been restored, they are to be treated like anyone else. The appropriate test for the restoration of the balance of justice (that is, fulfillment of the requirements of compensatory justice) is determined by the set of criteria for just compensation that would be mutually acceptable to all who understand the unjust practice and who view the matter disinterestedly (following Rawls, as before).

III

Does the foregoing view entail that, in the given society, *each individual* who is not a C-person has a duty to make reparation to *every* C-person he happens to be able to benefit in some way? This would seem to be unfair, since the individual who is claimed to have such a duty might not himself have intentionally or knowingly participated in the discriminatory social practice, and might even have done what he could to oppose it. It also seems unfair to C-persons, who would then be compensated only under the contingency that particular non-C individuals happen to be in a position of being able to benefit them. We must here face the questions: To whom is owed the compensatory treatment, that is, who has the right to reparation? And upon whom does the obligation corresponding to that right fall?

If we consider such compensatory policies as Affirmative Action and the Equal Opportunity Program to be appropriate ways of restoring the balance of justice, a possible answer to our questions becomes apparent. For such programs are, within the framework of democratic institutions, social policies carried out by organized agencies of a central government representing the whole people. They are not directed toward any "assignable" individual (to use Bentham's apt phrase), but rather are directed toward any member of an "assignable" group (the class of C-persons) who wishes to take advantage of, or to qualify for, the compensatory benefits offered to the group as a whole. The obligation to offer such benefits to the group as a whole is an obligation that falls on society in general, not on any particular person. For it is the society in general that, through its established social practice, brought upon itself the obligation.

To bring out the moral significance of this, consider the case in which an individual has himself treated a particular C-person unjustly. By so acting, the individual in question has brought upon himself a special obligation which he owes to that particular C-person. This obligation is above and beyond the duty he has—along with everyone else—to support and comply with the social policy of reverse discrimination being carried out by his government. For everyone in the society (if it is just) contributes his fair share to the total cost of that policy, whether or not he has, personally, done an injustice to a C-person. So the individual who commits such an injustice himself has a special duty, and his victim has a special right, in contrast to the general duty of everyone to do his share (by obeying laws, paying taxes, etc.) in supporting the policy of reverse discrimination directed toward the class of C-persons as a whole, and in contrast to the general right on the part of any C-person to benefit from such a policy if he wishes to take advantage of its provisions.

The issue of the justifiability of reverse discrimination does not have to do with an individual's making up for his own acts of injustice done to this or that person. It has to do with righting the wrongs committed as an integral part of an organized social practice whose very essence was discrimination against C-persons as such. In this sense the perpetrator of the original injustice was the whole society (other than the class of C-persons). The victim was the class of C-persons as a group, since they were the *collective target* of an institutionalized practice of unjust treatment. It is for this reason that Cowan's concluding remarks do not stand up. At the end of his article he makes the following statements regarding the present members of a group which has been discriminated against in the past:

> They should most certainly be treated like everyone else. But this does not mean "their" individual histories should be ignored. As with anyone else, injustices done "them" as individuals should be prevented or rectified insofar as possible. But past or future discrimination and injustice done "them" as a group and special advantages to them as a group are both out of the question, since in the moral context there is no such group. (pp. 11–12 [7])

But there is such a group. It is the group that was, as it were, *created* by the original unjust practice. To deny the existence of the group is to deny a social reality—a reality which cannot morally be ignored as long as the wrongs that created it are not corrected.

Cowan's position assumes that compensatory justice applies to the relations of one individual to another, but not to organized social practices and whole classes of persons with respect to whom the goals and methods of the practices are identified and pursued. This assumption, however, completely disregards what, morally speaking, is the most hideous aspect of the injustices of human history: those carried out systematically and directed toward whole groups of men and women *as groups*.

My conclusion is that society is morally at fault if it ignores the group which it has discriminated against. Even if it provides for compensation to each member of the group, not *qua* member of the group but *qua* person who has been unjustly treated (for whatever reason), it is leaving justice undone. For it is denying the specific obligation it owes to, and the specific right it has created in, the group as such. This obligation and this right follow from the society's past use of a certain characteristic or set of characteristics as the criterion for identification of the group, membership in which was taken as a ground for unjust treatment. Whatever duties of justice are owed by individuals to other individuals, institutionalized injustice demands institutionalized compensation.

4

Reparations to Wronged Groups

Michael D. Bayles

If a group of people (blacks, women) has been wronged by its members' being discriminated against on the basis of a morally irrelevant characteristic, is it morally permissible to use that characteristic as a basis for providing special considerations or benefits as reparations? It is frequently argued that since the characteristic is morally irrelevant, its use as a basis for providing reparations must also constitute wrongful discrimination.

James W. Nickel contends that such reparations are not wrong because they are not based on the morally irrelevant characteristic. Being black, for example, is a morally irrelevant characteristic for discriminating against or for a person. However, Nickel claims that if a black man receives special consideration as reparation for past discrimination the basis is not the morally irrelevant characteristic of his being black. Instead, it is the morally relevant one of his having been "subject to unfair treatment because he was black" (p. 114 [4]).

J. L. Cowan criticizes Nickel for even including the morally irrelevant characteristic as part of the complex predicate on the basis of which reparations are given. It is not a man's having been subject to unfair treatment because he was black which is the basis of reparation, Cowan contends, "but rather simply the fact that, and the extent to which, he was unjustly discriminated against for whatever reason" (p. 11 [6]). We would not, Cowan points out, wish to favor a person who has been discriminated

Reprinted from *Analysis* 33 (1973) by permission of Mrs. Marjorie Bayles.

against for being black over another who has been discriminated against for being Jewish. He further claims that the problem of using a morally irrelevant characteristic as the basis for reparation

> arises when rather than individuals it is the group which is intended, and individuals are regarded merely as members of that group rather than in their individuality. This creates a contradiction, since the original premise of the moral irrelevance of blackness on the basis of which the original attribution of unjust discrimination rests implies that there is and can be no morally relevant group which could have suffered or to which retribution could now be made. (p. 11 [6])

The solution of the problem proposed by Nickel and Cowan, that the reparation is based on a characteristic other than the morally irrelevant one, is spurious. By parallel reasoning it can be argued that the original discrimination was not on the basis of a morally irrelevant characteristic. Racists do not discriminate against blacks simply because they are black. Rather, they claim that blacks as a class are inferior in certain relevant respects, e.g., they lack certain abilities and virtues such as industriousness, reliability, and cleanliness. Thus, reasoning similarly to Nickel and Cowan, racists could contend that they do not discriminate on the basis of a morally irrelevant characteristic, but the morally relevant ones which are thought to be associated with being black. Further, a reformed racist could contend that he was mistaken to believe blacks lacked such abilities and virtues. But, since it was a mistaken belief which was the basis of his discrimination, he was not responsible and owes no reparations. In short, if being black is not the basis for reparations, it was not the basis for the original discrimination.

However, there need be no contradiction involved in claiming that being black is both morally irrelevant for discriminating against people and morally relevant in discriminating in favor of people to provide reparations. One may simply hold that there is no justifiable moral rule which, when correctly applied, supports discriminating against blacks, but there is one which supports discriminating in favor of them. One may hold that people have an obligation to give reparations to groups they have wronged. By using the characteristic of being black as an identifying characteristic to discriminate against people, a person has wronged the group, blacks. He thus has an obligation to make reparations to the group. Since the obligation is to the group, no specific individual has a right to reparation. However, since the group is not an organized one like a state, church, or corporation, the only way to provide reparations to the group is to provide them to members of the group.

Being black can, thus, become morally relevant in distinguishing between those individuals who are members of the group to whom reparations are owed and those who are not. But being black is only derivatively morally relevant. It is not mentioned as a morally relevant characteristic in the rule requiring one to provide reparations to groups one has wronged. Instead, it becomes relevant by being the identifying characteristic of the group wronged. The way in which it is an identifying characteristic here differs from the way in which it is an identifying characteristic for the racist. Being black is an identifying characteristic for the racist only because he thinks it is contingently connected with other characteristics. But being black is not contingently connected with the group one has wronged. Rather, it is logically connected as the defining characteristic of members of the group.

Cowan has failed to distinguish the relevance of being black as applied to groups and individuals. One may hold that one owes reparations to the group, blacks, not because the group is the group of blacks, but because the group has been wronged. But with respect to individuals, one may, as reparation, discriminate in their favor on the basis of their being black. One discriminates in favor of individuals because they are black, but one owes reparations to the group, blacks, because it has been wronged. Nor does such a position commit one to favoring individual blacks over individuals who belong to another wronged group, e.g., women. One has a morally relevant reason to favor each on the basis of their being black and female respectively. It does not follow that either should be preferred over the other.

Nothing has been said to support accepting any moral rules or principles applying to groups. (As a matter of fact, most people appear to accept one such rule, namely, that genocide is wrong.) Nor has anything been said to support accepting the rule that one has an obligation to provide reparations to groups one has wronged. These remarks have only indicated how being black can derivatively be a morally relevant characteristic for discriminating in favor of individuals if such a rule is accepted.

17

5

Individuals, Groups, and Inverse Discrimination

Roger A. Shiner

Many morally sensitive people find themselves faced with the following dilemma. On the one hand, they are persuaded by the argument that if being black, e.g., is morally irrelevant, then it is morally irrelevant and no more justifies favorable inverse discrimination than it justifies unfavorable discrimination. On the other hand, this move seems to open the way to neglect, whether benign or malign, of genuine social injustices. James W. Nickel and J. L. Cowan have done much to bring the logic of this situation to the surface. I shall not resist their general strategy of showing that the above is a false dilemma. My concern is with Cowan's diagnosis of the trouble as consisting in the illegitimacy of the thought that blacks as a group deserve inverse discrimination. His view is that one cannot argue that blacks *as a group* deserve retribution without also implying blackness as such is a morally relevant characteristic. This is false.

In the first place, it simply is not true that sense can never be made of the thought that a group as such deserves inverse discrimination. Consider these cases. (1) The Illyrians, through the incompetence of their negotiators, entered the European Economic Community under extremely unfair conditions. Later on, an E.E.C. Council member argues, "We ought now to give the Illyrians especially favorable consideration," and recommends inverse discrimination. (2) Form 3B are not allowed to go on the school outing because there are 35 in the class—or so they are told, and this is not a

Reprinted from *Analysis* 34 (1974), by permission of the author.

matter of the school bus size or the tickets available. The form master argues later, "3B should be given special consideration," and recommends inverse discrimination.

The objection might be raised that Form 3B is not really a group in a sense relevant to the problem at issue. It is an individual member of the group "classes in elementary schools," and an individual school-class may deserve inverse discrimination because of unfair treatment in the same way as an individual black or woman. However, there are many educators who argue that a disproportionate amount of money has been spent in recent years on secondary and post-secondary education, and that we now need to spend an equally disproportionate amount of money on elementary schools and schoolchildren as a group. But my argument need not turn on the accuracy of this remark, for the Illyrians are not a closed formally defined group as is Form 3B, nor are they members of some wider group.

Now it might be said that statements about Illyria or the Illyrian nation are reducible without remainder to statements about individual Illyrians. So I still have not presented a counter-example to the thesis that a group as such cannot deserve inverse discrimination. But this is a highly contentious philosophical thesis, and the debate about whether it is true remains unresolved. It cannot be that the present question about inverse discrimination is simply this old chestnut in a new guise, and indeed Cowan does not talk as though this is what he has in mind. Those who wish to support inverse discrimination draw on the stock of available collective nouns, and frequently speak of the Black/Indian/Jewish nation/race/people and of the female sex.

These points show, then, I submit, that talk about groups deserving inverse discrimination, as opposed to similar talk about individuals, cannot be simply ruled out as nonsensical, nor will it do to rule it in purely on the basis of some reductionist theory about nations. If we are to get at what is peculiar about the thought that blacks as a group deserve inverse discrimination, we must try a different tack.

Consider these remarks—(3) "My car ought to go in for repair, because it is a 1970 Ford"; (4) "George deserves inverse discrimination, because he is black." Cowan and Nickel are upset about (4), because it is logically of a piece with (5) "George deserves to be discriminated against, because he is black," and we want to reject that inference, on the grounds that the feature mentioned is irrelevant. But why should my car's being a 1970 Ford and just exactly that mean that it ought to go in for repair? We explain a case like (3) by treating it as an elliptical argument, with a missing premiss (3*) to the effect that all 1970 Fords have been recalled by the maker and ought to go in for repair. We can then underpin (4) in the same way, by supplying a premise (4*) to the effect that all blacks have been discriminated against unjustly in the past and deserve discrimination now.

This is pretty clearly the kind of point Cowan wants to make, but to show that (4) won't do unless underpinned with (4*) is not to show what if anything is wrong with (4') "Blacks as a group deserve inverse discrimination," still less that it is the introduction of the notion of a group deserving inverse discrimination that is problematic. As I have implied, to get from the need for (4*) to the illegitimacy of (4'), we will at least need to grapple with the reductionist position outlined above.

Nonetheless, the need for (4*) will enable us to get a correct picture of the peculiarity of the bald inference (4). Compare (3)/(3*) and (4)/(4*) with (6) "The figure is a rectangle, because it has equal diagonals." (6) to the same degree seems to need (6*) "All figures with equal diagonals are rectangle." However, although the (3) and (4) sets and the (6) set are in this respect structurally similar, there is an important difference in their content. (3*) and (4*) are, if true, then *a posteriori* true. (6*), on the other hand is true and moreover *a priori* true. Thus, the arguments constituted by the (3) set and the (4) set will only be sound as well as valid if (3*) and (4*) are as a matter of empirical fact true. The difference between the (6) set and the (3) and (4) sets is that there is an *a priori* and conceptual connection between being a rectangle and having equal diagonals, whereas there is *no a priori* and conceptual connection between being a 1970 Ford and needing to go in for repair, nor between being a black and deserving inverse discrimination.

This, then, I take to be the fundamental point about the moral irrelevancy of the characteristic of being a black. It is not a matter of whether it is a group or an individual that is held to have the characteristic. It is instead a matter of the kind of link that exists between the possession of that characteristic and the possession of some other moral characteristic. The moral irrelevancy of being a black is a matter of the absence of the appropriate *a priori* link.[1] Contrast (7) "Fred deserves inverse discrimination, because he is socio-economically disadvantaged," and the corresponding (7*) "The socio-economically disadvantaged deserve inverse discrimination." In this case, many philosophers would be prepared to concede that, if (7*) were part of a plausible moral theory, e.g., *à la* Rawls, (7*) would state a conceptual connection.

In short, my thesis in this paper is that, if we want to get clear why being a black is morally irrelevant though blacks deserve inverse discrimination, then the individual/group distinction is a red herring. We need instead the *a posteriori* connection/*a priori* connection distinction. The absence of the latter connection means that any claim to the effect that blacks, whether as a group or as individuals, deserve inverse discrimination must stand, not simply on their being blacks, but on the facts of history. If, that is to say, blacks as a group deserve inverse discrimination, it will be because some claim like (4*) is true. But if (4*) is true, then one can reasonably argue that blacks as a group deserve retribution *without* also implying blackness as such is a morally relevant characteristic. I suspect the facts of history can stand the weight thus put on them.

6

Reverse Discrimination

William A. Nunn III

In his recent article supporting the policy of reverse discrimination, Paul W. Taylor ("Reverse Discrimination and Compensatory Justice") argued, roughly, that when a certain group of persons within a given society is discriminated against because of some non-moral characteristic (e.g., skin color), and such discrimination is essentially tied to a pervasive social practice, the characteristic upon which the discrimination is based takes on a moral quality; consequently it becomes the moral duty of the society to make reparation to that group. Although I find it difficult to disagree with the allegation that in some sense institutionalized injustice demands institutionalized compensation, I think that Taylor's argument contains two fundamental flaws. First, he has not concerned himself with the task of making reasonably clear some of the essential terms he employs—among them "institutionalized injustice" and "institutionalized compensation." Secondly, a consistent application of his thesis to a given society is more likely to perpetuate than eliminate the injustices of discrimination.

I

There are a good many different kinds of organized social practices in every society, most of which in one way or another are discriminatory. Cer-

Reprinted from *Analysis* 34 (1974), by permission of the author.

tain religious groups, for example, either forbid or actively discourage intermarriage between their members and those of other religious groups. Although I think it unlikely that this sort of discriminatory practice could be justified by disinterested observers who understood it, it is on quite a different level from, say, a governmental prohibition against inter-racial marriage in the form of an anti-miscegenation statute. Both of these social practices embody a form of discrimination which is both institutionalized and unjust. Yet it is arguable that no society has the right to interfere with the former, whereas the latter ought not to be tolerated by any society. Again, the policy of not a few social and professional organizations excluding certain persons from membership solely on the basis of race, sex, or other non-moral criterion is clearly not on all fours with an overt or covert sanction of discrimination by a government on the same grounds. The difficulty, then, is to determine which discriminatory social practices fall under Taylor's concept of institutionalized injustice and which do not. Once that problem is resolved, we may turn our attention to the nature and scope of the required compensation—a subject he dismisses with a vague reference to the "restoration of the balance of justice" (p. 180). Clearly a democratic government, in its capacity of representing all the people, has a duty to rectify discriminatory legislation and enforcement of the law. It may also have a duty to abolish certain forms of private discrimination in which it has a compelling interest. It is not clear that private organizations have a duty to abolish and make reparation for their discriminatory practices. Nor is it clear that in every case of unjust discrimination some form of compensation is either desirable or possible. The appropriate compensation for an unjust tax might include a refund with interest; or for the unjust taking of private property a restitution of the property itself or, that not being possible, an award of damages for its value. But it is doubtful whether the concept of compensation is at all meaningful in the case of an anti-miscegenation statute. The appropriate remedy for the last form of discrimination is repeal—not an award of damages (how would damages be measured?) or the enactment of a statute requiring that henceforth all marriages be interracial.

Taylor has not offered a clue as to whether he thinks all unjust social practices must be abolished or, if not all, how to differentiate between those that should and those that need not be abolished. Nor has he demonstrated the necessity or even possibility of compensation in such cases. The vagueness of his use of these important terms gives rise to a suspicion that the phrase, "institutionalized injustice demands institutionalized compensation," may be little more than a high-sounding but vacuous slogan.

II

Assuming *arguendo* that the meaning of the above-discussed terms is reasonably clear and that there are no logical difficulties involved in their application, compensation for past discrimination is nevertheless unjustifiable if it incorporates reverse discrimination. By "reverse discrimination" I refer to a policy of according favored treatment to a group of persons unjustly discriminated against in the past because of some non-moral characteristic C possessed by each member of the group (hereafter the C-group), and corresponding unfavored treatment to a group of persons no member of which possesses the characteristic C (hereafter the C'-group). As Taylor correctly argues, individual moral desert is not relevant to the application of such a policy. It is both justifiable and necessary, he believes, even though it is possible (indeed probable) that not every C-person suffered and there are C'-persons who neither caused, condoned, practiced, nor benefited from the initial discrimination. The reason it is justifiable, he explains, is that the original discrimination created the C-group's right to reparation—not as individuals, but as a class—and the existence of that right entails reverse discrimination. In short, the C-group must be compensated at the expense of the C'-group.

In applying the policy, it seems to me that whatever good is accomplished by compensating members of the C-group for past wrongs is vitiated by the corresponding denial of benefits to the C'-group. Where before the entire C-group was victimized for the benefit of individual C'-persons, now the entire C'-group has been substituted as a victim for the benefit of individual C-persons. The criterion for discrimination is no longer C but C'. Thus while certain C-persons are compensated for the wrongs done them or other members of the C-group, the C'-group is unjustly discriminated against as a class. It follows that a right to reparation is created within the C'-group—not as individuals, but as a class—and the existence of this right entails what we might call reverse reverse discrimination. It is not difficult to see where this path leads.

The theory of compensatory justice, as explained by Taylor, will not do insofar as it incorporates reverse discrimination. The best way of avoiding the injustices of discrimination is to avoid unjust discrimination in the first place. The second-best method is to avoid making the same mistake twice.

7

Should Reparations Be to Individuals or to Groups?

James W. Nickel

The discussion occasioned by my note "Discrimination and Morally Relevant Characteristics" has helped to clarify some of the available positions on the justification of special benefits for victims of discrimination. J. L. Cowan ("Inverse Discrimination") agrees that the justification for special help lies in the fact that one has been wronged, not in the fact, say, that one is black. But he thinks that it is important to emphasize that the special benefits which are due to many blacks are due only because they are individuals who have been wronged, not because of any fact relating to their race. In his view, "reparations for blacks" must be understood as "reparations for wronged individuals who happen to be black." P. W. Taylor and M. D. Bayles criticize my approach from the opposite direction. They think that my approach pays insufficient attention to the moral status of wronged groups. In what follows I shall attempt to point out some weaknesses in my critics' positions and to elaborate further my own.

The "reverse discrimination argument" alleges that special benefits for blacks are unjust because they continue to base special treatment on an irrelevant characteristic (viz., being black) and hence continue to discriminate. The counter-argument that I offered has two premises:

Reprinted from *Analysis* 34 (1974), by permission of the author.

P₁: For differential treatment to be discriminatory (and unjust for that reason) it must be based on a morally irrelevant characteristic.

P₂: Differential treatment of blacks for purposes of reparations is not based on an irrelevant characteristic (as it would be if it were based on race instead of the fact of having been wronged).

From these premises I drew the conclusion that differential treatment of blacks for purposes of reparations is not unjust on account of being discriminatory.

Cowan's criticism is that the formulation of the argument is ambiguous because it fails to make clear whether it is defending special help to individuals or special help to groups:

> Nickel's reasoning thus does not really, as it might be taken to do, provide any support at all for the kind of self-contradictory thinking the original argument was surely intended to rebut. This is the reasoning that since blacks…have suffered unjust discrimination we should now give them special treatment to make it up to them. Once again there is no problem insofar as this simply means that where individual blacks have suffered injustice it should, as with anyone else, insofar as possible be made up to those individuals who have so suffered. The fallacy arises when rather than individuals it is the group which is intended, and individuals are regarded merely as members of that group rather than in their individuality. (p. 11 [6])

But it was indeed my intention to provide support for the kind of thinking that Cowan finds contradictory. I intended to suggest that since almost all American blacks have been victimized by discrimination it would be justifiable to design and institute programs of special benefits for blacks. Such programs, which are probably the only effective and administratively feasible way to provide reparations to blacks, would be justified in terms of the injuries that almost all of the recipients have suffered—not in terms of the race of the recipients. To make this clearer one needs to distinguish between the justifying and the administrative basis for a program.[1] The justifying basis for such a program would be the injuries that many blacks suffer and the special needs that many blacks have because of discrimination. The administrative basis for distributing the program's benefits might be the presence in an individual of these needs and injuries, but it is more likely that it would be some other characteristics (such as race and present income) which were easier to detect and which were highly correlated with the justifying basis. My assumption here is that it is sometimes justifiable for reasons of administrative efficiency to use as part of the administrative basis for a program of benefits a characteristic such as race which would be implausible as a justifying basis. Cowan argues that special advantages to blacks as a group are "out of the question, since in the moral context there is no such group" (p. 12 [7]). I agree with the premise that there is no such group insofar as this means that race or ancestry can never be a justifying basis for differential treatment. But I do not agree that race or ancestry can never serve as a morally acceptable administrative basis for a program of differential treatment which provides compensation for past wrongs, and hence I reject the unqualified conclusion that special advantages to blacks as a group are out of the question.

Bayles and Taylor want to go further than this. They want to give direct moral status to the defining characteristics of wronged groups, and argue that special help to blacks as a group can be justified in terms of a principle requiring reparations to wronged groups. They hold the view, paradoxical but not contradictory, that although race is irrelevant in a context where persons of a given race are being unjustly harmed, it is not irrelevant in a context where the obligation to give reparations to wronged groups is being met. Bayles, unlike Taylor, does not offer positive grounds for his own view; he simply offers it as an alternative to my approach—which he thinks can be discredited by refutation by analogy. In response to my claim that having been wronged rather than being black is the justifying basis for special help, he says,

> By parallel reasoning it can be argued that the original discrimination was not on the basis of a morally irrelevant characteristic. Racists do not discriminate against blacks simply because they are black. Rather they claim that blacks as a class are inferior in certain relevant respects, e.g., they lack certain abilities and virtues such as industriousness, reliability, and cleanliness. Thus, reasoning similarly to Nickel and Cowan, racists could contend that they do not discriminate on the basis of a morally irrelevant characteristic, but the morally relevant ones which are thought to be associated with being black. (p. 183 [16])

Bayles' complaint is that if those who favor reparations can use this argument, then so can racists. He thinks that if it works for the one then it will work for the other. And since it is obvious that it won't work for the racist as a way of showing that he doesn't discriminate, he concludes that it won't work for those who favor reparations.

One response to this complaint is to argue that the second premise of my counter-argument to the "reverse discrimination argument" would not be true when used by the racist. The racist's version of the second premise would be:

RP$_2$: My differential treatment of blacks is not based on an irrelevant characteristic (as it would be if it were based on race
instead of the fact of being lazy, unreliable, and unclean).

In most cases this would not be, I submit, a true claim. It would rather be a self-serving rationalization. In B. A. O. Williams' words, the racist is "paying, in very poor coin, the homage of irrationality to reason."[2] Most racists could not use this defense of their differential treatment of blacks because its premise about their real reasons would not be true.

But to avoid being doctrinaire about this we must allow that some racists might be able to make this claim about their real reasons without falsehood and rationalization. And Bayles is right in suggesting that this possibility requires me to modify or give up my counter-argument. Bayles' approach is to give up this defense and use a much stronger principle about reparations to wronged groups to defend programs of reparations to blacks from the charge of unjust discrimination. But before adopting Bayles' approach we will do well, I think, to consider modifying the first premise of my counter-argument. This premise holds that for differential treatment to be discriminatory (and unjust for that reason) it must be based on an irrelevant characteristic. But it should be changed to one which holds that for differential treatment to be discriminatory (and unjust for that reason) it is necessary that it be based on an irrelevant characteristic *or* on a false claim about the correlation between characteristics. This is, in effect, to modify one's definition of "discrimination." When this modification is made, the defender of reparations is not able to move directly from the fact that preferential treatment was not based on an irrelevant characteristic to the conclusion that it was not unjustly discriminatory. To get to this conclusion he would also have to show that there was in fact a very high correlation between being an American black and being a victim of discriminatory and harmful treatment. I think that the defender of reparations can do this, but the racist cannot make the analogous move. He cannot show that there is in fact a high correlation between being black and lacking industry, reliability, and cleanliness, and hence his actions are based on false beliefs about correlations between characteristics and can—under the modified premise—be condemned as discriminatory. Hence the defender of reparations can use this defense without making an equally good defense available to the racist.

Taylor agrees with Bayles's claim that the justification of special benefits to blacks requires us to appeal to a moral principle about compensation for wronged *groups*. He formulates this principle as follows:

> The principle of compensatory justice is that, in order to restore the balance of justice when an injustice has been committed to a group of persons, some form of compensation or reparation must be made to that group. (p. 179 [11])

When there has been institutionalized discrimination against persons who have a certain morally irrelevant characteristic, the effect of this principle is to *make* this characteristic relevant for purposes of reparations. Taylor insists that in such a case reparations is due to the group, not just to those of its members who were harmed by the discriminatory practice. Since the characteristic which defines the group was essentially involved in the discriminatory practice, reparations must be made available to all those who have this characteristic.

An interesting aspect of Taylor's paper is his suggestion that the principles of compensatory justice can be chosen from the perspective which John Rawls advocates for choosing principles of distributive justice. If it can be argued plausibly that persons in the Rawlsian original position would choose compensatory principles which include a principle providing benefits directly to wronged groups, then any lingering suspicion that Taylor's principle is *ad hoc* and has been invented specifically to deal with the issue of special benefits for blacks could be laid to rest.

Rawls has very little to say about compensatory and retributive justice in *A Theory of Justice*, but the principles of distributive justice which he thinks would be chosen in the original position would themselves require a good deal of compensatory activity on the part of government. These principles embody a general conception of justice which holds that "all social values...are to be distributed equally unless an unequal distribution of any, or all, of these values is to everyone's advantage" (*A Theory of Justice*, p. 62). A consequence of this is that heavier-than-average burdens are unjust unless they can be justified by showing that even the person who suffers the most from bearing the burden would be worse off if that kind of burden were shifted or compensated. But it will be impossible to show this with regard to many types of burdens, and hence these will have to be shifted to others with lighter loads or compensated. Since it is often impossible to shift such burdens (e.g., a heavy work load resulting from skills which are much in demand, or disabilities resulting from an accident), compensation in the form of balancing benefits will be required in many cases by Rawls' principles of distributive justice. This applies to all unjustifiable burdens, no matter what their origin, and would include unequal burdens resulting from discrimination. The latter, being unjustifiable, would have to be shifted or compensated. It appears, therefore, that Rawls' principles of distributive justice by themselves would take us some distance towards remedying the effects of discrimination.

Since the compensation of unjustifiable burdens would be required by Rawls' principles of distributive justice, it is not entirely clear that *any* distinct principles of compensatory justice would be chosen by persons in the original position. From the Rawlsian perspective, such principles would not be chosen merely because it was thought to be "fitting" that wrongdoers should repay their victims. They would be chosen only if their use would maximize the life prospects of those who would live in the projected society.

But assume, for purposes of argument, that persons in the original position would choose to have compensatory principles among their principles of justice. These principles would require persons and institutions to compensate the victims of their wrong-doing and negligence, and would require government to provide compensation when the wrongdoer was financially unable. The question, then, is whether persons in the original position would also choose a principle which would compensate *groups* as such for injuries suffered by their members as members. Since the members of these groups could obtain compensation as individuals under the other reparations principles, would there be any reason to provide compensation to groups as such?

I am unable to think of any such reason, and I think that the reason that Taylor presents is unsound. He contends that a program of reparations which is justified by reference to the wrongs suffered by individuals "completely disregards what, morally speaking, is the most hideous aspect of the injustices of human history: those carried out systematically against whole groups of men and women *as groups*" (pp. 181–82 [14]). If Taylor is right in claiming that providing reparations to groups as groups is the only alternative to ignoring these hideous injustices, then persons in the original position would have a reason for choosing principles requiring such reparations. One function of requiring the performance of acts of reparations is to provide a symbolic denunciation of the evil that was done and to provide the wrongdoer with an opportunity to declare in a concrete and meaningful way his turning away from that evil. Perhaps it is this element that those, like Taylor, who demand reparations to blacks as a group feel would be missing in any approach to reparations which proceeded on an individual basis. A person of strong moral feeling may hold that such an approach allows America to bury its racist past rather than to confront it and repent of it. A symbolic denunciation of racism is desired, and it is held that only a program of reparations to blacks as a group can do this.

But surely Taylor presents us with a false dilemma when he suggests that compensation to groups as such is the only alternative to disregarding the injustices of institutionalized discrimination against groups. We can give great emphasis to the injustices involved in such discrimination through means other than those of imitating the structure of such injustices in our compensatory mechanisms. We can denounce such practices, teach our children to notice their silent but sinister operations and avoid them, make them illegal and provide effective enforcement mechanisms, and provide reparations to their victims which is justified—but not necessarily administered—on an individual basis. If we succeed in doing these things then it can scarcely be said that we have disregarded the most hideous aspects of institutionalized discrimination against groups. Direct compensation to groups of the sort advocated by Taylor is not the only effective way of demonstrating our aversion to this kind of injustice.

The upshot of this is that there do not seem to be any reasons why the life prospects of persons in the original position would be bettered by their choosing a principle requiring reparations to wronged groups. Furthermore, there is at least one reason for thinking that these prospects would be worsened. This is that there might well be cases in which the result of following Taylor's principle would be to waste resources on substantial numbers of persons who were completely unaffected by discrimination directed against a group to which they belonged. Suppose that there was a group which was evenly distributed throughout the country but which was subject to discriminatory treatment in only some sections, and as a result of this half of the members of this group were completely unaffected by this discrimination—even though it was based on a characteristic which all of them shared.[3] Would we be willing to agree with the conclusion of Taylor's principle that all of them should receive compensation whether they had been harmed or not? This problem does not arise in the case of American blacks since all, or almost all, of them have suffered significantly from discrimination, and hence there is no great unfairness or waste of resources if benefits are provided for all. But in dealing with a group in which only a portion of the members had been affected by the discrimination it is far from clear that a principle requiring compensation to all would be desirable.

8

Reparations to Individuals or Groups?

Alan H. Goldman

James Nickel bases his latest argument for reparations to groups upon a distinction between the justifying and administrative basis for a program of reparations. I have argued against compensatory hiring for groups elsewhere,[1] but had not considered there this most recent argument. Its novelty lies in the shift from abstract or ideal principles of compensatory justice to the necessity in practice of balancing claims so as to maximize (imperfect) justice. The justification for favored treatment for groups according to Nickel derives from the administrative feasibility of such a program by comparison with the high cost and impracticality of administering compensatory justice in this area on an individual basis. Thus while there is only a high correlation between being black, for example, and having been discriminated against and so deserving compensation (justifying basis), so that preferential treatment for the group will occasionally result in undeserved benefits for individuals, the balance of justice in practice favors such treatment. The viable alternatives seem to be either award of deserved compensation in the great majority of cases and occasional undeserved benefit and hence injustice to white job applicants, or compensation on an individual basis, which would require demonstration of past injustice in court or before a special administrative body, so that the cost and difficulty of the operation would result in far fewer awards of deserved reparation. It is better, the argument holds, to have compensation which is only almost always de-

Reprinted from *Analysis* 35 (1975), reprinted by permission of the author.

served than a program which in practice would amount to almost no compensation at all, so that a policy which would not be accepted in an ideally just world (a world which became ideally just after compensation was paid) becomes best in the present situation.

In reply, one would first of all like to ask how high the correlation between group membership and past discrimination, and hence the proportion of deserved to underserved compensation, must be. Presumably a ratio of fifty-one to forty-nine will not do, since in the case of compensation by preferential hiring policies, there are two injustices involved in every case of undeserved compensation: first the payment for the undeserved benefit made by society in accepting less efficient service (since the candidate will not be as competent if hired only because of preferred treatment), but, more important, the injustice to the white male applicant who is best qualified.[2] The correlation is presumably not as high in the case of women as a group as in the case of blacks, and not as high for middle class as for lower class blacks. The latter comparison suggests narrowing the specification of the group so as to maximize the correlation, but of course at the limit of such narrowing is a program administered on an individual basis.

Thus far it still seems we must balance ideal theory against practice, but the far more serious point completely forgotten in Nickel's argument is the effect of the operation of market criteria upon hiring even within a compensatory program of preferential treatment. Since hiring within the preferred group still depends upon relative qualifications and hence upon past opportunities for acquiring qualifications, there is in fact an inverse ratio established between past discrimination and present benefits, so that those who benefit most from the program, those who actually obtain jobs, are those who deserve to least. Given that those individuals will always be hired first who have suffered least from prior discrimination, this effect of competence requirements completely destroys the rationale of arguing by correlation unless the correlation is extremely close to perfect, for as long as there are some members in the market who have not unfairly lost opportunities, they will be the ones getting the jobs. But the establishment of such high correlation for a specific group, or the narrowing of specifications for group membership until virtually all members have been treated unjustly, amounts to administering a program on an individual basis. It will have to be determined for each individual whether he belongs to the narrowly specified group and have to be determined for individuals within that group whether virtually all have been discriminated against and thereby suffered harm.[3] These two steps, when the group is sufficiently narrowly specified, will I suspect be as difficult as handling cases on an individual basis from the beginning.

Since Nickel's argument wrongly assumes that the majority of compensation cases will tend to be fair if the correlation of past injustice to group membership is above fifty percent, it is unsound. Nor can the practice of hiring by competence itself be blamed or held therefore unjust. If efficiency is Nickel's basis for arguing for group compensation, he cannot condemn a general practice which in the long run results in more goods for all in favor of some less efficient alternative. It would at least be strange to recommend hiring the least competent as a general practice within some preferred group, and in this case efficiency would be gained not lost by moving away from a group program. In order then not to create a policy which in practice singles out for benefits within a generally unjustly treated minority just that minority which has not been unjustly treated, and thus does treat unfairly members of the "majority group" applying for jobs, a compensatory program of preferential hiring must be administered on an individual basis. Where there are significant departures from this toward preferential treatment for loosely defined large groups, we must suspect further injustice not only to "majority group" members, but to members of the minority who have suffered previous injustice and are now passed over in favor of other members who have at least suffered less. There are surely degrees of injustice, and the market here will invert the ratio of past injustice to present compensation if the program is directed toward a group.

8

What's Wrong with Discrimination?

Paul Woodruff

The trouble with compensatory discrimination in favor of a group, say its critics, is that it is discrimination. It is morally wrong because it accords differential treatment on morally irrelevant grounds—it distributes reparations on the basis of group membership, whereas if reparations are to be made, they should be made to the individuals who have been wronged (William A. Nunn and Alan H. Goldman). The defenders of compensatory discrimination for groups tend to deny that its criteria are morally irrelevant. A person's membership in a group, they say, may become morally relevant when there has been systematic discrimination against that group (Paul W. Taylor).

No one, it seems, stops to consider the relevance of moral relevance to the issue. The important question is why discrimination is wrong when it is wrong. When we know the answer to that we shall know who it is that is wronged by it.

For brevity's sake, and because it is the hardest case to make out, I shall consider only discrimination in hiring by private employers. The problem is that it does not always seem to be wrong. Suppose a private banker hires his cousin in preference to a better qualified applicant from another family. Hiring bankers this way is discriminatory, for it uses a criterion (kinship) that is irrelevant to banking. Is it morally wrong?

Reprinted from *Analysis* 36 (1976), reprinted by permission of the author.

We need to know more about the case. Suppose that our banker's bank is the only bank in the country, that it is entirely a family affair, and that it dominates the modern economy of the country. Then, whenever our banker hires a cousin, he helps to exclude those outside his family from power and to raise over them a class with birthright privileges. He participates in a pattern of discrimination that wrongs *everyone* who is not a member of his family by making their parentage a reason for failure. This is insulting to every member of the excluded class, and damages their self-respect and the respect in which they are held by others.

On the other hand, if our banker's bank was a small business in a land of many and various banks, which were not in general ruled by a privileged class, then what moral wrong would he commit in hiring his cousin? If the cousin is idle, it is foolish to hire him. If an applicant is disappointed, it is sad not to hire him. But I am not aware that it is generally wrong to disappoint people.

The disappointed applicant may have valid complaints against the banker that have nothing to do with discrimination. For example, in advertising the job, our banker may have promised to give it to the best applicant. Or using customary hiring practices like interviews may oblige him to hire the best applicant. But he can discriminate without violating obligations of that sort. Also, it may turn out that no one hires the applicant. Whatever the cause of this, and whether or not discrimination was involved, his unemployment may be a social injustice. If so, the banker does wrong by contributing to that injustice. But discrimination and the fate to which it may bring its victims are wrong in different ways. For example, it does not matter how people are made slaves; their slavery is an injustice whether they came to it by stupidity, conquest, discrimination, or an impartial lottery. Slavery is an injustice to the slaves. But enslaving people *for their race* would add a wrong to slavery, and not to slaves only, but to every member of the insulted race.

Notice that the moral relevance of the criteria used is not decisive. Kinship would be morally relevant to our banker's decision if he himself had benefited from the hiring of cousins. But what really matters is whether or not it is right to hire cousins.

I suggest that an act of discrimination is wrong when it is wrong not simply because it is discriminatory, but because it is part of a pattern of discrimination that is wrong. A pattern of discrimination is wrong when it makes membership in a group burdensome by unfairly reducing the respect in which the group is held. It may accomplish this, for example, by making group membership a *prima facie* reason for failure. One act of discrimination cannot do that. If an applicant fails at one bank because of his race, and at other banks for other reasons, his race is not the reason for his unemployment, and his failure is not an insult to his race. Discriminating, like walking on the grass, is to be judged with reference to how much of it is being done. Walking on the grass is harmful only if enough people are in the habit of doing it to ruin the grass. So it is with walking over the feelings of a group.

My account of discrimination yields two conclusions for the debate on compensatory discrimination.

(1) The objection that compensatory discrimination is wrong because it is discriminatory may be dismissed. Compensatory discrimination is not part of a pattern that is wrong. Since it is compensatory it is limited to a scale which will not reduce *unfairly* the respect in which the compensating group is held. Though it may cause certain people to be unemployed, it does not increase unemployment, which is an evil however it is distributed.

I do not consider the objection that compensatory discrimination violates the principle that the best people deserve the best jobs (the meritocratic principle). The merits of that principle are much in question, and raise too large an issue for this brief note. In any case, the chief complaints against discrimination are based not on that principle but on egalitarian beliefs. I have tried to make the burden of those complaints precise.

(2) It is now clear that compensation for discrimination is owed to all members of the relevant group in virtue of their membership in that group. An individual disappointed by discrimination has no special claim to redress on that score. He has been wronged, not because he has been disappointed, but because he is a member of a group that has been wronged. Every member of the group finds membership in the group unfairly burdensome as a result of the pattern of discrimination; every member has an equal claim to compensation. Conversely, every member is benefited equally by an act that tends to break the pattern. Our banker would do well by the non-cousins if he hires even a privileged non-cousin, one who has not yet been disappointed, if in doing so he increases the accessibility of bank jobs to non-cousins.

Of course in the history of any pattern of discrimination there are usually at least two wrongs to be righted. Thus if people have been enslaved on the basis of race, then (i) every member of the race deserves redress for discrimination, and (ii) every slave deserves redress for enslavement. Slavery, poverty, and the like are borne by individuals; discrimination is borne by groups.

But what precisely is a group for our purposes? Consider the group of those who are either black women or hold degrees in law from Harvard. Few of its members in proportion to its number enjoy jobs of importance. Yet no white Harvard lawyer is wronged by the snubbing of a black woman, and it would be no consolation to black women to see a Harvard lawyer advanced to a good job, if he is white. We need to restrict what counts as a group for our purposes. As consistent egalitarians, we must avoid certain moral and natural criteria for grouphood, on pain of undermining our objection to discrimination. The relevant group in each case is the group that has been insulted. What that is is a question for social scientists.

II. Justice and Compensation

10

Preferential Hiring

Judith Jarvis Thomson

Many people are inclined to think preferential hiring an obvious injustice.[1] I should have said "feel" rather than "think": it seems to me the matter has not been carefully thought out, and that what is in question, really, is a gut reaction.

I am going to deal with only a very limited range of preferential hirings: that is, I am concerned with cases in which several candidates present themselves for a job, in which the hiring officer finds, on examination, that all are equally qualified to hold that job, and he then straightway declares for the black, or for the woman, because he or she *is* a black or a woman. And I shall talk only of hiring decisions in the universities, partly because I am most familiar with them, partly because it is in the universities that the most vocal and articulate opposition to preferential hiring is now heard— not surprisingly, perhaps, since no one is more vocal and articulate than a university professor who feels deprived of his rights.

I suspect that some people may say, Oh well, in *that* kind of case it's all right, what we object to is preferring the less qualified to the better qualified. Or again, What we object to is refusing even to consider the qualifications of white males. I shall say nothing at all about these things. I think that the argument I shall give for saying that preferential hiring is not unjust in the cases I do concentrate on can also be appealed to to justify it out-

Reprinted from *Philosophy and Public Affairs* 2 (1973). Copyright © 1973 by Princeton University Press. Reprinted by permission of Princeton University Press.

side that range of cases. But I won't draw any conclusions about cases outside it. Many people do have that gut reaction I mentioned against preferential hiring in any degree or form; and it seems to me worthwhile bringing out that there is good reason to think they are wrong to have it. Nothing I say will be in the slightest degree novel or original. It will, I hope, be enough to set the relevant issues out clearly.

I

But first, something should be said about qualifications.

I said I would consider only cases in which the several candidates who present themselves for the job are equally qualified to hold it; and there plainly are difficulties in the way of saying precisely how this is to be established, and even what is to be established. Strictly academic qualifications seem at a first glance to be relatively straightforward: the hiring officer must see if the candidates have done equally well in courses (both courses they took, and any they taught), and if they are recommended equally strongly by their teachers, and if the work they submit for consideration is equally good. There is no denying that even these things are less easy to establish than first appears: for example, you may have a suspicion that Professor Smith is given to exaggeration, and that his "great student" is in fact less strong than Professor Jones's "good student"—but do you *know* that this is so? But there is a more serious difficulty still: as blacks and women have been saying, strictly academic indicators may themselves be skewed by prejudice. My impression is that women, white and black, may possibly suffer more from this than black males. A black male who is discouraged or down-graded for being black is discouraged or down-graded out of dislike, repulsion, a desire to avoid contact; and I suspect that there are very few teachers nowadays who allow themselves to feel such things, or, if they do feel them, to act on them. A woman who is discouraged or down-graded for being a woman is not discouraged or down-graded out of dislike, but out of a conviction she is not serious, and I suspect that while there are very few teachers nowadays who allow themselves to feel that women generally are not serious, there are many who allow themselves to feel of the particular individual women students they confront that Ah, this one isn't serious, and in fact that one isn't either, nor is that other one— women generally are, of course, one thing, but these particular women, really they're just girls in search of husbands, are quite another. And I suspect that this will be far harder to root out. A teacher could not face himself in the mirror of a morning if he had down-graded anyone out of dislike; but a teacher can well face himself in the mirror if he down-grades someone out of a conviction that that person is not serious: after all, life is serious, and jobs and work, and who can take the unserious seriously? Who pays attention to the dilettante? So the hiring officer must read very very carefully between the lines in the candidates' dossiers even to assess their strictly academic qualifications.

And then of course there are other qualifications besides the strictly academic ones. Is one of the candidates exceedingly disagreeable? A department is not merely a collection of individuals, but a working unit; and if anyone is going to disrupt that unit, and to make its work more difficult, then this counts against him—he may be as well qualified in strictly academic terms, but he is not as well qualified. Again, is one of the candidates incurably sloppy? Is he going to mess up his records, is he going to have to be nagged to get his grades in, and worse, is he going to lose students' papers? This too would count against him: keeping track of students' work, records, and grades, after all, is part of the job.

What seems to me to be questionable, however, is that a candidate's race or sex is itself a qualification. Many people who favor preferential hiring in the universities seem to think it is; in their view, if a group of candidates is equally well qualified in respect of those measures I have already indicated, then if one is of the right race (black) or of the right sex (female), then that being itself a qualification, it tips the balance, and that one is the best qualified. If so, then of course no issue of injustice, or indeed of any other impropriety, is raised if the hiring officer declares for that one of the candidates straightway.

Why does race or sex seem to many to be, itself, a qualification? There seem to be two claims in back of the view that it is. First, there is the claim that blacks learn better from a black, women from a woman. One hears this less often in respect of women; blacks, however, are often said to mistrust the whites who teach them, with the result that they simply do not learn as well, or progress as far, as they would if taught by blacks. Secondly, and this one hears in respect of women as well as blacks, what is wanted is *role models*. The proportion of black and women faculty members in the larger universities (particularly as one moves up the ladder of rank) is very much smaller than the proportion of blacks and women in the society at large—even, in the case of women, than the proportion of them amongst recipients of Ph.D. degrees from those very same universities. Black and women students suffer a constricting of ambition because of this. They need to see members of their race or sex who are accepted, successful professionals. They need concrete evidence that those of their race or sex *can* become accepted, successful professionals.

And perhaps it is thought that it is precisely by virtue of having a role model right in the classroom that blacks do learn better from a black, women from a woman.

Now it is obviously essential for a university to staff its classrooms with people who can teach, and so from whom its students can learn, and indeed learn as much and as well as possible—teaching, after all, is, if not the whole of the game, then anyway a very large part of it. So if the first claim is true, then race and sex *do* seem to be qualifications. It obviously would not follow that a university should continue to regard them as qualifications indefinitely; I suppose, however, that it would follow that it should regard them as qualifications at least until the proportion of blacks and women on the faculty matches the proportion of blacks and women among the students.

But in the first place, allowing this kind of consideration to have a bearing on a hiring decision might make for trouble of a kind that blacks and women would not be at all happy with. For suppose it could be made out that white males learn better from white males? (I once, years ago, had a student who said he really felt uncomfortable in a class taught by a woman, it was interfering with his work, and did I mind if he switched to another section?) I suppose we would feel that this was due to prejudice, and that it was precisely to be discouraged, certainly not encouraged by establishing hiring ratios. I don't suppose it is true of white males generally that they learn better from white males; I am concerned only with the way in which we should take the fact, if it were a fact, that they did—and if it would be improper to take it to be reason to think being a white male is a qualification in a teacher, then how shall we take its analogue to be reason to think being black, or being a woman, is a qualification in a teacher?

And in the second place, I must confess that, speaking personally, I do not find the claim we are looking at borne out in experience; I do not think that as a student I learned any better, or any more, from the women who taught me than from the men, and I do not think that my own women students now learn any better or any more from me than they do from my male colleagues. Blacks, of course, may have, and may have had, very different experiences, and I don't presume to speak for them—or even for women generally. But my own experience being what it is, it seems to *me* that any defense of preferential hiring in the universities which takes this first claim as premise is so far not an entirely convincing one.

The second claim, however, does seem to me to be plainly true: black and women students do need role models, they do need concrete evidence that those of their race or sex can become accepted, successful, professionals—plainly, you won't try to become what you don't believe you can become.

But do they need these role models right there in the classroom? Of course it might be argued that they do: that a black learns better from a black teacher, a woman from a woman teacher. But we have already looked at this. And if they are, though needed, not needed in the classroom, then is it the university's job to provide them?

For it must surely be granted that a college, or university, has not the responsibility—or perhaps, if it is supported out of public funds, even the right—to provide just *any* service to its students which it might be good for them, or even which they may need, to be provided with. Sports seem to me plainly a case in point. No doubt it is very good for students to be offered, and perhaps even required to become involved in, a certain amount of physical exercise; but I can see no reason whatever to think that universities should be expected to provide facilities for it, or taxpayers to pay for those facilities. I suspect others may disagree, but my own feeling is that it is the same with medical and psychiatric services: I am sure that at least some students need medical and psychiatric help, but I cannot see why it should be provided for them in the universities, at public expense.

So the further question which would have to be answered is this: granting that black and female students need black and female role models, why should the universities be expected to provide them within their faculties? In the case of publicly supported universities, why should taxpayers be expected to provide them?

I don't say these questions can't be answered. But I do think we need to come at them from a quite different direction. So I shall simply sidestep this ground for preferential hiring in the universities. The defense I give will not turn on anyone's supposing that of two otherwise equally well qualified candidates, one may be better qualified for the job by virtue, simply, of being of the right race or sex.

II

I mentioned several times in the preceding section the obvious fact that it is the taxpayers who support public universities. Not that private universities are wholly private: the public contributes to the support of most of them, for example by allowing them tax-free use of land, and of the dividends and capital gains on investments. But it will be the public universities in which the problem appears most starkly: as I shall suggest, it is the fact of public support that makes preferential hiring in the universities problematic.

For it seems to me that—other things being equal—there is no problem about preferential hiring in the case of a wholly private college or university, that is, one which receives no measure of public support at all, and which lives simply on tuition and (non-tax-deductible) contributions.

The principle here seems to me to be this: no perfect stranger has a right to be given a benefit which is yours to dispose of; no perfect stranger even has a right to be given an equal chance at getting a benefit which is yours to dispose of. You not only needn't give the benefit to the first perfect stranger who walks in and asks for it, you needn't even give him a chance at it, as, e.g., by tossing a coin.

I should stress that I am here talking about *benefits*, that is, things which people would like to have, which would perhaps not merely please them, but improve their lives, but which they don't actually *need*. (I suspect the same holds true of things people do actually need, but many would disagree, and as it is unnecessary to speak here of needs, I shall not discuss them.) If I have extra apples (they're mine: I grew them, on my own land, from my own trees), or extra money, or extra tickets to a series of lectures I am giving on How to Improve Your Life through Philosophy, and am prepared to give them away, word of this may get around, and people may present themselves as candidate recipients. I do not have to give to the first, or to proceed by letting them all draw straws; if I really do own the things, I can give to whom I like, on any ground I please, and in so doing, I violate no one's *rights*, I treat no one *unjustly*. None of the candidate recipients has a right to the benefit, or even to a chance at it.

There are four caveats. (1) Some grounds for giving or refraining from giving are less respectable than others. Thus, I might give the apples to the first who asks for them simply because he is the first who asks for them. Or again, I might give the apples to the first who asks for them because he is black, and because I am black and feel an interest in and concern for blacks which I do not feel in and for whites. In either case, not merely do I do what it is within my rights to do, but more, my ground for giving them to that person is a not immoral ground for giving them to him. But I might instead give the apples to the sixth who asks, and this because the first five were black and I hate blacks—or because the first five were white and I hate whites. Here I do what I have a right to do (for the apples are *mine*), and I violate no one's rights in doing it, but my ground for disposing of the apples as I did was a bad one; and it might even, more strongly, be said that I ought not to have disposed of the apples in the way I did. But it is important to note that it is perfectly consistent, on the one hand, that a man's ground for acting as he did was a bad one, and even that he ought not have done what he did, and, on the other hand, that he had a right to do what he did, that he violated no one's rights in doing it, and that no one can complain he was unjustly treated.

The second caveat (2) is that although I have a right to dispose of my apples as I wish, I have no right to harm, or gratuitously hurt or offend. Thus I am within my rights to refuse to give the apples to the first five because they are black (or because they are white); but I am not within my rights to say to them "I refuse to give you apples because you are black (or white) and because those who are black (or white) are inferior."

And (3) if word of my extra apples, and of my willingness to give them away, got around because I advertised, saying or implying First Come First Served Till Supply Runs Out, then I cannot refuse the first five because they are black, or white. By so advertising I have *given* them a right to a chance at the apples. If they come in one at a time, I must give out apples in order, till the supply runs out; if they come in together, and I have only four apples, then I must either cut up the apples, or give them each an equal chance, as, e.g., by having them draw straws.

And lastly (4), there may be people who would say that I don't really, or don't fully own those apples, even though I grew them on my own land, from my own trees, and therefore that I don't have a right to give them away as I see fit. For after all, I don't own the police who protected my land while those apples were growing, or the sunlight because of which they grew. Or again, wasn't it just a matter of luck for me that I was born with a green thumb?—and why should I profit from a competence that I didn't deserve to have, that I didn't earn? Or perhaps some other reason might be put forward for saying that I don't own those apples. I don't want to take this up here. It seems to me wrong, but I want to let it pass. If anyone thinks that I don't own the apples, or, more generally, that no one really or fully owns anything, he will regard what I shall say in the remainder of this section, in which I talk about what may be done with what is privately owned, as an idle academic exercise. I'll simply ask that anyone who does think this be patient: we will come to what is publicly owned later.

Now what was in question was a job, not apples: and it may be insisted that to give a man a job is not to give him a benefit, but rather something he needs. Well, I am sure that people do need jobs, that it does not fully satisfy people's needs to supply them only with food, shelter, and medical care. Indeed, I am sure that people need, not merely jobs, but jobs that interest them, and that they can therefore get satisfaction from the doing of. But on the other hand, I am not at all sure that any candidate for a job in a university needs a job in a university. One would very much like it if all graduate students who wish it could find jobs teaching in universities; it is in some measure a tragedy that a person should spend three or four years preparing for a career, and then find there is no job available, and that he has in consequence to take work which is less interesting than he had hoped and prepared for. But one thing seems plain: no one *needs* that work which would interest him most in all the whole world of work. Plenty of people have to make do with work they like less than other work—no economy is rich enough to provide everyone with the work he likes best of all— and I should think that this does not mean they lack something they *need*. We are all of us prepared to tax ourselves so that no one shall be in need; but I should imagine that we are not prepared to tax ourselves (to tax barbers, truck drivers, salesclerks, waitresses, and factory workers) in order that everyone who wants a university job, and is competent to fill it, shall have one made available to him.

All the same, if a university job is a benefit rather than something needed, it is anyway not a "pure" benefit (like an apple), but an "impure" one. To give a man a university job is to give him an opportunity to do work which is interesting and satisfying; but he will only be interested and satisfied if he actually does the work he is given an opportunity to do, and does it well.

What this should remind us of is that certain cases of preferential hiring might well be utterly irrational. Suppose we have an eating club, and need a new chef; we have two applicants, a qualified French chef, and a Greek who happens to like to cook, though he doesn't do it very well. We are fools if we say to ourselves "We like the Greeks, and dislike the French, so let's hire the Greek." We simply won't eat as well as we could have, and eating, after all, was the point of the club. On the other hand, it's *our* club, and so *our* job. And who shall say it is not within a man's rights to dispose of what really is his in as foolish a way as he likes?

And there is no irrationality, of course, if one imagines that the two applicants are equally qualified French chefs, and one is a cousin of one of our members, the other a perfect stranger. Here if we declare directly for the cousin, we do not act irrationally, we violate no one's rights, and indeed do not have a morally bad ground for making the choice we make. It's not a morally splendid ground, but it isn't a morally bad one either.

Universities differ from eating clubs in one way which is important for present purposes: in an eating club, those who consume what the club serves are the members, and thus the owners of the club themselves—by contrast, if the university is wholly private, those who consume what it serves are not among the owners. This makes a difference: the owners of the university have a responsibility not merely to themselves (as the owners of an eating club do), but also to those who come to buy what it offers. It could, I suppose, make plain in its advertising that it is prepared to allow the owners' racial or religious or other preferences to outweigh academic qualifications in its teachers. But in the absence of that, it must, in light of what a university is normally expected to be and to aim at, provide the best teachers it can afford. It does not merely act irrationally, but indeed violates the rights of its student-customers if it does not.

On the other hand, this leaves it open to the university that in case of a choice between equally qualified candidates, it violates no one's rights if it declares for the black because he is black, or for the white because he is white. To the wholly *private* university, that is, for that is all I have so far been talking of. Other things being equal—that is, given it has not advertised the job in a manner which would entitle applicants to believe that all who are equally qualified will be given an equal chance at it, and given it does not gratuitously give offense to those whom it rejects—the university may choose as it pleases, and violates no one's rights in doing so. Though no doubt its grounds for choosing may be morally bad ones, and we may even wish to say, more strongly, that it ought not choose as it does.

What will have come out in the preceding is that the issue I am concerned with is a moral, and not a legal one. My understanding is that the law does prevent an employer wholly in the private sector from choosing a white rather than a black on ground of that difference alone—though not from choosing a black rather than a white on ground of that difference alone. Now if, as many people say, legal rights (or perhaps, legal rights in a relatively just society) create moral rights, then even a moral investigation should take the law into account; and indeed, if I am not mistaken as to the law, it would have to be concluded that blacks (but not whites) do have rights of the kind I have been denying. I want to sidestep all this. My question can be re-put: would a private employer's choosing a white (or black) rather than a black (or white) on ground of that difference alone be a violation of anyone's rights if there were no law making it illegal? And the answer seems to me to be: it would not.

III

But hardly any college or university in America is purely private. As I said, most enjoy some public support, and the moral issues may be affected by the extent of the burden carried by the public. I shall concentrate on universities which are entirely publicly funded, such as state or city universities, and ignore the complications which might arise in case of partial private funding.

The special problem which arises here, as I see it, is this: where a community pays the bills, the community owns the university.

I said earlier that the members, who are therefore the owners, of a private eating club may declare for whichever chef they wish, even if the man they declare for is not as well qualified for the job as some other; in choosing amongst applicants, they are *not* choosing amongst fellow members of the club who is to get some benefit from the club. But now suppose, by contrast, that two of us who are members arrive at the same time, and there is only one available table. And suppose also that this has never happened before, and that the club has not voted on any policy for handling it when it does happen. What seems to me to be plain is this: the headwaiter cannot indulge in preferential seating, he cannot simply declare for one or the other of us on just any ground he pleases. He must randomize: as it might be, by tossing a coin.

Or again, suppose someone arrives at the dining room with a gift for the club: a large and very splendid apple tart. And suppose that this, too, has never happened before, and that the club has not voted on any policy for handling it when it does happen. What seems to me plain is this: the headwaiter cannot distribute that tart in just any manner, and on any ground he pleases. If the tart won't keep till the next meeting, and it's impossible to convene one now, he must divide the tart amongst us equally.

Consideration of these cases might suggest the following principle: every owner of a jointly owned property has a right to either an equal chance at, or an equal share in, any benefit which that property generates, and which is available for distribution amongst the owners—equal chance rather than equal share if the benefit is indivisible, or for some reason is better left undivided.

Now I have all along been taking it that the members of a club jointly own the club, and therefore jointly own whatever the club owns. It seems to me possible to view a community in the same way: to suppose that its members jointly own it, and therefore jointly own whatever it owns. If a community is properly viewed in this way, and if the principle I set out above is true, then every member of the community is a joint owner of whatever the community owns, and so in particular, a joint owner of its university; and therefore every member of the community has a right to an equal chance at, or equal share in, any benefit which the university generates, which is available for distribution amongst the owners. And that includes university jobs, if, as I argued, a university job is a benefit.

Alternatively, one might view a community as an imaginary Person: one might say that the members of that community are in some sense participants in that Person, but that they do not jointly own what the Person owns. One might in fact say the same of a club: that its members do not jointly own the club or anything which the club owns, but only in some sense participate in the Person which owns the things. And then the cases I mentioned might suggest an analogous principle: every "participant" in a Person (Community-Person, Club-Person) has a right to either an equal chance at, or an equal share in, any benefit which is generated by a property which that Person owns, which is available for distribution amongst the "participants."

On the other hand, if we accept any of this, we have to remember that there are cases in which a member may, without the slightest impropriety, be deprived of this equal chance or equal share. For it is plainly not required that the university's hiring officer decide who gets the available job by randomizing amongst *all* the community members, however well- or ill-qualified, who want it. The university's student-customers, after all, have rights too; and their rights to good teaching are surely more stringent than each member's right (if each has such a right) to an equal chance at the job. I think we do best to reserve the term "violation of a right" for cases in which a man is unjustly deprived of something he has a right to, and speak rather of "overriding a right" in cases in which, though a man is deprived of something he has a right to, it is not unjust to deprive him of it. So here the members' rights to an equal chance (if they have them) would be, not violated, but merely overridden.

It could of course be said that these principles hold only of benefits of a kind I pointed to earlier, and called "pure" benefits (such as apples and apple tarts), and that we should find some other, weaker, principle to cover "impure" benefits (such as jobs).

Or it could be said that a university job is not a benefit which is available for distribution amongst the community members—that although a university job is a benefit, it is, in light of the rights of the students, available for distribution only amongst those members of the community who are best qualified to hold it. And therefore that they alone have a right to an equal chance at it.

It is important to notice, however, that unless *some* such principle as I have set out is true of the publicly owned university, there is no real problem about preferential hiring in it. Unless the white male applicant who is turned away had a right that this should not be done, doing so is quite certainly not violating any of his rights. Perhaps being joint owner of the university (on the first model) or being joint participant in the Person which owns the university (on the second model), do not give him a right to an equal chance at the job; perhaps he is neither joint owner nor joint participant (some third model is preferable), and it is something else which gives him his right to an equal chance at the job. Or perhaps he hasn't a right to an equal chance at the job, but has instead some other right which is violated by declaring for the equally qualified black or woman straightway. It is here that it seems to me it emerges most clearly that opponents of preferential hiring are merely expressing a gut reaction against it: for they have not asked themselves precisely what right is in question, and what it issues from.

Perhaps there is lurking in the background some sense that everyone has a right to "equal treatment," and that it is this which is violated by preferential hiring. But what on earth right is this? Mary surely does not have to decide between Tom and Dick by toss of a coin, if what is in question is marrying. Nor even, as I said earlier, if what is in question is giving out apples, which she grew on her own land, on her own trees.

It could, of course, be argued that declaring for the black or woman straightway isn't a violation of the white male applicant's rights, but is all the same wrong, bad, something which ought not be done. As I said, it is perfectly consistent that one ought not do something which it is, nevertheless, no violation of anyone's rights to do. So perhaps opponents of preferential hiring might say that rights are not in question, and still argue against it on other grounds. I say they *might*, but I think they plainly do better not to. If the white male applicant has no rights which would be violated, and appointing the black or woman indirectly benefits other blacks or women (remember that need for role models), and thereby still more indirectly benefits us all (by widening the available pool of talent), then it is very hard to see how it could come out to be morally objectionable to declare for the black or woman straightway.

I think we should do the best we can for those who oppose preferential hiring: I think we should grant that the white male applicant has a right to an equal chance at the job, and see what happens for preferential hiring if we do. I shall simply leave open whether this right issues from considerations of the kind I drew attention to, and so also whether or not every member of the community, however well- or ill-qualified for the job, has the same right to an equal chance at it.

Now it is, I think, widely believed that we may, without injustice, refuse to grant a man what he has a right to only if *either* someone else has a conflicting and more stringent right, *or* there is some very great benefit to be obtained by doing so—perhaps that a disaster of some kind is thereby averted. If so, then there really is trouble for preferential hiring. For what more stringent right could be thought to override the right of the white male applicant for an equal chance? What great benefit obtained, what disaster averted, by declaring for the black or the woman straightway? I suggested that benefits are obtained, and they are not small ones. But are they large enough to override a right? If these questions cannot be satisfactorily answered, then it looks as if the hiring officer does act unjustly, and does violate the rights of the white males, if he declares for the black or woman straightway.

But in fact there are other ways in which a right may be overriden. Let's go back to that eating club again. Suppose that now it has happened that two of us arrive at the same time when there is only one available table; we think we had better decide on some policy for handling it when it happens. And suppose that we have of late had reason to be especially grateful to one of the members, whom I'll call Smith: Smith has done a series of very great favors for the club. It seems to me we might, out of gratitude to Smith, adopt the following policy: for the next six months, if two members arrive at the same time, and there is only one available table, then Smith gets in first, if he's one of the two; whereas if he's not, then the headwaiter shall toss a coin.

We might even vote that for the next year, if he wants apple tart, he gets more of it than the rest of us.

It seems to me that there would be no impropriety in our taking these actions—by which I mean to include that there would be no injustice in our taking them. Suppose another member, Jones, votes No. Suppose he says, "Look. I admit we all benefited from what Smith did for us. But still, I'm a member, and a member in as good standing as Smith is. So I have a right to an equal chance (and equal share), and I demand what I have a right to." I think we may rightly feel that Jones merely shows insensitivity: he does not adequately appreciate what Smith did for us. Jones, like all of us, has a right to an equal chance at such benefits as the club has available for distribution to the members; but there is no injustice in a majority's refusing to grant the members this equal chance, in the name of a debt of gratitude to Smith.

It is worth noticing an important difference between a debt of gratitude and debts owed to a creditor. Suppose the club had borrowed $1,000 from Dickenson, and then was left as a legacy a painting appraised at $1,000. If the club has no other saleable assets, and if no member is willing to buy the painting, then I take it that justice would precisely require *not* randomizing amongst the members who is to get that painting, but would instead require our offering it to Dickenson. Jones could not complain that to offer it to Dickenson is to treat him, Jones, unjustly: Dickenson has a right to be paid back, and that right is more stringent than any member's right to an equal chance at the painting. Now Smith, by contrast, did not have a right to be given anything, he did not have a right to our adopting a policy of preferential seating in his favor. If we fail to do anything for Dickenson, we do him an injustice; if we fail to do anything for Smith, we do *him* no injustice—our failing is, not injustice, but ingratitude. There is no harm in speaking of debts of gratitude and in saying that they are owed to a benefactor, by analogy with debts owed to a creditor; but it is important to remember that a creditor has, and a benefactor does not have, a right to repayment.

To move now from clubs to more serious matters, suppose two candidates for a civil service job have equally good test scores, but that there is only one job available. We could decide between them by cointossing. But in fact we do allow for declaring for A straightway, where A is a veteran, and B is not.[2] It may be that B is a nonveteran through no fault of his own: perhaps he was refused induction for flat feet, or a heart murmur. That is, those things in virtue of which B is a nonveteran may be things which it was no more in his power to control change than it is in anyone's power to control or change the color of his skin. Yet the fact is that B is not a veteran and A is. On the assumption that the veteran has served his country,[3] the country owes him something. And it seems plain that giving him preference is a not unjust way in which part of that debt of gratitude can be paid.

And now, finally, we should turn to those debts which are incurred by one who wrongs another. It is here we find what seems to me the most powerful argument for the conclusion that the preferential hiring of blacks and women is not unjust.

I obviously cannot claim any novelty for this argument: it's a very familiar one. Indeed, not merely is it familiar, but so are a battery of objections to it. It may be granted that if we have wronged A, we owe him something: we should make amends, we should compensate him for the wrong done him. It may even be granted that if we have wronged A, we must make amends, that justice requires it, and that a failure to make amends is not merely callousness, but injustice. But (a) are the young blacks and women who are amongst the current applicants for university jobs amongst the blacks and women who were wronged? To turn to particular cases, it might happen that the black applicant is middle class, son of professionals, and has had the very best in private schooling; or that the woman applicant is plainly the product of feminist upbringing and encouragement. Is it proper, much less required, that the black or woman be given preference over a white male who grew up in poverty, and has to make his own way and earn his encouragements? Again, (b), did we, the current members of the community, wrong any blacks or women? Lots of people once did; but then isn't it for them to do the compensating? That is, if they're still alive. For presumably nobody now alive owned any slaves, and perhaps nobody now alive voted against women's suffrage. And (c) what if the white male applicant for the job has never in any degree wronged any blacks or women? If so, *he* doesn't owe any debts to them, so why should *he* make amends to them?

These objections seem to me quite wrong-headed.

Obviously the situation for blacks and women is better than it was a hundred and fifty, fifty, twenty-five years ago. But it is absurd to suppose that the young blacks and women now of an age to apply for jobs have not been wronged. Large-scale, blatant, overt wrongs have presumably disappeared; but it is only within the last twenty-five years (perhaps the last ten years, in the case of women) that it has become at all widely agreed in this country that blacks and women must be recognized as having, not merely this or that particular right normally recognized as belonging to white males, but all of the rights and respect which go with full membership in the community. Even young blacks and women have lived through down-grading for being black or female: they have not merely not been given that very equal chance at the benefits generated by what the community owns which is so firmly insisted on for white males, they have not until lately even been felt to have a right to it.

And even those were not themselves down-graded for being black or female have suffered the consequences of the down-grading of other blacks and women: lack of self-confidence, and lack of self-respect. For where a community accepts that a person's being black, or being a woman, are right and proper grounds for denying that person full membership in the community, it can hardly be supposed that any but the most extraordinarily independent black or woman will escape self-doubt. All but the most extraordinarily independent of them have had to work harder—if only against self-doubt—than all but the most deprived white males, in the competition for a place amongst the best qualified.

If any black or woman has been unjustly deprived of what he or she has a right to, then of course justice does call for making amends. But what of the blacks and women who haven't actually been deprived of what they have a right to, but only made to suffer the consequences of injustice to other blacks and women? *Perhaps* justice doesn't require making amends to them as well; but common decency certainly does. To fail, at the very least, to make what counts as public apology to all, and to take positive steps to show that it is sincerely meant, is, if not injustice, then anyway a fault at least as serious as ingratitude.

Opting for a policy of preferential hiring may of course mean that some black or woman is preferred to some white male who as a matter of fact has had a harder life than the black or woman. But so may opting for a policy of veterans' preference mean that a healthy, unscarred, middle class veteran is preferred to a poor, struggling, scarred, nonveteran. Indeed, opting for a policy of settling who gets the job by having all equally qualified candidates draw straws may also mean that in a given case the candidate with the hardest life loses out. Opting for any policy other than hard-life preference may have this result.

I have no objection to anyone's arguing that it is precisely hard-life preference that we ought to opt for. If all, or anyway all of the equally qualified, have a right to an equal chance, then the argument would have to draw attention to something sufficiently powerful to override that right. But perhaps this could be done along the lines I followed in the case of blacks and women: perhaps it could be successfully argued that we have wronged those who have had hard lives, and therefore owe it to them to make amends. And then we should have in more extreme form a difficulty already present: how are these preferences to be ranked? shall we place the hard-lifers ahead of blacks? both ahead of women? and what about veterans? I leave these questions aside. My concern has been only to show that the white male applicant's right to an equal chance does not make it unjust to opt for a policy under which blacks and women are given preference. That a white male with a specially hard history may lose out under this policy cannot possibly be any objection to it, in the absence of a showing that hard-life preference is not unjust, and, more important, takes priority over preference for blacks and women.

Lastly, it should be stressed that to opt for such a policy is not to make the young white male applicants themselves make amends for any wrongs done to blacks and women. Under such a policy, no one is asked to give up a job which is already his; the job for which the white male competes isn't his, but is the community's, and it is the hiring officer who gives it to the black or woman in the community's name. Of course the white male is asked to give up his equal chance at the job. But that is not something he pays to the black or woman by way of making amends; it is something the community takes away from him in order that *it* may make amends.

Still, the community does impose a burden on him: it is able to make amends for its wrongs only by taking something away from him, something which, after all, we are supposing he has a right to. And why should *he* pay the cost of the community's amends-making?

If there were some appropriate way in which the community could make amends to its blacks and women, some way which did not require depriving anyone of anything he has a right to, then that would be the best course of action for it to take. Or if there were anyway some way in which the costs could be shared by everyone, and not imposed entirely on the young white male job applicants, then that would be, if not the best, then anyway better than opting for a policy of preferential hiring. But in fact the nature of the wrongs done is such as to make jobs the best and most suitable form of compensation. What blacks and women were denied was full membership in the community; and nothing can more appropriately make amends for that wrong than precisely what will make them feel they now finally have it. And that means jobs. Financial compensation (the cost of which could be shared equally) slips through the fingers; having a job, and discovering you do it well, yield—perhaps better than anything else—that very self-respect which blacks and women have had to do without.

But of course choosing this way of making amends means that the costs are imposed on the young white male applicants who are turned away. And so it should be noticed that it is not entirely inappropriate that those applicants should pay the costs. No doubt few, if any, have themselves, individually, done any wrongs to blacks and women. But they have profited from the wrongs the community did. Many may actually have been direct beneficiaries of policies which excluded or down-graded blacks and women—perhaps in school admissions, perhaps in access to financial aid, perhaps elsewhere; and even those who did not directly benefit in this way had, at any rate, the advantage in the competition which comes of confidence in one's full membership, and of one's rights being recognized as a matter of course.

Of course it isn't only the young white male applicant for a university job who has benefited from the exclusion of blacks and women; the older white male, now comfortably tenured, also benefited, and many defenders of preferential hiring feel that he should be asked to share the costs. Well, presumably we can't demand that he give up his job, or share it. But it seems to me in place to expect the occupants of comfortable professorial chairs to contribute in some way, to make some form of return to the young white male who bears the cost, and is turned away. It will have been plain that I find the outcry now heard against preferential hiring in the universities objectionable; it would also be objectionable that those of us who are now securely situated should placidly defend it, with no more than a sigh of regret for the young white male who pays for it.

IV

One final word: "discrimination." I am inclined to think we so use it that if anyone is convicted of discriminating against blacks, women, white males, or what have you, then he is thereby convicted of acting unjustly. If so, and if I am right in thinking that preferential hiring in the restricted range of cases we have been looking at is *not* unjust, then we have two options: (a) we can simply reply that to opt for a policy of preferential hiring in those cases is not to opt for a policy of discriminating against white males, or (b) we can hope to get usage changed—e.g., by trying to get people to allow that there is discriminating against and discriminating against, and that some is unjust, but some is not.

Best of all, however, would be for that phrase to be avoided altogether. It's at best a blunt tool: there are all sorts of nice moral discriminations [*sic*] which one is unable to make while occupied with it. And that bluntness itself fits it to do harm: blacks and women are hardly likely to see through to what precisely is owed them while they are being accused of welcoming what is unjust.

11

Preferential Hiring: A Reply To Judith Jarvis Thomson

Robert Simon

Judith Jarvis Thomson has recently defended preferential hiring of women and black persons in universities.[1] She restricts her defense of the assignment of preference to only those cases where candidates from preferred groups and their white male competitors are equally qualified, although she suggests that her argument can be extended to cover cases where the qualifications are unequal as well. The argument in question is compensatory; it is because of pervasive patterns of unjust discrimination against black persons and women that justice, or at least common decency, requires that amends be made.

While Thomson's analysis surely clarifies many of the issues at stake, I find it seriously incomplete. I will argue that even if her claim that compensation is due victims of social injustice is correct (as I think it is), it is questionable nevertheless whether preferential hiring is an acceptable method of distributing such compensation. This is so, even if, as Thomson argues, compensatory claims override the right of the white male applicant to equal consideration from the appointing officer. For implementation of preferential hiring policies may involve claims, perhaps even claims of right, other than the above right of the white male applicant. In the case of the claims I have in mind, the best that can be said is that where preferential hiring is concerned, they are arbitrarily ignored. If so, and if such

Reprinted from *Philosophy and Public Affairs* 3 (1974). Copyright © 1974 by Princeton University Press. Reprinted by permission of Princeton University Press.

claims are themselves warranted, then preferential hiring, while *perhaps* not unjust, is open to far more serious question than Thomson acknowledges.

I

A familiar objection to special treatment for blacks and women is that, if such a practice is justified, other victims of injustice or misfortune ought to receive special treatment too. While arguing that virtually all women and black persons have been harmed, either directly or indirectly, by discrimination, Thomson acknowledges that in any particular case, a white male may have been victimized to a greater extent than have the blacks or women with which he is competing. However, she denies that other victims of injustice or misfortune ought automatically to have priority over blacks and women where distribution of compensation is concerned. Just as veterans receive preference with respect to employment in the civil service, as payment for the service they have performed for society, so can blacks and women legitimately be given preference in university hiring, in payment of the debt owed them. And just as the former policy can justify hiring a veteran who in fact had an easy time of it over a non-veteran who made great sacrifices for the public good, so too can the latter policy justify hiring a relatively undeprived member of a preferred group over a more disadvantaged member of a nonpreferred group.

But surely if the reason for giving a particular veteran preference is that he performed a service for his country, that same preference must be given to anyone who performed a similar service. Likewise, if the reason for giving preference to a black person or to a woman is that the recipient has been injured due to an unjust practice, then preference must be given to anyone who has been similarly injured. So, it appears, there can be no relevant *group* to which compensation ought to be made, other than that made up of and only of those who have been injured or victimized.[2] Although, as Thomson claims, all blacks and women may be members of that latter group, they deserve compensation *qua* victim and not *qua* black person or woman.

There are at least two possible replies that can be made to this sort of objection. First, it might be agreed that anyone injured in the same way as blacks or women ought to receive compensation. But then, "same way" is characterized so narrowly that it applies to no one except blacks and women. While there is nothing logically objectionable about such a reply, it may nevertheless be morally objectionable. For it implies that a nonblack male who has been terribly injured by a social injustice has less of a claim to compensation than a black or woman who has only been minimally injured. And this implication may be morally unacceptable.

A more plausible line of response may involve shifting our attention from compensation of individuals to collective compensation of groups.[3] Once this shift is made, it can be acknowledged that as individuals, some white males may have stronger compensatory claims than blacks or women. But as compensation is owed the group, it is group claims that must be weighed, not individual ones. And surely, at the group level, the claims of black persons and women to compensation are among the strongest there are.

Suppose we grant that certain groups, including those specified by Thomson, are owed collective compensation. What should be noted is that the conclusion of concern here—that preferential hiring policies are acceptable instruments for compensating groups—does not directly follow. To derive such a conclusion validly, one would have to provide additional premises specifying the relation between collective compensation to groups and distribution of that compensation to individual members. For it does not follow from the fact that some group members are compensated that the group is compensated. Thus, if through a computer error, every member of the American Philosophical Association was asked to pay additional taxes, then if the government provided compensation for this error, it would not follow that it had compensated the Association. Rather, it would have compensated each member *qua* individual. So what is required, where preferential hiring is concerned, are plausible premises showing how the preferential award of jobs to group members counts as collective compensation for the group.

Thomson provides no such additional premises. Moreover, there is good reason to think that if any such premises were provided, they would count against preferential hiring as an instrument of collective compensation. This is because although compensation is owed to the group, preferential hiring policies award compensation to an arbitrarily selected segment of the group; namely, those who have the ability and qualifications to be seriously considered for the jobs available. Surely, it is far more plausible to think that collective compensation ought to be equally available to all group members, or at least to all kinds of group members.[4] The claim that although compensation is owed collectively to a group, only a special sort of group member is eligible to receive it, while perhaps not incoherent certainly ought to be rejected as arbitrary, at least in the absence of an argument to the contrary.

Accordingly, the proponent of preferential hiring faces the following dilemma. Either compensation is to be made on an individual basis, in which case the fact that one is black or a woman is irrelevant to whether one ought to receive special treatment, or it is made on a group basis, in which case it is far from clear that preferential hiring policies are acceptable compensatory instruments. Until this dilemma is resolved, assuming it can be resolved at all, the compensatory argument for preferential hiring is seriously incomplete at a crucial point.

II

Even if the above difficulty could be resolved, however, other problems remain. For example, once those entitled to compensatory benefits have been identified, questions arise concerning how satisfactorily preferential hiring policies honor such entitlements.

Consider, for example, a plausible principle of compensatory justice which might be called the Proportionality Principle (PP). According to the PP, the strength of one's compensatory claim, and the quantity of compensation one is entitled to is, *ceteris paribus*, proportional to the degree of injury suffered. A corollary of the PP is that equal injury gives rise to compensatory claims of equal strength. Thus, if X and Y were both injured to the same extent, and both deserve compensation for their injury, then, *ceteris paribus*, each has a compensatory claim of equal strength and each is entitled to equal compensation.

Now, it is extremely unlikely that a hiring program which gives preference to blacks and women will satisfy the PP because of the arbitrariness implicit in the search for candidates on the open market. Thus, three candidates, each members of previously victimized groups, may well wind up with highly disparate positions. One may secure employment in a prestigious department of a leading university while another may be hired by a university which hardly merits the name. The third might not be hired at all.

The point is that where the market place is used to distribute compensation, distribution will be by market principles, and hence only accidentally will be fitting in view of the injury suffered and compensation provided for others. While any compensation may be better than none, this would hardly appear to be a satisfactory way of making amends to the victimized.

"Compensation according to ability" or "compensation according to marketability" surely are dubious principles of compensatory justice. On the contrary, those with the strongest compensatory claims should be compensated first (and most). Where compensatory claims are equal, but not everybody can actually be compensated, some fair method of distribution should be employed, e.g., a lottery. Preferential hiring policies, then, to the extent that they violate the PP, *arbitrarily* discriminate in favor of some victims of past injustice and against others. The basis on which compensation is awarded is independent of the basis on which it is owed, and so distribution is determined by application of principles which are irrelevant from the point of view of compensatory justice.

Now, perhaps this is not enough to show that the use of preferential hiring as a compensatory instrument is unjust, or even unjustified. But perhaps it is enough to show that the case for the justice or justification of such a policy has not yet been made. Surely, we can say, at the very least, that a policy which discriminates in the arbitrary fashion discussed above is not a particularly satisfactory compensatory mechanism. If so, the direction in which considerations of compensatory justice and common decency point may be far less apparent than Thomson suggests.

III

So far, I have considered arbitrariness in the distribution of compensatory benefits by preferential hiring policies. However, arbitrariness involved in the assessment of costs is also of concern.

Thus, it is sometimes argued that preferential hiring policies place the burden of providing compensation on young white males who are just entering the job market. This is held to be unfair, because, first, there is no special reason for placing the burden on that particular group and, second, because many members of that group are not responsible for the injury done to blacks and women. In response to the first point, Thomson acknowledges that it seems to her "in place to expect the occupants of comfortable professorial chairs to contribute in some way, to make some form of return to the young white male who bears the cost" (p. 384 [61]). In response to the second point, Thomson concedes that few, if any, white male applicants to university positions individually have done any wrong to women or black persons. However, she continues, many have profited by the wrongs inflicted by others. So it is not unfitting that they be asked to make sacrifices now.

However, it is far from clear, at least to me, that this reply is satisfactory. For even if the group which bears the cost is expanded to include full professors, why should that new group be singled out? The very same consideration that required the original expansion would seem to require a still wider one. Indeed, it would seem this point can be pressed until costs are assessed against society as a whole. This is exactly the position taken by Paul Taylor, who writes, "The obligation to offer such benefits to (the previously victimized) group ... is an obligation that falls on society in general, not on any particular person. For it is the society in general, that through its established (discriminatory) social practice, brought upon itself the obligation."[5]

Perhaps, however, the claim that preferential hiring policies arbitrarily distribute burdens can be rebutted. For presumably the advocate of preferential hiring does not want to restrict such a practice to universities but rather would wish it to apply throughout society. If so, and *if* persons at the upper echelons are expected to share costs with young white male job applicants, then perhaps a case can be made that burdens are equitably distributed throughout society.

Even here, however, there are two points an opponent of preferential hiring can make. First, he can point out that burdens are not equitably distributed now. Consequently, to the extent that preferential policies are employed at present, then to that extent are burdens arbitrarily imposed now. Second, he can question the assumption that if someone gains from an unjust practice for which he is not responsible and even opposes, the gain is not really his and can be taken from him without injustice. This assumption is central to the compensatory argument for preferential hiring since if it is unacceptable, no justification remains for requiring "innocent bystanders" to provide compensation.

If X benefits at the expense of Y because of the operation of an unjust social institution, then is the benefit which accrues to X really deserved by Y? It seems to me that normally the answer will be affirmative. But it also seems to me that there is a significant class of cases where an affirmative response *may* not be justified. Suppose X himself is the victim of a similarly unjust social practice so that Z benefits at his expense. In such circumstances, it is questionable whether X ought to compensate Y, especially if X played no personal role in the formation of the unjust institutions at issue. Perhaps *both* X and Y ought to receive (different degrees of) compensation from Z.

If this point is sound, it becomes questionable whether *all* members of nonpreferred groups are equally liable (or even liable at all) for provision of compensation. It is especially questionable in the case where the individual from the nonpreferred group has been unjustly victimized to a far greater extent than the individual from the preferred group. Hence, even if it were true that all members of non-preferred groups have profited from discrimination against members of preferred groups, it does not automatically follow that all are equally liable for providing compensation. In so far as preferential hiring policies do not take this into account, they are open to the charge of arbitrariness in assessing the costs of compensation.

One more point seems to require mention here. If preferential hiring policies are expanded, as Thomson suggests, to cases where the candidates are not equally qualified, a further difficulty arises. To the extent that lowering quality lowers efficiency, members of victimized groups are likely to lose more than others. This may be particularly important in educational contexts. Students from such groups may have been exposed to poorer instruction than was made available to others. But they might have greater need for better instruction than, say, middle class students from affluent backgrounds.[6]

Suppose that members of previously discriminated against groups deserve special support in developing their capacities and talents. Then, it would seem that educational institutions charged with promoting such development have a corresponding obligation to develop those capacities and talents to the best of their ability. Presumably, this requires hiring the best available faculty and administration.

What we seem to have here is a conflict within the framework of compensatory justice itself. Even if preferential hiring is an acceptable method for distributing compensation, the compensation so distributed may decrease the beneficial effects of education. And this may adversely affect more members of the preferred groups than are helped by the preferential policy.[7]

IV

The argument of this paper is not directed against the view that victims of grave social injustice in America deserve compensation. On the contrary, a strong case can be made for providing such compensation.[8] Rather, I have tried to show that the case for using preferential hiring as a *means* of providing such compensation is incomplete at three crucial points:

(1) It is not clear to whom compensation should be made, groups or individuals. If the former, it has not been shown that preferential hiring compensates the group. If the latter, it has not been shown why membership in a group (other than that composed of, and only of, the victimized) is relevant to determining who should be compensated.

(2) It has not been shown that compensation should be awarded on grounds of marketability, grounds that certainly seem to be irrelevant from the compensatory point of view.

(3) It has not been shown that arbitrariness and inequity are or can be avoided in distributing the costs of preferential hiring policies of the sort in question.

If these charges have force, then whether or not preferential hiring can be justified on other grounds, the compensatory argument for such a practice is far more doubtful than Thomson's article suggests.

12

Justifying Reverse Discrimination in Employment

George Sher

A currently favored way of compensating for past discrimination is to afford preferential treatment to the members of those groups which have been discriminated against in the past. I propose to examine the rationale behind this practice when it is applied in the area of employment. I want to ask whether, and if so under what conditions, past acts of discrimination against members of a particular group justify the current hiring of a member of that group who is less than the best qualified applicant for a given job. Since I am mainly concerned about exploring the relations between past discrimination and present claims to employment, I shall make the assumption that each applicant is at least minimally competent to perform the job he seeks; this will eliminate the need to consider the claims of those who are to receive the services in question. Whether it is ever justifiable to discriminate in favor of an incompetent applicant, or a less than best qualified applicant for a job such as teaching, in which almost any increase in employee competence brings a real increase in services rendered, will be left to be decided elsewhere. Such questions, which turn on balancing the claim of the less than best qualified applicant against the competing claims of those who are to receive his services, are not as basic as the question of whether the less than best qualified applicant ever *has* a claim to employment.[1]

Reprinted from *Philosophy and Public Affairs* 4 (1975). Copyright © 1975 by Princeton University Press. Reprinted by permission of Princeton University Press.

I

It is sometimes argued, when members of a particular group have been barred from employment of a certain kind, that since this group has in the past received *less* than its fair share of the employment in question, it now deserves to receive *more* by way of compensation.[2] This argument, if sound, has the virtue of showing clearly why preferential treatment should be extended even to those current group members who have not themselves been denied employment: if the point of reverse discrimination is to compensate a wronged *group*, it will presumably hardly matter if those who are preferentially hired were not among the original victims of discrimination. However, the argument's basic presupposition, that groups as opposed to their individual members are the sorts of entities that can be wronged and deserve redress, is itself problematic.[3] Thus the defense of reverse discrimination would only be convincing if it were backed by a further argument showing that groups can indeed be wronged and have deserts of the relevant sort. No one, as far as I know, has yet produced a powerful argument to this effect, and I am not hopeful about the possibilities. Therefore I shall not try to develop a defense of reverse discrimination along these lines.

Another possible way of connecting past acts of discrimination in hiring with the claims of current group members is to argue that even if these current group members have not (yet) been denied *employment*, their membership in the group makes it very likely that they have been discriminatorily deprived of *other* sorts of goods. It is a commonplace, after all, that people who are forced to do menial and low-paying jobs must often endure corresponding privations in housing, diet, and other areas. These privations are apt to be distributed among young and old alike, and so to afflict even those group members who are still too young to have had their qualifications for employment bypassed. It is, moreover, generally acknowledged by both common sense and law that a person who has been deprived of a certain amount of one sort of good may sometimes reasonably be compensated by an equivalent amount of a good of another sort. (It is this principle, surely, that underlies the legal practice of awarding sums of money to compensate for pain incurred in accidents, damaged reputations, etc.) Given these facts and this principle, it appears that the preferential hiring of current members of discriminated-against groups may be justified as compensation for the *other* sorts of discrimination these individuals are apt to have suffered.[4]

But, although this argument seems more promising than one presupposing group deserts, it surely cannot be accepted as it stands. For one thing, insofar as the point is simply to compensate individuals for the various sorts of privations they have suffered, there is no special reason to use reverse discrimination rather than some other mechanism to effect compensation. There are, moreover, certain other mechanisms of redress which seem prima facie preferable. It seems, for instance, that it would be most appropriate to compensate for past privations simply by making preferentially available to the discriminated-against individuals equivalent amounts of the very same sorts of goods of which they have been deprived; simple cash settlements would allow a far greater precision in the adjustment of compensation to privation than reverse discriminatory hiring ever could. Insofar as it does not provide any reason to adopt reverse discrimination rather than these prima facie preferable mechanisms of redress, the suggested defense of reverse discrimination is at least incomplete.

Moreover, and even more important, if reverse discrimination is viewed simply as a form of compensation for past privations, there are serious questions about its fairness. Certainly the privations to be compensated for are not the sole responsibility of those individuals whose superior qualifications will have to be bypassed in the reverse discriminatory process. These individuals, if responsible for those privations at all, will at least be no more responsible than others with relevantly similar histories. Yet reverse discrimination will compensate for the privations in question at the expense of these individuals alone. It will have no effect at all upon those other, equally responsible persons whose qualifications are inferior to begin with, who are already entrenched in their jobs, or whose vocations are noncompetitive in nature. Surely it is unfair to distribute the burden of compensation so unequally.[5]

These considerations show, I think, that reverse discriminatory hiring of members of groups that have been denied jobs in the past cannot be justified simply by the fact that each group member has been discriminated against in other areas. If this fact is to enter into the justification of reverse discrimination at all, it must be in some more complicated way.

II

Consider again the sorts of privations that are apt to be distributed among the members of those groups restricted in large part to menial and low-paying jobs. These individuals, we said, are apt to live in substandard homes, to subsist on improper and imbalanced diets, and to receive inadequate educations. Now, it is certainly true that adequate housing, food, and education are goods in and of themselves; a life without them is certainly less pleasant and less full than one with them. But, and crucially, they are also goods in a different sense entirely. It is an obvious and well-documented fact that (at least) the sorts of nourishment and education a person receives as a child will causally affect the sorts of skills and capacities he will have as an adult—including, of course, the very skills which are needed if he is to compete on equal terms for jobs and other goods. Since this is so, a child who is deprived of adequate food and education may lose not only the immediate enjoyments which a comfortable and stimulating environment bring but also the subsequent ability to compete equally for other things of intrinsic value. But to lose this ability to compete is, in essence, to lose one's access to the goods that are being competed for; and this, surely, is itself a privation to be compensated for if possible. It is, I think, the key to an adequate justification of reverse discrimination to see that practice, not as the redressing of *past* privations, but rather as a way of neutralizing the *present* competitive disadvantage *caused* by those past privations and thus as a way of restoring equal access to those goods which society distributes competitively.[6] When reverse discrimination is justified in this way, many of the difficulties besetting the simpler justification of it disappear.

For whenever someone has been irrevocably deprived of a certain good and there are several alternative ways of providing him with an equivalent amount of another good, it will ceteris paribus be preferable to choose whichever substitute comes closest to actually replacing the lost good. It is this principle that makes preferential access to decent housing, food, and education especially desirable as a way of compensating for the experiential impoverishment of a deprived childhood. If, however, we are concerned to compensate not for the experiential poverty, but for the effects of childhood deprivations, then this principle tells just as heavily for reverse discrimination as the proper form of compensation. If the lost good is just the *ability* to compete on equal terms for first-level goods like desirable jobs, then surely the most appropriate (and so preferable) way of substituting for what has been lost is just to remove the *necessity* of competing on equal terms for these goods—which, of course, is precisely what reverse discrimination does.

When reverse discrimination is viewed as compensation for lost ability to compete on equal terms, a reasonable case can also be made for its fairness. Our doubts about its fairness arose because it seemed to place the entire burden of redress upon those individuals whose superior qualifications are bypassed in the reverse discriminatory process. This seemed wrong because these individuals are, of course, not apt to be any more responsible for past discrimination than others with relevantly similar histories. But, as we are now in a position to see, this objection misses the point. The crucial fact about these individuals is not that they are more *responsible* for past discrimination than others with relevantly similar histories (in fact, the dirty work may well have been done before any of their generation attained the age of responsibility), but rather that unless reverse discrimination is practiced, they will *benefit* more than the others from its effects on their competitors. They will benefit more because unless they are restrained, they, but not the others, will use their competitive edge to claim jobs which their competitors would otherwise have gotten. Thus, it is only because they stand to *gain* the most from the relevant effects of the *original* discrimination, that the bypassed individuals stand to *lose* the most from *reverse* discrimination.[7] This is surely a valid reply to the charge that reverse discrimination does not distribute the burden of compensation equally.

III

So far, the argument has been that reverse discrimination is justified insofar as it neutralizes competitive disadvantages caused by past privations. This may be correct, but it is also oversimplified. In actuality, there are many ways in which a person's environment may affect his ability to compete; and there may well be logical differences among these ways which affect the degree to which reverse discrimination is called for. Consider, for example, the following cases:

(1) An inadequate education prevents someone from acquiring the degree of a certain skill that he would have been able to acquire with a better education.

(2) An inadequate diet, lack of early intellectual stimulation, etc., lower an individual's ability, and thus prevent him from acquiring the degree of competence in a skill that he would otherwise have been able to acquire.

(3) The likelihood that he will not be able to use a certain skill because he belongs to a group which has been discriminated against in the past leads a person to decide, rationally, not even to try developing that skill.

(4) Some aspect of his childhood environment renders an individual incapable of putting forth the sustained effort needed to improve his skills.

These are four different ways in which past privations might adversely affect a person's skills. Ignoring for analytical purposes the fact that privation often works in more than one of these ways at a time, shall we say that reverse discrimination is equally called for in each case?

It might seem that we should say it is, since in each case a difference in the individual's environment would have been accompanied by an increase in his mastery of a certain skill (and, hence, by an improvement in his competitive position with respect to jobs requiring that skill). But this blanket counterfactual formulation conceals several important distinctions. For one thing, it suggests (and our justification of reverse discrimination seems to require) the possibility of giving *just enough* preferential treatment of the disadvantaged individual in each case to restore to him the competitive position that he would have had, had he not suffered his initial disadvantage. But in fact, this does not seem to be equally possible in all cases. We can roughly calculate the difference that a certain improvement in education or intellectual stimulation would have made in the development of a person's skills if his efforts had been held constant (cases 1 and 2); for achievement is known to be a relatively straightforward compositional function of ability, environmental factors, and effort. We cannot, however, calculate in the same way the difference that improved prospects or environment would have made in degree of *effort* expended; for although effort is affected by environmental factors, it is not a known compositional function of them (or of anything else). Because of this, there would be no way for us to decide how much preferential treatment is just enough to make up for the efforts that a particular disadvantaged individual would have made under happier circumstances.

There is also another problem with (3) and (4). Even if there were a way to afford a disadvantaged person just enough preferential treatment to make up for the efforts he was prevented from making by his environment, it is not clear that he *ought* to be afforded that much preferential treatment. To allow this, after all, would be to concede that the effort he *would* have made under other conditions is worth just as much as the effort that his rival actually *did* make; and this, I think, is implausible. Surely a person who *actually has* labored long and hard to achieve a given degree of a certain skill is more deserving of a job requiring that skill than another who is equal in all other relevant respects, but who merely *would* have worked and achieved the same amount under different conditions. Because actual effort creates desert in a way that merely possible effort does not, reverse discrimination to restore precisely the competitive position that a person would have had if he had not been prevented from working harder would not be desirable even if it were possible.

There is perhaps also a further distinction to be made here. A person who is rationally persuaded by an absence of opportunities not to develop a certain skill (case 3) will typically not undergo any sort of character transformation in the process of making this decision. He will be the same person after his decision as before it, and, most often, the same person without his skill as with it. In cases such as (4), this is less clear. A person who is rendered incapable of effort by his environment does in a sense undergo a character transformation; to become truly incapable of sustained effort is to become a different (and less meritorious) person from the person one would otherwise have been. Because of this (and somewhat paradoxically, since his character change is itself apt to stem from factors beyond his control), such an individual may have less of a claim to reverse discrimination than one whose lack of effort does not flow from even an environmentally induced character fault, but rather from a justified rational decision.[8]

IV

When reverse discrimination is discussed in a nontheoretical context, it is usually assumed that the people most deserving of such treatment are blacks, members of other ethnic minorities, and women. In this last section, I shall bring the results of the foregoing discussion to bear on this assumption. Doubts will be raised both about the analogy between the claims of blacks and women to reverse discrimination and about the propriety, in absolute terms, of singling out either group as the proper recipient of such treatment.

For many people, the analogy between the claims of blacks and the claims of women to reverse discrimination rests simply upon the undoubted fact that both groups have been discriminatorily denied jobs in the past. But on the account just proposed, past discrimination justifies reverse discrimination only insofar as it has adversely affected the competitive position of present group members. When this standard is invoked, the analogy between the claims of blacks and those of women seems immediately to break down. The exclusion of blacks from good jobs in the past has been only one element in an interlocking pattern of exclusions and often has resulted in a poverty issuing in (and in turn reinforced by) such other privations as inadequate nourishment, housing, and health care, lack of time to provide adequate guidance and intellectual stimulation for the young, dependence on (often inadequate) public education, etc. It is this whole complex of privations that undermines the ability of the young to compete; and it is largely because of its central causal role in this complex that the past unavailability of good jobs for blacks justifies reverse discrimination in their favor now. In the case of women, past discrimination in employment simply has not played the same role. Because children commonly come equipped with both male *and* female parents, the inability of the female parent to get a good job need not, and usually does not, result in a poverty detracting from the quality of the nourishment, education, housing, health, or intellectual stimulation of the female child (and, of course, when such poverty does result, it affects male and female children indifferently). For this reason, the past inaccessibility of good jobs for women does not seem to create for them the same sort of claim on reverse discrimination that its counterpart does for blacks.

Many defenders of reverse discrimination in favor of women would reply at this point that although past discrimination in employment has of course not played the *same* causal role in the case of women which it has in the case of blacks, it has nevertheless played *a* causal role in both cases. In the case of women, the argument runs, that role has been mainly psychological: past discrimination in hiring has led to a scarcity of female "role-models" of suitably high achievement. This lack, together with a culture which in many other ways subtly inculcates the idea that women should not or cannot do the jobs that men do, has in turn made women psychologically less able to do these jobs. This argument is hard to assess fully, since it obviously rests on a complex and problematic psychological claim.[9] The following objections, however, are surely relevant. First, even if it is granted without question that cultural bias and absence of suitable role-models do have some direct and pervasive effect upon women, it is not clear that this effect must take the form of a reduction of women's *abilities* to do the jobs men do. A more likely outcome would seem to be a reduction of women's *inclinations* to do these jobs—a result whose proper compensation is not preferential treatment of those women who have sought the jobs in question, but rather the encouragement of others to seek those jobs as well. Of course, this disinclination to do these jobs may in turn lead some women not to develop the relevant skills; to the extent that this occurs, the competitive position of these women will indeed be affected, albeit indirectly, by the scarcity of female role models. Even here, however, the resulting disadvantage will not be comparable to those commonly produced by the poverty syndrome. It will flow solely from lack of effort, and so will be of the sort (cases 3 and 4) that neither calls for nor admits of full equalization by reverse discrimination. Moreover, and conclusively, since there is surely the same dearth of role-models, etc., for blacks as for women, whatever psychological disadvantages accrue to women because of this will beset blacks as well. Since blacks, but not women, must also suffer the privations associated with poverty, it follows that they are the group more deserving of reverse discrimination.

Strictly speaking, however, the account offered here does not allow us to speak this way of *either* group. If the point of reverse discrimination is to compensate for competitive disadvantages caused by past discrimination, it will be justified in favor of only those group members whose abilities have actually been reduced; and it would be most implausible to suppose that *every* black (or *every* woman) has been affected in this way. Blacks from middle-class or affluent backgrounds will surely have escaped many, if not all, of the competitive handicaps besetting those raised under less fortunate circumstances; and if they have, our account provides no reason to practice reverse discrimination in their favor. Again, whites from impoverished backgrounds may suffer many, if not all, of the competitive handicaps besetting their black counterparts; and if they do, the account provides no reason *not* to practice reverse discrimination in their favor. Generally, the proposed account allows us to view racial (and sexual) boundaries only as roughly suggesting which individuals are likely to have been disadvantaged by past discrimination. Anyone who construes these boundaries as playing a different and more decisive role must show us that a different defense of reverse discrimination is plausible.

13

Preferential Hiring and Compensation

Robert K. Fullinwider

> If a man shall steal an ox, or a sheep, and kill it,
> or sell it; he shall restore five oxen for an ox, and
> four sheep for a sheep.
>
> ———Exodus 22

Persons have rights; but sometimes a right may justifiably be overridden. Can we concede to all job applicants a right to equal consideration, and yet support a policy of preferentially hiring female over white male applicants?

Judith Thomson, in her article "Preferential Hiring,"[1] appeals to the principle of compensation as a ground which justifies us in sometimes overriding a person's rights. She applies this principle to a case of preferential hiring of a woman in order to defend the claim that such preferential hiring is not unjust. Her defense rests upon the contention that a debt of compensation is owed to women, and that the existence of this debt provides us with a justification of preferential hiring of women in certain cases even though this involves setting aside or overriding certain rights of white male applicants.

Although she is correct in believing that the right to compensation sometimes allows us or requires us to override or limit other rights, I shall argue that Thomson has failed to show that the principle of compensation

Reprinted from *Social Theory and Practice* 3 (1975), by permission of the journal and the author.

justifies preferential hiring in the case she constructs. Thus, by implication, I argue that she has failed to show that preferential hiring of women in such cases is not unjust. I proceed by setting out Thomson's argument, by identifying the crucial premise. I then show that Thomson fails to defend the premise, and that, given her statement of the principle of compensation, the premise is implausible.

2. Thomson's Case

Thomson asks us to imagine the following case. Suppose for some academic job a white male applicant (WMA) and a female applicant (FA) are under final consideration.[2] Suppose further that we grant that WMA and FA each have a *right to equal consideration* by the university's hiring officer. This means that each has a right to be evaluated for the job solely in terms of his or her possession of job related qualifications. Suppose, finally, that the hiring officer hires FA because she is a woman. How can the hiring officer's choice avoid being unjust?

Since being a woman is, by hypothesis, not a job related qualification in this instance, the hiring officer's act of choosing FA because she is a woman seems to violate WMA's right to equal consideration. The hiring officer's act would not be unjust only if in this situation there is some sufficient moral ground for setting aside or overriding WMA's right.

Consider, Thomson asks us, "those debts which are incurred by one who wrongs another. *It is here that we find what seems to me the most powerful argument for the conclusion that preferential hiring of women is not unjust*" (emphasis added).[3] We are promised that the basis for justly overriding WMA's acknowledged right is to be found in the principle of compensation. But, at this crucial point in her paper, Thomson stops short of setting out the actual derivation of her conclusion from the application of the principle of compensation to her imagined case. The reader is left to construct the various steps in the argument. From remarks Thomson makes in dealing with some objections to preferential hiring, I offer the following as a fair construction of the argument she intends.

Women, as a group, are owed a debt of compensation. Historically women, because they were women, have been subject to extensive and damaging discrimination, socially approved and legally supported. The discriminatory practices have served to limit the opportunities for fulfillment open to women and have disadvantaged them in the competition for many social benefits. Since women have been the victims of injustice, they have a moral right to be compensated for the wrongs done to them.

The compensation is owed by the community. The community as a whole is responsible, since the discriminatory practices against women have not been limited to isolated, private actions. These practices have been widespread, and public as well as private. Nowhere does Thomson argue that the case for preferring FA over WMA lies in a debt to FA directly incurred by WMA. In fact, Thomson never makes an effort to show any direct connection between FA and WMA. The moral relationship upon which Thomson's argument must rely exists between women and the community. The sacrifice on WMA's part is exacted from him by the community so it may pay its debt to women. This is a crucial feature of Thomson's case, and creates the need for the next premise: The right to compensation on the part of women justifies the community in overriding WMA's right to equal consideration. This premise is necessary to the argument. If the setting aside of WMA's right is to be justified by appeal to the principle of compensation, and the debt of compensation exists between the community and women, then something like the fourth premise is required to gain the application of the principle of compensation to WMA. This premise grounds the justness of WMA's sacrifice in the community's debt.

In short, Thomson's argument contains the following premises:

1. Women, as a group, are owed a debt of compensation.
2. The compensation is owed to women by the community.
3. The community exacts a sacrifice from WMA (i.e., sets aside his right to equal consideration) in order to pay its debt.[4]
4. The right to compensation on the part of women against the community justifies the community in setting aside WMA's right.

If we assume that the community may legitimately discharge its debt to women by making payments to *individual women*, then from premises 1–4 the conclusion may be drawn that WMA's right to equal consideration may be overridden in order to prefer FA, and, hence, that it is not unjust for the hiring officer to choose FA because she is a woman.

I shall not quarrel with premises 1–3, nor with the assumption that *groups* can be wronged and have rights.[5] My quarrel here is with premise 4. I shall show that Thomson offers no support for 4, and that it does not involve a correct application of the principle of compensation as used by Thomson. I will examine the case for premise 4 in section 4. In the next section I pause to look at Thomson's statement of the principle of compensation.

3. The Principle of Compensation

In the passage quoted earlier, Thomson speaks of those debts incurred by one who wrongs another. These are the debts of compensation. Using

Thomson's own language, we may formulate the principle of compensation as the declaration that *he who wrongs another owes the other.*[6] The principle of compensation tells us that, for some person B, B's act of wronging some person A creates a special moral relationship between A and B. The relationship is a species of the relationship of *being indebted to.* In the case of compensation, the indebtedness arises as a result of a wrongdoing, and involves the wrongdoer owing the wronged. To say that B owes something to A is to say that B's liberty of action with respect to what is owed is limited. B is under an obligation to yield to A what he owes him, and A has a right to it.[7] *What* B must yield will be a matter of the kind of wrong he has done A, and the optional means of compensation open to him. Thus, it is clearly the case that debts of compensation are grounds for limiting or overriding rights. But our being owed compensation by someone, though giving us some purchase on his liberty, does not give us carte blanche in limiting his rights. The debt is limited to what makes good our loss (restores our right), and is limited to us, his victims.

It might be that, for some reason, WMA directly owes FA compensation. If so, it would immediately follow that FA has a moral claim against WMA which limits WMA's liberty with respect to what he owes her. Furthermore, the nature of WMA's wrong may be such as to require a form of compensation interfering with the particular right we are focusing on—his right to equal consideration. Suppose the wrong done by WMA involved his depriving FA of fair opportunities for employment. Such a wrong might be the basis for requiring WMA, in compensation, to forego his right to equal consideration if he and FA were in direct competition for some job. This case would conform precisely to the model of Thomson's stated principle of compensation.

Thomson makes no effort to show that WMA has interfered with FA's chances at employment, or done her any other harm. She claims that it is "wrongheaded" to dwell upon the question of whether WMA has wronged FA or any other woman.[8] As we have already seen, Thomson maintains that the relevant moral relationship exists between *women* and the *community*. Consequently, the full weight of her argument rests on premise 4, and I now turn to it.

4. Applying the Principle of Compensation to Groups

Thomson asserts that there is a relationship of indebtedness between the community and women. Yet it is the overriding of WMA's right which is purportedly justified by this fact. The sacrifice imposed upon WMA is not due to his directly owing FA. The community owes FA (as a woman), and exacts the sacrifice from WMA in order that *it* may pay its debt. This is supposed to be justified by premise 4.

May the community take *any* act it sees fit in order to pay its debts?[9] This question goes to the heart of Thomson's case: what support is there for her premise 4? What is the connection between the community's liability to women (or FA), and WMA's membership in the community? Can we find in the fact that the community owes something to women a moral justification for overriding WMA's right? In this section I explore two attempts to provide a positive answer to this last question. These are not Thomson's attempts; I consider her own words in the next section.

First, one might attempt to justify the imposition of a sacrifice on WMA by appeal to distributive liability. It might be urged that since the community owes FA, then every member of the community owes FA and thus WMA owes FA. This defense of premise 4 is unconvincing. While it is true that if the community owes FA then its members collectively owe FA, it does not follow that they distributively owe FA. It is not the case that, as a general rule, distributive liability holds between organized groups and their members.[10] What reason is there to suppose it does in this case?

Though this attempt to defend premise 4 is unsatisfactory, it is easy to see why it would be very appealing. Even though the indebtedness is established, in the first instance, between the community and FA, if distributive liability obtained we could derive a debt WMA owed to FA, a debt that arose as a result of the application of the principle of compensation to the community. In imposing a sacrifice on WMA, the community would be enforcing *his* (derived) obligation to FA.

Second, imagine a 36 hole, 2 round, golf tournament among FA, WMA, and a third party, sanctioned and governed by a tournament organizing committee. In previous years FA switched to a new model club, which improved her game. Before the match the third player surreptitiously substitutes for FA's clubs a set of the old type. This is discovered after 18 holes have been played. If we suppose that the match cannot be restarted or cancelled, then the committee is faced with the problem of compensating FA for the unfair disadvantage caused her by the substitution. By calculating her score averages over the years, the committee determines that the new clubs have yielded FA an average two-stroke improvement per 18 holes over the old clubs. The committee decides to compensate FA by penalizing the third player by two strokes in the final 18 holes.

But the committee must also penalize WMA two strokes. If FA has been put at a disadvantage by the wrongful substitution, she has been put at a disadvantage with respect to every player in the game. She is in competition with all the players; what the third player's substitution has done is to deprive her of a fair opportunity to defeat all the other players. That opportunity is not restored by penalizing the third player alone. If the committee is to rectify in mid-match the wrong done to FA, it must penalize WMA as well, though WMA had no part in the wrong done to FA.

Now, if it is right for the committee to choose this course of action, then this example seems promising for Thomson's argument. Perhaps in it can be found a basis for defending premise 4. This example seems appropriately similar to Thomson's case: in it an organization penalizes WMA to compensate FA, though WMA is innocent of any wrong against FA. If the two situations are sufficiently alike and in the golfing example it is not unjust for the committee to penalize WMA, then by parity of reasoning it would seem that the community is not unjust in setting aside WMA's right.

Are the committee's action and the community's action to be seen in the same light? Does the committee's action involve setting aside any player's rights? The committee constantly monitors the game, and intervenes to balance off losses or gains due to infractions or violations. Unfair gains are nullified by penalties; unfair losses are offset by awards. In the end no player has a complaint because the interventions ensure that the outcome has not been influenced by illegitimate moves or illegal actions. Whatever a player's position at the end of the game, it is solely the result of his own unhindered efforts. In penalizing WMA two strokes (along with the third player), the committee does him no injustice nor overrides any of his rights.

The community, or its government, is responsible for preserving fair employment practices for its members. It can penalize those who engage in unfair discrimination; it can vigorously enforce fair employment rules; and, if FA has suffered under unfair practices, it may consider some form of compensation for FA. However, compensating FA by imposing a burden on WMA, when he is not culpable, is *not* like penalizing WMA in the golf match. The loss imposed by the community upon WMA is not part of a game-like scheme, carefully regulated and continuously monitored by the community, wherein it intervenes continually to offset unfair losses and gains by distributing penalties and advantages, ensuring that over their lifetimes WMA's and FA's chances at employment have been truly equal. WMA's loss may endure; and there is no reason to believe that his employment position at the end of his career reflects only his unhindered effort. If the community exacts a sacrifice from WMA to pay FA, *it merely redistributes losses and gains without balancing them.*

Even though the golfing example looked promising as a source of clues for a defense of premise 4, on examination it seems not to offer any support for that premise. Indeed, in seeing how the golfing case is different from the hiring case, we may become even more dubious that Thomson's principle of compensation can justify the community in overriding WMA's right to equal consideration in the absence of his culpability.[11]

5. Thomson's Words

Since Thomson never explicitly expresses premise 4 in her paper, she never directly addresses the problem of its defense. In the one place where she seems to take up the problem raised by premise 4, she says:

> Still, the community does impose a burden upon him (WMA): it is able to make amends for its wrongs only by taking something away from him, something which, after all, we are supposing he has a right to. And why should *he* pay the cost of the community's amends-making?
>
> If there were some appropriate way in which the community could make amends to its … women, some way which did not require depriving anyone of anything he has a right to, then that would be the best course of action to take. Or if there were anyway some way in which the costs could be shared by everyone, and not imposed entirely on the young white male applicants, then that would be, if not the best, then anyway better than opting for a policy of preferential hiring. But in fact *the nature of the wrongs done is such as to make jobs the best and most suitable form of compensation (emphasis added).*[12]

How does this provide an answer to our question? Is this passage to be read as suggesting, in support of premise 4, the principle that a group may override the rights of its (nonculpable) members in order to pay the "best" form of compensation?[13] If WMA's right to equal consideration stood in the way of the community's paying best compensation to FA, then this principle would entail premise 4. This principle, however, will not withstand scrutiny.

Consider an example: Suppose that you have stolen a rare and elaborately engraved hunting rifle from me. Before you can be made to return it, the gun is destroyed in a fire. By coincidence, however, your brother possesses one of the few other such rifles in existence; perhaps it is the only other model in existence apart from the one you stole from me and which was destroyed. From my point of view, having my gun back, or having one exactly like it, is the best form of compensation I can have from you. No other gun will be a suitable replacement, nor will money serve satisfactorily to compensate me for my loss. I prized the rifle for its rare and unique qualities, not for its monetary value. You can pay me the best form of compensation by giving me your brother's gun. However, this is clearly not a morally justifiable option. I have no moral title to your brother's gun, nor are you (solely in virtue of your debt to me) required or permitted to take your brother's gun to give to me. The gun is not yours to give; and nothing about the fact that you owe me justifies you in taking it.

In this example it is clear that establishing what is the best compensation (best makes up the wrongful loss) does not determine what is the morally appropriate form of compensation. Thus, as a defense of premise 4, telling us that preferential hiring is the best compensation begs the question.

The question of the best form of compensation may properly arise only after we have determined who owes whom, and what are the morally permissible means of payment open to the debtor. The question of the best form of compensation arises, in other words, only after we have settled the moral justifiability of exacting something from someone, and settled the issue of what it is that the debtor has that he can pay.

The case of preferential hiring seems to me more like the case of the stolen rifle than like the case of the golfing match. If WMA has a right to equal consideration, then he, not the community, owns the right. In abridging his right in order to pay FA, the community is paying in stolen coin, just as you would be were you to expropriate your brother's rifle to compensate me. The community is paying with something that does not belong to it. WMA has not been shown by Thomson to owe anybody anything. Nor has Thomson defended or made plausible premise 4, which on its face ill fits her own expression of the principle of compensation. If we reject the premise, then Thomson has not shown what she claimed—that it is not unjust to engage in preferential hiring of women. I fully agree with her that it would be appropriate, if not obligatory, for the community to adopt measures of compensation to women.[14] I cannot agree, on the basis of her argument, that it may do so by adopting a policy of preferential hiring.

6. Benefit and Innocence

Thomson seems vaguely to recognize that her case is unconvincing without a demonstration of culpability on the part of WMA. At the end of her paper, after having made her argument without assuming WMA's guilt, she assures us that after all WMA is not so innocent, and it is not unfitting that he should bear the sacrifice required in preferring FA.

> It is not entirely inappropriate that those applicants (like WMA) should pay the costs. No doubt few, if any, have themselves, individually, done any wrongs to ... women. But they have profited from the wrongs the community did. Many may actually have been direct beneficiaries of policies which excluded or down-graded ... women —perhaps in school admissions, perhaps in access to financial aid,

perhaps elsewhere; and even those who did not directly benefit in this way had, at any rate, the advantage in the competition which comes of confidence in one's full membership, and of one's rights being recognized as a matter of course.[15]

Does this passage make a plausible case for WMA's diminished "innocence," and the appropriateness of imposing the costs of compensation on him? The principle implied in the passage is, "He who benefits from a wrong shall pay for the wrong." Perhaps Thomson confuses this principle with the principle of compensation itself ("He who wrongs another shall pay for the wrong"). At any rate, the principle, "He who benefits from a wrong shall pay for the wrong," is surely suspect as an acceptable moral principle.

Consider the following example. While I am away on vacation, my neighbor contracts with a construction company to repave his driveway. He instructs the workers to come to his address, where they will find a note describing the driveway to be repaired. An enemy of my neighbor, aware somehow of this arrangement, substitutes for my neighbor's instructions a note describing *my* driveway. The construction crew, having been paid in advance, shows up on the appointed day while my neighbor is at work, finds the letter, and faithfully following its instructions paves my driveway. In this example my neighbor has been wronged and damaged. He is out a sum of money, and his driveway is unimproved. I benefited from the wrong, for my driveway is considerably improved. Yet, am I morally required to compensate my neighbor for the wrong done him? Is it appropriate that the costs of compensating my neighbor fall on me? I cannot see why. My paying the neighbor the cost he incurred in hiring the construction company would be an act of supererogation on my part, not a discharge of an obligation to him. If I could afford it, it would be a decent thing to do; but it is not something I *owe* my neighbor. I am not less than innocent in this affair because I benefited from my neighbor's misfortune; and no one is justified in exacting compensation from me.

The very obvious feature of the situation just described which bears on the fittingness of compensation is the fact of *involuntariness*. Indeed I benefited from the wrong done my neighbor, but the benefit was involuntary and undesired. If I knowingly and voluntarily benefit from wrongs done to others, though I do not commit the wrongs myself, then perhaps it is true to say that I am less than innocent of these wrongs, and perhaps it is morally fitting that I bear some of the costs of compensation. But it is not like this with involuntary benefits.

Though young white males like WMA have undeniably benefited in many ways from the sexist social arrangements under which they were reared, to a large extent, if not entirely, these benefits are involuntary. From an early age the male's training and education inculcate in him the attitudes and dispositions, the knowledge and skills, which give him an advantage over women in later life. Such benefits are unavoidable (by him) and ineradicable. Most especially is this true of "that advantage…which comes of confidence in one's full membership [in the community] and of one's rights being recognized as a matter of course."

The principle, "He who *willingly* benefits from wrong must pay for the wrong," may have merit as a moral principle. To show a person's uncoerced and knowledgeable complicity in wrongdoing is to show him less than innocent, even if his role amounts to no more than ready acceptance of the fruits of wrong. Thomson makes no effort to show such complicity on WMA's part. The principle that she relies upon, "He who benefits from a wrong must pay for the wrong," is without merit. So, too, is her belief that "it is not entirely inappropriate" that WMA (and those like him) should bear the burden of a program of compensation to women. What Thomson ignores is the moral implication of the fact that the benefits of sexism received by WMA may be involuntary and unavoidable. This implication cannot be blinked, and it ruins Thomson's final pitch to gain our approval of a program which violates the rights of some persons.[16]

14

Compensatory Justice: The Question of Costs

Robert Amdur

An adequate theory of compensatory justice should include answers to two sets of questions. First, who is to receive compensation, and how much should they receive? Second, who should pay the costs of compensation, and how much should each pay?

In the literature on preferential hiring, reverse discrimination, and affirmative action, the first set of questions has received far more attention than the second. Several writers have argued in favor of preferential treatment without considering the costs of compensation at all—suggesting either that the distribution of costs is not a major issue or that the solution to the problem is too obvious to require discussion. Others have dealt with the question of who should pay, but only briefly, after detailed and rigorous examinations of who should be compensated. By the time these writers reach the question of distribution of costs, everything else, including the proper mode of compensation, has been decided on. At this point, there are very few options left: the mode of compensation determines how the burden will be distributed.

I want to suggest that the question of who should pay is a fundamental one. It is too important to be postponed until after the rest of the problems concerning compensatory justice have been settled. In Part I of this essay, I put forward three principles intended to regulate distribution of the costs of

Reprinted from *Political Theory* 7 (1979). Copyright © 1979 by *Political Theory*. Reprinted by permission of Sage Publications, Inc.

compensation. In Parts II and III, I ask whether these principles can be satisfied by programs involving preferential treatment for blacks and women.

I

Assume that it will sometimes be necessary to compensate certain individuals or groups, either for past injustices committed against them or for present competitive disadvantages resulting from past injustices. Who should pay the costs of compensation? There are two obvious answers:

> *First principle:* Compensation should be paid by the perpetrators of injustice, those whose unjust actions gave rise to the need for compensation.
>
> *Second principle:* Compensation should be paid by those who benefited from injustice, whether directly or indirectly (for example, inheriting wealth originally acquired by unjust means).

These principles do not comprise a complete theory of just compensation; at best, they provide the beginnings of such a theory. I want to comment briefly on four issues that require further attention: identification of the perpetrators of injustice; the question of intentions; the distribution of costs among perpetrators (or among beneficiaries); and the relationship between the two principles.

(1) The first principle is intended to impose costs on those persons responsible for injustice. But how do we determine who was responsible for instituting and perpetuating a particular unjust practice? Discussing the theft of Indian lands, Robert E. Litan observes: "Certainly more individuals were responsible...than just those in the U.S. Army. What about the political leaders who founded such activities, individuals who voted for these leaders, and the like?" "Where," Litan asks, "does the buck of responsibility come to rest?"[1]

To answer this question, information about who did what to whom is necessary, but not sufficient. Whether we are responsible for starvation in Bangladesh depends in part on the history of our relations with that country. But it also depends on whether we have a duty to supply starving people with food. To answer Litan's question, we would need both historical information *and* a theory of responsibility, a theory that tells us when individuals are obliged to act to alleviate suffering and when they are to be held accountable for their actions or failures to act. Although philosophers have begun to address these questions,[2] a satisfactory theory of responsibility does not yet exist.

In the absence of such a theory, it is not surprising that there is little agreement (even among supporters of compensatory programs) about who is responsible for injustice against blacks and women in America. According to one view, the perpetrators of injustice are those individuals who have engaged in overt racial or sexual discrimination, particularly hiring discrimination. At the opposite extreme is the view that every person has a duty to struggle against injustice wherever it exists, and hence that anyone not currently fighting for equality is a perpetrator of injustice. As Alison Jaggar puts it, "Everyone who acquiesces in a racist and sexist system helps to "cause' discrimination."[3] Most supporters of compensation fall somewhere between these extremes; they see the perpetrators of injustice as including all those who have engaged in a variety of social and economic practices which tend to perpetuate the inferior position of blacks and women.[4]

(2) Several writers have endorsed the second principle but suggested that it should apply only to those who have benefited intentionally or voluntarily. According to Robert K. Fullinwider,

> If I knowingly and voluntarily benefit from wrongs done to others, though I do not commit the wrongs myself, then perhaps it is true to say that I am less than innocent of these wrongs, and perhaps it is morally fitting that I bear some of the costs of compensation. But it is not like this with involuntary benefits.[5]

Is such a restriction necessary? If we were concerned with guilt and innocence, blame and responsibility, then Fullinwider would undoubtedly be correct: intention would be a relevant consideration. But most of the writers who endorse the second principle are not concerned with guilt and innocence. For them, the idea behind the second principle is not that those who are to blame for an injustice should be made to pay. Rather, they are interested in restoring the competitive balance that would have existed had the injustice in question never taken place. They believe that the natural way to accomplish this goal is simply to ask those who have gained from injustice to give up what they have gained. Whether the beneficiaries are "innocent of these wrongs" is, according to this view, irrelevant.

(3) Another issue involves the distribution of costs *among* beneficiaries or perpetrators. While many people may benefit from an unjust practice or policy, some are likely to benefit more than others. Responsibility raises more complicated problems, but most theorists seem to agree that it too can be divided unevenly. Here it seems reasonable to amend the first and second principles in the following manner: in applying these principles, the costs of compensation should be distributed in proportion to the degree of responsibility or to the benefits received. In some instances a demand for

strict proportionality will make little sense, but even in these cases it is appropriate that those who are more responsible (those who have contributed more to initiating or perpetuating unjust policies) or those who have benefited more should pay a larger share. If for some reason it becomes necessary to assign the costs of compensation to some group within the general population of beneficiaries and/or perpetrators, costs ought to be assigned to those who have benefited most, or those most responsible. When an individual is asked to pay part of the costs of compensation, while others who benefited more than he did from the injustice in question are *not* being asked to pay a share of the costs, he may rightly complain that he is being singled out unfairly. He is justified in asking "Why me?" In this case, it is not sufficient to answer, "Because you did, after all, benefit from injustice."

(4) Finally, what is the relationship between the two principles? We might want to apply both principles at the same time (with a proviso to deal with perpetrators of injustice who are also beneficiaries). Alternatively, we could specify a priority rule—for example: apply the first principle whenever possible; in other cases, apply the second. I am not sure how the two principles should fit together, though clearly this is a question that a comprehensive theory of compensation would have to answer.

Although many details have yet to be worked out, I believe that the principles discussed above should ideally regulate allocation of the costs of compensating individuals or groups for the effects of past injustice. Not surprisingly, these principles have been put forward, in one form or another, in many discussions of compensatory justice. The problem is that it is extremely difficult—perhaps impossible—to apply these principles, in any rigorous way, to actual cases.

This is probably clearer with regard to the second principle. It is never easy to determine exactly who has benefited from a particular social practice or policy; witness the ongoing debates on the left over whether members of the white working class gain or lose from racial discrimination and economic imperialism. When a practice and its effects extend over several generations, the difficulties become more serious and the possibilities of error increase. Where we must not only identify gainers and losers but also determine how much different individuals have gained, the problems become still more complex.[6] To apply the second principle to an historical case, one would have to answer an enormous number of questions not only about what in fact happened but also about what *would have* happened under a different set of social practices. Efforts to determine who benefited (and how much) from discriminatory practices are likely to yield results too crude to serve as a just basis for decisions about the allocation of costs.[7]

When we turn to the first principle, the problems are no less serious. Given a generally accepted theory of responsibility and a detailed knowledge of the relevant historical facts, it will often be possible to identify the perpetrators of injustice. However, many of the most interesting cases are likely to involve unjust practices carried out over a long period of time, or past injustices, the effects of which are still being felt. All or nearly all of the perpetrators (particularly those who appear most responsible for initiating and maintaining the unjust practices in question) are likely to be dead. Since responsibility (unlike benefits) cannot be inherited, it will often be impossible to apply the first principle, even in those cases where the perpetrators can be identified. In general, it will be difficult to apply this principle when the most important injustices requiring compensation, and the compensation itself, do not take place within the same generation.

These considerations give rise to the question: who should pay the costs of compensation in those cases where it is not possible to assign costs either to the perpetrators or to the beneficiaries of injustice? One possible answer is that in situations of this sort no one should pay. From this point on, it might be argued, we should prohibit all racial and sexual discrimination. We should guarantee those individuals previously victimized by injustice an equal opportunity to advance as far as their talents will carry them. But that is all we should do. If we are unable to assign the costs to the "right" people, then there should be no compensation at all. The results of past injustice must be allowed to fall wherever they happen to fall.

This position might be described as the libertarian solution to the problem of costs. In some ways it is an appealing solution. It is the only alternative which guarantees that no one will be treated unfairly by the compensation process itself. That is to say, it is the only alternative which guarantees that the process of compensation will not make anyone worse off than he would have been if there had never been any injustice in the first place. As such, it must recommend itself to anyone opposed to using some people as means to promote the good of others.

Nevertheless, there are good reasons for rejecting the libertarian position. I want to emphasize two of these. First, the effects of past injustice generally do not "wash away" with time; frequently, the disadvantages resulting from unjust practices are transmitted from one generation to the next. Contrary to the expectations of many nineteenth- and early-twentieth-century egalitarians, formal equality of opportunity is not sufficient to eliminate the effect of past privations on the present generation. At least in many cases, victims of injustice who do not receive some sort of compensation are likely to remain seriously disadvantaged, despite the existence of equality of opportunity.

The second point concerns the arbitrariness involved in compensating some victims of injustice, but not others. Imagine two victimized groups, both equally (and seriously) disadvantaged as a result of past wrongs. In one case it is possible to identify the perpetrators (and/or beneficiaries) of injustice; in the other case it is not—we have no knowledge about them, or our knowledge is not sufficiently certain, or we know the class to which they belong but cannot identify particular individuals. Most of us will agree that if the first group of victims is entitled to compensation, then so is the second. Their claim to receive compensation should depend on the nature of the injustice they have suffered and the effects of that injustice, not on whether it is possible to locate the perpetrators of injustice and hold them accountable. If the victims ought to receive compensation when the perpetrators of injustice can be found, then it will seem unfair to deny them compensation in those cases where the perpetrators cannot be found.

I believe these considerations are sufficient to outweigh the arguments in favor of the libertarian position. The most plausible alternative is close to the mirror image of the libertarian view.

> *Third principle:* When it is not possible to assign the costs of compensation either to the perpetrators or to the beneficiaries of injustice, those costs should be distributed evenly among the entire community.

In short, everyone should pay. The costs of compensation should be divided so as to equalize sacrifice as nearly as possible; they should be distributed, in other words, just the way we distribute the costs of any public good.[8]

This suggestion is not original; a number of writers have argued in favor of having the entire community pay the costs of compensation. Generally, however, those who take this position couch their arguments in terms of collective responsibility. Thus, according to Paul W. Taylor, when injustice has resulted from a discriminatory social practice, "the obligation to compensate for the past injustice does not fall upon any particular individual but upon the society as a whole," excepting, of course, the victims of past discrimination. Taylor believes that "the perpetrator of the original injustice was the whole society," therefore, "society is morally at fault if it ignores the group which it has discriminated against." The duty to provide compensation follows from "the society's past use of a certain characteristic or set of characteristics as the criterion for identification of the group, membership in which was taken as a ground for unjust treatment."[9]

When the case for payment by the entire community is made in this fashion, there is an obvious reply. "The society in general" is made up of a large number of individuals, many of whom will not have engaged in discriminatory or otherwise unjust behavior. What about recent immigrants?

What about those who were children when the discriminatory acts took place? What about those people who disapproved of unjust practices and fought to eliminate them? What about persons who simply had no opportunity to engage in discrimination? Even if one takes a very broad view concerning the locus of responsibility for social practices, it will be impossible to maintain that *everyone* is responsible for *every* unjust practice. When we talk about "society as a whole" perpetrating injustices or using certain characteristics as a basis for unjust treatment, we are using a kind of shorthand. That shorthand may be appropriate for some purposes, but not for assigning responsibility. When we are concerned with assigning responsibility, we are necessarily concerned with individuals.

These objections are, in my view, persuasive. Even if there are cases in which (nearly) everyone bears responsibility for an unjust social practice, there will be many cases in which responsibility is far less widely diffused. For that reason, it is not possible to base the demand for equal sacrifice on a notion of collective responsibility. If something like the third principle can be defended, it must be defended on the ground that an even distribution of costs among the entire community is simply more equitable (or perhaps less inequitable) than any other distribution that might be suggested, given the impossibility of assigning the costs to the "right" people. It is difficult to make a positive argument for this position. On the other hand, once we are agreed that *someone* will have to pay the costs of compensation, it seems equally difficult to think of another principle of distribution that is, on its face, superior.

It is important to emphasize that distributing costs *evenly* is very different from distributing costs *randomly*. At first glance, the two may seem to be based on the same philosophical principle; and some of those who have written about compensatory justice appear to believe that payment by the community and payment by a random sample of the community are equivalent.[10] But payment by randomly selected individuals is different from payment by the entire community, and, from a moral point of view, distinctly inferior.

We can support this conclusion, and thereby strengthen the case for the third principle, on either utilitarian or Rawlsian grounds. There are two utilitarian reasons for preferring to have costs spread out as evenly as possible. First, if we accept the standard utilitarian assumptions about diminishing marginal utility, "equality of sacrifice" is likely to be superior to any principle that assigns costs to a randomly selected few; small sacrifices by large numbers of people will have a less serious impact on overall utility than larger sacrifices by smaller numbers.[11] Second, a scheme that distributes costs evenly among the entire community is most likely to allow people to plan their lives in a rational manner. On the other hand, a program that assigns larger burdens to a few randomly selected individuals will make planning more difficult, and life more insecure, for everyone.

From a Rawlsian perspective, the case for equal sacrifice is also compelling. Rawls ignores compensation in *A Theory of Justice*, along with most other branches of what he calls non-ideal theory. But he acknowledges that a comprehensive theory of justice would include principles to regulate compensation, and he clearly believes that such principles would have to be chosen in the original position. It is, of course, one of his major contentions that the features of the original position force the hypothetical contractees to choose conservatively; when we place ourselves behind the veil of ignorance, we will feel constrained "to adopt the alternative, the worst outcome of which is superior to the worst outcomes of the others."[12] When the parties in the original position meet to choose non-ideal principles, each will seek to avoid the risk of having to pay a disproportionate share of the costs of compensation. This should lead to a unanimous preference for equal sacrifice over any principle that assigns larger costs to fewer people.

The point of the third principle is to divide costs as evenly as possible among the entire community, not to assign costs by lot. It is grossly unfair to impose the costs of compensation on individuals chosen at random from the population. Nor is the injustice mitigated by the fact that every person has an equal chance to be among those selected.

What if we cannot avoid assigning costs to a smaller group? In such situations it may be necessary to select people at random. But the third principle suggests that we should try to avoid situations of this sort whenever possible. In choosing among alternative modes of compensation, the possibility of dividing costs evenly should be an important consideration. Other things being equal, one mode of compensation is superior to another if its costs can be spread evenly among the entire community rather than assigned to any smaller group (except, of course, those groups identified by the first two principles). Even when other things are not equal, the need to distribute costs evenly may be an overriding consideration. It may be enough to tip the scales in favor of a mode of compensation which is, in all other respects, second best.

II

Can programs requiring preferential treatment for blacks or women satisfy the first two principles? If one takes a narrow view of the injustice requiring rectification, then it might be possible to imagine a preferential hiring program that assigned costs to the perpetrators and beneficiaries of injustice. In universities, in particular, it may be possible to identify those persons who have engaged in or benefited from discriminatory hiring practices. They will be some, though obviously not all, of the white males currently holding faculty and administrative positions. If we were concerned solely with compensating for (fairly recent) university hiring discrimination, we might be able to devise a scheme that would force the beneficiaries and perpetrators of injustice to give up their jobs, to be replaced by the most qualified black and female candidates currently available. Even in this case our task would not be easy: how can we be certain which professors would have achieved their present positions under a perfectly just selection procedure; how can we know whether professor x voted against candidate y for unjust reasons? Still, such a program might be feasible. It would, of course, be different from anything yet instituted in an American university—or anything seriously recommended in the literature on preferential treatment.

What about the sorts of preferential hiring and preferential admissions programs that have been proposed and implemented during the past decade? Is it possible to justify *these* programs in terms of the first two principles discussed above? In his article "Justifying Reverse Discrimination in Employment," George Sher tries to defend preferential hiring by an appeal to something close to the second principle. Sher begins by suggesting that

> if reverse discrimination is viewed simply as a form of compensation for past privations, there are serious questions about its fairness. Certainly the privations to be compensated for are not the sole responsibility of those individuals whose superior qualifications will have to be bypassed in the reverse discriminatory process. These individuals, if responsible for those privations at all, will at least be no more responsible than others with relevantly similar histories. Yet reverse discrimination will compensate for the privations in question at the expense of these individuals alone. It will have no effect at all upon those other, equally responsible persons.... Surely it is unfair to distribute the burden of compensation so unequally.[13]

But this does not mean that we should abandon reverse discrimination. Rather, we should view "that practice, not as the redressing of *past* privations, but rather as a way of neutralizing the *present* competitive disadvantage *caused* by those past privations and thus as a way of restoring equal access to those goods which society distributes competitively." Sher continues:

> When reverse discrimination is viewed as compensation for lost ability to compete on equal terms, a reasonable case can also be made

for its fairness. Our doubts about its fairness arose because it seemed to place the entire burden of redress upon those individuals whose superior qualifications are bypassed in the reverse discriminatory process. This seemed wrong because these individuals are, of course, not apt to be any more responsible for past discrimination than others with relevantly similar histories. But, as we are now in a position to see, this objection misses the point. The crucial fact about these individuals is not that they are more *responsible* for past discrimination than others with relevantly similar histories (in fact, the dirty work may well have been done before any of their generation attained the age of responsibility), but rather that unless reverse discrimination is practiced, they will *benefit* more than the others from its effects on their competitors. They will benefit more because unless they are restrained, they, but not the others, will use their competitive edge to claim jobs which their competitors would otherwise have gotten. Thus, it is only because they stand to *gain* the most from the relevant effects of the *original* discrimination, that the bypassed individuals stand to *lose* the most from *reverse* discrimination. This is surely a valid reply to the charge that reverse discrimination does not distribute the burden of compensation equally.[14]

Is it? The answer depends at least in part on whether the people who are bypassed in the reverse discrimination process are the same ones who would not have gotten jobs had there been no past discrimination. If they are, then we can say to those people: look, if not for past discrimination, there would be a larger number of highly qualified applicants today, and you would not be in line for jobs at all. The crucial word in this sentence is "you." It is *not* sufficient to say: look, if not for past discrimination, there would be a larger number of highly qualified applicants today, and *some* white males would not be in line for jobs at all. Though he is not explicit, Sher does seem to believe that today's marginal applicants are exactly the same people who would have lost out in the competition for jobs had there been no history of discrimination. I find this assumption implausible. It is extremely difficult to determine what society would look like today if radically different social practices had been instituted a century ago. Surely, it is reasonable to think that racial injustice has affected whites differentially: that some who are now advantaged would have been less well off under a different set of rules and that some who are now "marginal" would have been better off. At the very least, Sher's assumption seems open to question.

Even if we accept Sher's assumption, one feature of his argument remains puzzling. Why allow the present generation of white male job applicants to bear *all* the costs of compensation? In a footnote Sher concedes that "many who are now entrenched in their jobs (tenured professors, for example) have already benefited from the effects of past discrimination at least as much as the currently best qualified applicant will if reverse discrimination is not practiced." But he sees that as "largely irrelevant."[15] He appears to believe that we ought to assist disadvantaged members of this generation by depriving contemporaries who would otherwise benefit at their expense. But why is such symmetry desirable? Why should all compensation be intragenerational? Intuitively it seems that those who "have already benefited from the effects of past discrimination" should be asked to sacrifice as much as those who were about to benefit, before the advent of reverse discrimination. Perhaps they should be asked to bear *more* of the costs since they, at least, have had an opportunity to enjoy their benefits.

III

If it is not possible to assign the costs of compensation either to the perpetrators or to the beneficiaries of injustice, then, according to the third principle, those costs should be divided as evenly as possible among all the members of the community. Obviously, no program of preferential hiring or preferential admissions will satisfy the requirement of equality of sacrifice. It is arguable that, by singling out young white males of lower-middle or working-class background, such programs assign the costs of compensation to those members of society *least* likely to have engaged in or benefited from past discrimination.[16] Whether or not that is true, it is clear that preferential programs do not distribute costs evenly and cannot be made to do so.

The programs that satisfy the third principle most easily are programs involving monetary compensation, paid for through taxation. The most interesting historical example is the program of reparations to Jews victimized by the Nazis, instituted in West Germany after World War II. Under this program large numbers of individual Jews received direct cash payments to compensate for the losses they had suffered under the Nazi regime. Individuals were eligible to receive payments if they could demonstrate damage to health, reduction of income, loss of freedom, property losses, or impairment of professional or economic advancement. Under certain circumstances, dependents of those killed by the Nazis also received compensation. In addition to the payments to individuals, beginning in 1953 the German Federal Republic paid hundreds of millions of dollars in reparations to the state of Israel and to an international claims conference which was responsible for the relief, rehabilitation, and resettlement of non-Israeli Jews.[17]

It should be noted that the German political leaders who supported reparations did not attempt to justify those payments in terms of collective guilt. Nearly every participant in the parliamentary debates over reparations explicitly rejected the argument that all Germans were responsible for the crimes of the Nazis. Several speakers echoed Konrad Adenauer's assertion that "the overwhelming majority of the German people abominated the crimes committed against the Jews, and did not participate in them." Nevertheless, the leaders of nearly all of Germany's postwar political parties agreed on two points: first, compensation for the Jews was morally necessary, and second, the community as a whole would have to bear the cost.[18]

Boris Bittker provides a second (hypothetical) example in *The Case for Black Reparations*. Bittker advances a number of plans designed to compensate black Americans for damages inflicted by slavery and subsequent racial discrimination. One alternative would involve money payments to blacks, "graduated by reference to a few readily ascertainable characteristics (such as the claimant's age and marital status)."[19] Another alternative would entail payments not to individuals but to representative groups, to be used for projects beneficial to the black community as a whole. It is also possible to imagine various combinations. Whatever alternative might be selected, Bittker believes that the payments would have to be at least large enough to "close the economic gap between blacks and whites"; that is to say, they would have to be sufficient to erase the current disparities both in income and in net worth. He is also sympathetic to additional allowances to compensate for "the humiliation inflicted by segregation."[20] As with the West German reparations program, the necessary money would be raised by taxation.

If my argument is correct, there is a presumption in favor of programs such as these and against preferential hiring and preferential admissions. Are there any reasons to override this presumption? Judith Jarvis Thomson has argued that there are. Her argument deserves close examination, for she is one of the few supporters of preferential hiring programs to acknowledge that there is a strong case for equality of sacrifice.

Thomson believes that "if there were ... some way in which costs could be shared by everyone, and not imposed on the young white male applicants, then that would be, if not the best, then anyway better than opting for a policy of preferential hiring." But she insists that

> the nature of the wrongs done is such as to make jobs the best and most suitable form of compensation. What blacks and women were denied was full membership in the community; and nothing can more appropriately make amends for that wrong than precisely what

will make them feel they now finally have it. And that means jobs. Financial compensation (the cost of which could be shared equally) slips through the fingers; having a job, and discovering you do it well, yield—perhaps better than anything else—that very self-respect which blacks and women have had to do without.[21]

This argument seems wrong on a number of crucial issues. It is not at all clear that the jobs provided by preferential hiring programs will make women and blacks feel they now have full membership in the community. These jobs *may* buttress the self-respect of the individual blacks and women who receive them, but these people are fairly certain to be a small group (and, arguably, not the ones whose self-respect is in greatest need of reinforcement).[22] There is little reason to believe that jobs for a few blacks and women will do anything for the self-respect of the majority; and this is especially true if, as Thomson asserts, "having a job, and discovering you do it well" is the key to self-respect.

Concerning the alternative to preferential hiring, it is also not clear what Thomson means by the assertion that "financial compensation... slips through the fingers." Clearly, very small amounts of money—such as, for example, the "fifteen dollars per nigger" demanded in the Black Manifesto of 1969—would do very little to improve the living conditions of blacks as a group. Such payments would undoubtedly be spent quickly, leaving their recipients no better off than before. If this is what Thomson means, she is right. But there is no reason to assume that compensatory payments would have to be so small. Bittker, in proposing to "close the economic gap between blacks and whites," clearly envisions payments much larger than those proposed in the Manifesto.

If Thomson is not simply pointing out that insignificant amounts of money are not very useful, what could she mean? Perhaps she has in mind something like E. C. Banfield's view that members of the "lower class" have an almost unlimited capacity to waste money.[23] If we accept this view as correct, then even a very ambitious program of money payments will indeed be pointless; it will make no positive long-term difference in the lives of recipients. If this is Thomson's argument, it is necessary to make two points in response. First, Banfield's assertion, and the larger theory of which it forms a part, have been widely criticized.[24] It is, to say the least, a matter of dispute whether large numbers of people actually display the attitudes and personality traits attributed by Banfield to the lower class. (Banfield himself appears to believe that the "radically improvident" constitute only 10 to 20% of those with incomes below the poverty line.) But second, if the claim under consideration is correct, it hardly does very much to advance the argument for preferential treatment. For if there are large numbers of people who should not receive transfer payments because of their lower-class attitudes, it is difficult to argue that those people ought to be given jobs teaching in universities, or places in law and medical schools.

In short, I do not believe Thomson has shown that jobs are a particularly appropriate, or transfer payments a particularly inappropriate, form of compensation. Perhaps others will offer more persuasive arguments to support these contentions. To make such an argument successfully, however, it would *not* be sufficient to demonstrate that provision of jobs (or places in professional schools) for blacks and women would achieve some desirable goal. It would also be necessary to show that the same goal could not be achieved by means of transfer payments. In discussion of the Bakke case, the most common argument for preferential admissions has focused on the need to improve medical care in the black community. This is obviously a worthwhile goal. But money payments on the scale envisioned by Bittker would almost certainly do more to improve medical care for blacks than any preferential admissions program that might be devised.

In any case, it should be emphasized that even if someone were to demonstrate convincingly that jobs are "the best and most suitable form of compensation" from the point of view of those to be compensated, that still would not clinch the argument in favor of preferential treatment. For the people being asked to pay *also* have claims that must be taken into account. In particular, they have a claim not to be singled out to pay the costs of compensation, unless they can be identified as either the perpetrators or the beneficiaries of injustice. Clearly, it would be unfair to the victims of discrimination not to provide compensation at all. But sometimes it may be necessary to choose a form of compensation other than the "best and most suitable" form, so as to avoid doing injustice to those who must pay the costs.

III. Equality and Diversity

15

The Morality of Reparation

Bernard R. Boxill

In "Black Reparations—Two Views,"[1] Michael Harrington rejected and Arnold Kaufman endorsed James Forman's demand for $500 million in reparation from Christian churches and Jewish synagogues for their part in the exploitation of black people. Harrington's position involves two different points; he argues that reparation is irrelevant and unwarranted because even if it were made, it would do little to "even up incomes"; and he maintains that the *demand* for reparation will be counterproductive, since it will "divert precious political energies from the actual struggle" to even up incomes. Now, though Kaufman seemed to show good reason that, contra Harrington, the demand for reparation could be productive, I shall in the ensuing, completely disregard that issue. Whether the demand for reparation is counterproductive or not is a question the answer to which depends on the assessment of a large number of consequences which cannot be answered by philosophy alone.

In this paper I shall take issue with what I have distinguished as the first of Harrington's points, viz. that reparation is unwarranted and irrelevant because it would do little to even up incomes. I assume that, by implication, Harrington is not averse to special compensatory programs which will effectively raise the incomes of the poor; what he specifically opposes is reparation. By a discussion of the justification and aims of reparation and compensation, I shall now try to show that, though both are parts of jus-

Reprinted from *Social Theory and Practice* 2 (1972), by permission of the journal and the author.

tice, they have different aims, and hence compensation cannot replace reparation.

Let me begin with a discussion of how compensation may be justified. Because of the scarcity of positions and resources relative to aspiring individuals, every society that refuses to resort to paternalism or a strict regimentation of aspirations must incorporate competition among its members for scarce positions and resources. Given that freedom of choice necessitates at least the possibility of competition, I believe that justice requires that appropriate compensatory programs be instituted both to ensure that the competition is fair, and that the losers be protected.

If the minimum formal requirement of justice is that persons be given equal consideration, then it is clear that justice requires that compensatory programs be implemented in order to ensure that none of the participants suffers from a removable handicap. The same reasoning supports the contention that the losers in the competition be given, if necessary, sufficient compensation to enable them to reenter the competition on equal terms with the others. In other words, the losers can demand equal opportunity as well as can the beginners.

In addition to providing compensation in the above cases, the community has the duty to provide compensation to the victims of accidents where no one was in the wrong, and to the victims of "acts of God" such as floods, hurricanes, and earthquakes. Here again, the justification is that such compensation is required if it is necessary to ensure equality of opportunity.

Now, it should be noted that, in all the cases I have stated as requiring compensation, no prior injustice need have occurred. This is clear, of course, in the case of accidents and "acts of God"; but it is also the case that in a competition, even if everyone abides by the rules and acts fairly and justly, some will necessarily be losers. In such a case, I maintain, if the losers are rendered so destitute as to be unable to compete equally, they can demand compensation from the community. Such a right to compensation does not render the competition nugatory; the losers cannot demand success—they can demand only the minimum necessary to reenter the competition. Neither is it the case that every failure has rights of compensation against the community. As we shall see, the right to compensation depends partly on the conviction that every individual has an equal right to pursue what he considers valuable; the wastrel or indolent man has signified what he values by what he has freely chosen to be. Thus, even if he seems a failure and considers himself a failure, he does not need or have a right of compensation. Finally, the case for compensation sketched is not necessarily paternalistic. It is not argued that society or government can decide what valuable things individuals should have and implement programs to see to it that they have them. Society must see to it that its members can pursue those things they consider valuable.

The justification of compensation rests on two premises: first, each individual is equal in dignity and worth to every other individual, and hence has a right, equal to that of any other, to arrange his life as he sees fit, and to pursue and acquire what he considers valuable; and second, the individuals involved must be members of a community. Both premises are necessary in order to show that compensation is both good and, in addition, mandatory or required by justice. One may, for example, concede that a man who is handicapped by some infirmity should receive compensation; but if the man is a member of no community, and if his infirmity is due to no injustice, then one would be hard put to find the party who could be legitimately forced to bear the cost of such compensation. Since persons can be legitimately compelled to do what justice dictates, then it would seem that in the absence of a community, and if the individual has suffered his handicap because of no injustice, that compensation cannot be part of justice. But given that the individual is a member of a community, then I maintain that he can legitimately demand compensation from that community. The members of a community are, in essential respects, members of a joint undertaking; the activities of the members of a community are interdependent and the community benefits from the efforts of its members even when such efforts do not bring the members what they individually aim at. It is legitimate to expect persons to follow the spirit and letter of rules and regulations, to work hard and honestly, to take calculated risks with their lives and fortunes, all of which helps society generally, only if such persons can demand compensation from society as a whole when necessary.

The case for rights of compensation depends, as I have argued above, on the fact that the individuals involved are members of a single community, the very existence of which should imply a tacit agreement on the part of the whole to bear the costs of compensation. The case for reparation, I shall try to show, is more primitive in the sense that it depends only on the premise that every person has an equal right to pursue and acquire what he values. Recall that the crucial difference between compensation and reparation is that whereas the latter is due only after injustice, the former may be due when no one has acted unjustly to anyone else. It is this relative innocence of all the parties concerned which make it illegitimate, in the absence of prior commitments, to compel anyone to bear the cost of compensation.

In the case of reparation, however, this difficulty does not exist. When reparation is due, it is not the case that no one is at fault, or that everyone is innocent; in such a case, necessarily, someone has infringed unjustly on another's right to pursue what he values. This could happen in several different ways, dispossession being perhaps the most obvious. When someone possesses something, he has signified by his choice that he values it. By taking it away from him one infringes on his equal right to pursue and possess what he values. On the other hand, if I thwart, unfairly, another's legitimate attempt to do or possess something, I have also acted unjustly; finally, an injustice has occurred when someone makes it impossible for others to pursue a legitimate goal, even if these others never actually attempt to achieve that goal. These examples of injustice differ in detail, but what they all have in common is that no supposition of prior commitment is necessary in order to be able to identify the parties who must bear the cost of reparation; it is simply and clearly the party who has acted unjustly.

The argument may, perhaps, be clarified by the ideas of a state of nature and a social contract. In the state of nature, as John Locke remarks, every man has the right to claim reparation from his injurer because of his right of self-preservation; if each man has a duty not to interfere in the rights of others, he has a duty to repair the results of his interference.[2] No social contract is required to legitimize compelling him to do so. But when compensation is due, i.e., when everyone has acted justly and has done his duty, then a social contract or a prior agreement to help must be appealed to in order to legitimately compel an individual to help another.

The case for reparation thus requires for its justification less in the way of assumptions than the case for compensation. Examination of the justifications of reparation and compensation also reveals the difference in their aims.

The characteristic of compensatory programs is that they are essentially "forward looking"; by that I mean that such programs are intended to alleviate disabilities which stand in the way of some *future* good, *however* these disabilities may have come about. Thus, the history of injustices suffered by black and colonial people is quite irrelevant to their right to compensatory treatment. What is strictly relevant to this is that such compensatory treatment is necessary if some future goods such as increased happiness, equality of incomes, and so on, are to be secured. To put it another way, given the contingency of causal connections, the present condition of black and colonial people could have been produced in any one of a very large set of different causal sequences. Compensation is concerned with the remedying of the present situation however it may have been produced; and to know the present situation, and how to remedy it, it is not, strictly speaking, necessary to know just how it was brought about, or whether it was brought about by injustice.

On the other hand, the justification of reparation is essentially "backward looking"; reparation is due only when a breach of justice *has* occurred. Thus, as opposed to the case of compensation, the case for reparation to black and colonial people depends precisely on the fact that such people have been reduced to their present condition by a history of injustice. In sum, while the aim of compensation is to procure some future good, that of reparation is to rectify past injustices; and rectifying past injustices may not insure equality of opportunity.

The fact that reparation aims precisely at correcting a prior injustice suggests one further important difference between reparation and compensation. Part of what is involved in rectifying an injustice is an acknowledgment on the part of the transgressor that what he is doing is required of him because of his prior error. This concession of error seems required by the premise that every person is equal in worth and dignity. Without the acknowledgment of error, the injurer implies that the injured has been treated in a manner that befits him; hence, he cannot feel that the injured party is his equal. In such a case, even if the unjust party repairs the damage he has caused, justice does not yet obtain between himself and his victim. For, if it is true that when someone has done his duty nothing can be demanded of him, it follows that if, in my estimation, I have acted dutifully even when someone is injured as a result, then I must feel that nothing can be demanded of me and that any repairs I may make are gratuitous. If justice can be demanded, it follows that I cannot think that what I am doing is part of justice.

It will be objected, of course, that I have not shown in this situation that justice cannot obtain between injurer and victim, but only that the injurer does not *feel* that justice can hold between himself and the one he injures. The objection depends on the distinction between the objective transactions between the individuals and their subjective attitudes, and assumes that justice requires only the objective transactions. The model of justice presupposed by this objection is, no doubt, that justice requires equal treatment of equals, whereas the view I take is that justice requires equal consideration between equals; that is to say, justice requires not only that we *treat* people in a certain way, for whatever reason we please, but that we treat them as equals precisely because we believe they are our equals. In particular, justice requires that we acknowledge that our treatment of others can be required of us; thus, where an unjust injury has occurred, the injurer reaffirms his belief in the other's equality by conceding that repair can be demanded of him, and the injured rejects the allegation of his inferiority contained in the other's behavior by demanding reparation.

Consequently, when injustice has reduced a people to indigency, compensatory programs alone cannot be all that justice requires. Since the avowed aim of compensatory programs is forward looking, such programs *necessarily* cannot affirm that the help they give is required because of a prior injustice. This must be the case even if it is the unjustly injuring party who makes compensation. Thus, since the acknowledgment of error is required by justice as part of what it means to give equal consideration, compensatory programs cannot take the place of reparation.

In sum, *compensation* cannot be substituted for *reparation* where reparation is due, because they satisfy two differing requirements of justice. In addition, practically speaking, since it is by demanding and giving justice where it is due that the members of a community continually reaffirm their belief in each other's equality, a stable and equitable society is not possible without reparation being given and demanded when it is due.

Consider now the assertion that the present generation of white Americans owes the present generation of black Americans reparation for the injustices of slavery inflicted on the ancestors of the black population by the ancestors of the white population. To begin, consider the very simplest instance of a case where reparation may be said to be due: Tom has an indisputable moral right to possession of a certain item, say a bicycle, and Dick steals the bicycle from Tom. Here, clearly, Dick owes Tom, at least the bicycle and a concession of error, in reparation. Now complicate the case slightly; Dick steals the bicycle from Tom and "gives" it to Harry. Here again, even if he is innocent of complicity in the theft, and does not know that his "gift" was stolen, Harry must return the bicycle to Tom with the acknowledgment that, though innocent or blameless, he did not rightfully possess the bicycle. Consider a final complication: Dick steals the bicycle from Tom and gives it to Harry; in the meantime Tom dies, but leaves a will clearly conferring his right to ownership of the bicycle to his son, Jim. Here again we should have little hesitation in saying that Harry must return the bicycle to Jim.

Now, though it involves complications, the case for reparation under consideration is essentially the same as the one last mentioned: the slaves had an indisputable moral right to the products of their labor; these products were stolen from them by the slave masters who ultimately passed them on to their descendants; the slaves presumably have conferred their rights of ownership to the products of their labor to their descendants; thus, the descendants of slave masters are in possession of wealth to which the descendants of slaves have rights; hence, the descendants of slave masters must return this wealth to the descendants of slaves with a concession that they were not rightfully in possession of it.

It is not being claimed that the descendants of slaves must seek reparation from those among the white population who happen to be descendants of slave owners. This perhaps would be the case if slavery had produced for the slave owners merely specific hoards of gold, silver, or diamonds, which could be passed on in a very concrete way from father to son. As a matter of fact, slavery produced not merely specific hoards, but wealth which has been passed down mainly to descendants of the white community to the relative exclusion of the descendants of slaves. Thus, it is the white community as a whole that prevents the descendants of slaves from exercising their rights of ownership, and the white community as a whole that must bear the cost of reparation.

The above statement contains two distinguishable arguments. In the first argument the assertion is that each white person, individually, owes reparation to the black community because membership in the white community serves to identify an individual as a recipient of benefits to which the black community has a rightful claim. In the second argument, the conclusion is that the white community as a whole, considered as a kind of corporation or company, owes reparation to the black community.

In the first of the arguments sketched above, individuals are held liable to make reparation even if they have been merely passive recipients of benefits; that is, even if they have not deliberately chosen to accept the benefits in question. This argument invites the objection that, for the most part, white people are simply not in a position to choose to receive or refuse benefits belonging to the descendants of slaves and are, therefore, not culpable or blameable and hence not liable to make reparation. But this objection misses the point. The argument under consideration simply does not depend on or imply the claim that white people are culpable or blameable; the argument is that merely by being white, an individual receives benefits to which others have at least partial rights. In such cases, whatever one's choice or moral culpability, reparation must be made. Consider an extreme case: Harry has an unexpected heart attack and is taken unconscious to the hospital. In the same hospital Dick has recently died. A heart surgeon transplants the heart from Dick's dead body to Harry without permission from Dick's family. If Harry recovers, he must make suitable reparation to Dick's family, conceding that he is not in rightful possession of Dick's heart even if he had no part in choosing to receive it.

The second of the arguments distinguished above concluded that for the purpose in question, the white community can be regarded as a corporation or company which, as a whole, owes reparation to the sons of slaves. Certainly the white community resembles a corporation or company in some striking ways; like such companies, the white community has interests distinct from, and opposed to, other groups in the same society, and joint action is often taken by the members of the white community to protect and enhance their interests. Of course, there are differences; people are generally born into the white community and do not deliberately choose their membership in it; on the other hand, deliberate choice is often the standard procedure for gaining membership in a company. But this difference is unimportant; European immigrants often deliberately choose to become part of the white community in the United States for the obvious benefits this brings, and people often inherit shares and so, without deliberate choice, become members of a company. What is important here is not how deliberately one chooses to become part of a community or a company; what is relevant is that one chooses to continue to accept the benefits which circulate exclusively within the community, sees such benefits as belonging exclusively to the members of the community, identifies one's interests with those of the community, viewing them as opposed to those of others outside the community, and finally, takes joint action with other members of the community to protect such interests. In such a case, it seems not unfair to consider the present white population as members of a company that incurred debts before they were members of the company, and thus to ask them justly to bear the cost of such debts.

It may be objected that the case for reparation depends on the validity of inheritance; for, only if the sons of slaves inherit the rights of their ancestors can it be asserted that they have rights against the present white community. If the validity of inheritance is rejected, a somewhat different, but perhaps even stronger, argument for reparation can still be formulated. For if inheritance is rejected with the stipulation that the wealth of individuals be returned to the whole society at their deaths, then it is even clearer that the white community owes reparation to the black community. For the white community has appropriated, almost exclusively, the wealth from slavery in addition to the wealth from other sources; but such wealth belongs jointly to all members of the society, white as well as black; hence, it owes them reparation. The above formulation of the argument is entirely independent of the fact of slavery and extends the rights of the black community to its just portion of the total wealth of the society.

16

Reverse Discrimination as Unjustified

Lisa H. Newton

I have heard it argued that "simple justice" requires that we favor women and blacks in employment and educational opportunities, since women and blacks were "unjustly" excluded from such opportunities for so many years in the not so distant past. It is a strange argument, an example of a possible implication of a true proposition advanced to dispute the proposition itself, like an octopus absent-mindedly slicing off his head with a stray tentacle. A fatal confusion underlies this argument, a confusion fundamentally relevant to our understanding of the notion of the rule of law.

Two senses of justice and equality are involved in this confusion. The root notion of justice, progenitor of the other, is the one that Aristotle (*Nichomachean Ethics* 5:6; *Politics* 1:2; 3:1) assumes to be the foundation and proper virtue of the political association. It is the condition which free men establish among themselves when they "share a common life in order that their association bring them self-sufficiency"—the regulation of their relationship by law, and the establishment, by law, of equality before the law. Rule of law is the name and pattern of this justice; its equality stands against the inequalities—of wealth, talent, etc.—otherwise obtaining among its participants, who by virtue of that equality are called "citizens." It is an achievement—complete, or, more frequently, partial—of certain people in certain concrete situations. It is fragile and easily disrupted by powerful individuals who discover that the blind equality of rule of law is

Reprinted from *Ethics* 83 (1973), by permission of the journal and the author.

inconvenient for their interests. Despite its obvious instability, Aristotle assumed that the establishment of justice in this sense, the creation of citizenship, was a permanent possibility for men and that the resultant association of citizens was the natural home of the species. At levels below the political association, this rule-governed equality is easily found; it is exemplified by any group of children agreeing together to play a game. At the level of the political association, the attainment of this justice is more difficult, simply because the stakes are so much higher for each participant. The equality of citizenship is not something that happens of its own accord, and without the expenditure of a fair amount of effort it will collapse into the rule of a powerful few over an apathetic many. But at least it has been achieved, at some times in some places; it is always worth trying to achieve, and eminently worth trying to maintain, wherever and to whatever degree it has been brought into being.

Aristotle's parochialism is notorious; he really did not imagine that persons other than Greeks could associate freely in justice, and the only form of association he had in mind was the Greek *polis*. With the decline of the *polis* and the shift in the center of political thought, his notion of justice underwent a sea change. To be exact, it ceased to represent a political type and became a moral ideal: the ideal of equality as we know it. This ideal demands that all men be included in citizenship—that one Law govern all equally, that all men regard all other men as fellow citizens, with the same guarantees, rights, and protections. Briefly, it demands that the circle of citizenship achieved by any group be extended to include the entire human race. Properly understood, its effect on our associations can be excellent: it congratulates us on our achievement of rule of law as a process of government but refuses to let us remain complacent until we have expanded the associations to include others within the ambit of the rules, as often and as far as possible. While one man is a slave, none of us may feel truly free. We are constantly prodded by this ideal to look for possible unjustifiable discrimination, for inequalities not absolutely required for the functioning of the society and advantageous to all. And after twenty centuries of pressure, not at all constant, from this ideal, it might be said that some progress has been made. To take the cases in point for this problem, we are now prepared to assert, as Aristotle would never have been, the equality of sexes and of persons of different colors. The ambit of American citizenship, once restricted to white males of property, has been extended to include all adult free men, then all adult males including ex-slaves, then all women. The process of acquisition of full citizenship was for these groups a sporadic trail of half-measures, even now not complete; the steps on the road to full equality are marked by legislation and judicial decisions which are only recently concluded and still often not enforced. But the fact that we can now discuss the possibility of favoring such groups in hiring shows that over the area that concerns us, at least, full equality is presupposed as a basis for discussion. To that extent, they are full citizens, fully protected by the law of the land.

It is important for my argument that the moral ideal of equality be recognized as logically distinct from the condition (or virtue) of justice in the political sense. Justice in this sense exists *among* a citizenry, irrespective of the number of the populace included in that citizenry. Further, the moral ideal is parasitic upon the political virtue, for "equality" is unspecified—it means nothing until we are told in what respect that equality is to be realized. In a political context, "equality" is specified as "equal rights"—equal access to the public realm, public goods and offices, equal treatment under the law—in brief, the equality of citizenship. If citizenship is not a possibility, political equality is unintelligible. The ideal emerges as a generalization of the real condition and refers back to that condition for its content.

Now, if justice (Aristotle's justice in the political sense) is equal treatment under law for all citizens, what is injustice? Clearly, injustice is the violation of that equality, discriminating for or against a group of citizens, favoring them with special immunities and privileges or depriving them of those guaranteed to the others. When the southern employer refuses to hire blacks in white-collar jobs, when Wall Street will only hire women as secretaries with new titles, when Mississippi high schools routinely flunk all black boys above ninth grade, we have examples of injustice, and we work to restore the equality of the public realm by ensuring that equal opportunity will be provided in such cases in the future. But of course, when the employers and the schools *favor* women and blacks, the same injustice is done. Just as the previous discrimination did, this reverse discrimination violates the public equality which defines citizenship and destroys the rule of law for the areas in which these favors are granted. To the extent that we adopt a program of discrimination, reverse or otherwise, justice in the political sense is destroyed, and none of us, specifically affected or not, is a citizen, a bearer of rights—we are all petitioners for favors. And to the same extent, the ideal of equality is undermined, for it has content only where justice obtains, and by destroying justice we render the ideal meaningless. It is, then, an ironic paradox, if not a contradiction in terms, to assert that the ideal of equality justifies the violation of justice; it is as if one should argue, with William Buckley, that an ideal of humanity can justify the destruction of the human race.

Logically, the conclusion is simple enough: all discrimination is wrong prima facie because it violates justice, and that goes for reverse discrimination too. No violation of justice among the citizens may be justified (may overcome the prima facie objection) by appeal to the ideal of equality, for that ideal is logically dependent upon the notion of justice. Reverse discrimination, then, which attempts no other justification than an appeal to equality, is wrong. But let us try to make the conclusion more plausible by suggesting some of the implications of the suggested practice of reverse discrimination in employment and education. My argument will be that the problems raised there are insoluble, not only in practice but in principle.

We may argue, if we like, about what "discrimination" consists of. Do I discriminate against blacks if I admit none to my school when none of the black applicants are qualified by the tests I always give? How far must I go to root out cultural bias from my application forms and tests before I can say that I have not discriminated against those of different cultures? Can I assume that women are not strong enough to be roughnecks on my oil rigs, or must I test them individually? But this controversy, the most popular and well-argued aspect of the issue, is not as fatal as two others which cannot be avoided: if we are regarding the blacks as a "minority" victimized by discrimination, what is a "minority"? And for any group—blacks, women, whatever—that has been discriminated against, what amount of reverse discrimination wipes out the initial discrimination? Let us grant as true that women and blacks were discriminated against, even where laws forbade such discrimination, and grant for the sake of argument that a history of discrimination must be wiped out by reverse discrimination. What follows?

First, are there other groups which have been discriminated against? For they should have the same right of restitution. What about American Indians, Chicanos, Appalachian Mountain whites, Puerto Ricans, Jews, Cajuns, and Orientals? And if these are to be included, the principle according to which we specify a "minority" is simply the criterion of "ethnic (sub) group," and we're stuck with every hyphenated American in the lower-middle class clamoring for special privileges for *his* group—and with equal justification. For be it noted, when we run down the Harvard roster, we find not only a scarcity of blacks (in comparison with the proportion in the population) but an even more striking scarcity of those second-, third-, and fourth-generation ethnics who make up the loudest voice of Middle America. Shouldn't they demand *their* share? And eventually, the WASPs will have to form their own lobby, for they too are a minority. The point is simply this: there is no "majority" in America who will not mind giving up just a bit of their rights to make room for a favored minority. There are only other minorities, each of which is discriminated against by the favoring. The initial injustice is then repeated dozens of times, and if each minority is granted the same right of restitution as the others, an entire area of rule governance is dissolved into a pushing and shoving match between self-interested groups. Each works to catch the public eye and political popularity by whatever means of advertising and power politics that lend themselves to the effort, to capitalize as much as possible on temporary popularity until the restless mob picks another group to feel sorry for. Hardly an edifying spectacle, and in the long run no one can benefit: the pie is no larger—it's just that instead of setting up and enforcing rules for getting a piece, we've turned the contest into a free-for-all, requiring much more effort for no larger a reward. It would be in the interests of all the participants to reestablish an objective rule to govern the process, carefully enforced and the same for all.

Second, supposing that we do manage to agree in general that women and blacks (and all the others) have some right of restitution, some right to a privileged place in the structure of opportunities for a while, how will we know when that while is up? How much privilege is enough? When will the guilt be gone, the price paid, the balance restored? What recompense is right for centuries of exclusion? What criterion tells us when we are done? Our experience with the Civil Rights movement shows us that agreement on these terms cannot be presupposed: a process that appears to some to be going at a mad gallop into a black takeover appears to the rest of us to be at a standstill. Should a practice of reverse discrimination be adopted, we may safely predict that just as some of us begin to see "a satisfactory start toward righting the balance," others of us will see that we "have already gone too far in the other direction" and will suggest that the discrimination ought to be reversed again. And such disagreement is inevitable, for the point is that we could not *possibly* have any criteria for evaluating the kind of recompense we have in mind. The context presumed by any discussion of restitution is the context of rule of law: law sets the rights of men and simultaneously sets the method for remedying the violation of those rights. You may exact suffering from others and/or damage payments for yourself if and only if the others have violated your rights; the suffering you have endured is not sufficient reason for them to suffer. And remedial rights exist only where there is law: primary human rights are useful guides to legislation but cannot stand as reasons for awarding remedies for injuries sustained. But then, the context presupposed by any discussion of restitution is the context of preexistent full citizenship. No remedial rights could exist for the excluded; neither in law nor in logic does there exist a right to *sue* for a standing to sue.

From these two considerations, then, the difficulties with reverse discrimination become evident. Restitution for a disadvantaged group whose rights under the law have been violated is possible by legal means, but restitution for a disadvantaged group whose grievance is that there was no law to protect them simply is not. First, outside of the area of justice defined by the law, no sense can be made of "the group's rights," for no law recognizes that group or the individuals in it, qua members, as bearers of rights (hence *any* group can constitute itself as a disadvantaged minority in some

119

sense and demand similar restitution). Second, outside of the area of protection of law, no sense can be made of the violation of rights (hence the amount of the recompense cannot be decided by any objective criterion). For both reasons, the practice of reverse discrimination undermines the foundation of the very ideal in whose name it is advocated; it destroys justice, law, equality, and citizenship itself, and replaces them with power struggles and popularity contests.

The Role Model Argument and Faculty Diversity

Anita L. Allen

Introduction

Proponents of faculty diversity in higher education sometimes advance the "role model" argument.[1] The argument is a familiar player in confrontations over race, gender, and the allocation of employment opportunities. In these contexts, the role model argument asserts that colleges and universities ought to hire females of all races and male members of minority groups to insure that undergraduate, graduate, and professional school students will have appropriate role models among their teachers.[2] The role model argument is popular because the belief that young people need role models is pervasive. In words so familiar that they bear the stigma of cliché, many say that if students are to realize their full potential as responsible adults, they need others in their lives whom they can emulate and by whom they will be motivated to do their best work.

Academic philosophers have seldom shown signs of taking the popular role model argument seriously. To be sure, philosophers who wrote about the moral foundations of civil rights policy in the 1970s and 80s invariably mentioned the argument.[3] But they mentioned it in passing as an argument—though not the most powerful or interesting argument—for a permissive, liberal stance toward policies they labelled "affirmative action," "preferential treatment," "reverse discrimination," or "quotas." Even

Reprinted from *The Philosophical Forum* 24 (1992-93), by permission of the journal.

philosophers like Bernard Boxill, who defended liberal, race-conscious policies for minority and female inclusion, gave the role model argument cursory treatment.[4] Everyone seemed content to regard the role model argument as ancillary to more powerful and interesting arguments for distributive and reparative justice. By the 1990s an apparent consensus had been reached in philosophical circles: the role model argument may reflect legitimate utilitarian concerns, but it does not deserve to be taken seriously as an independent argument for recruiting traditionally excluded minorities and white women.[5]

The persistent popularity of the role model argument in rationales for diversity and affirmative action have made it increasingly important to rethink the consensus. Accordingly, I will examine the power and limitations of the role model argument here. My focus will be the case for black female law teachers as role models for black female law students. The high standing of lawyers in American society justifies close attention to issues within *legal* education. I focus on *black women* in legal education for three reasons. First, black women are one of several groups in higher education still described as excluded or underrepresented. Second, according to one study, black and other minority women who manage to enter law teaching are "at the bottom" of their profession, "hindered by their sex rather than aided by it" when it comes to tenured teaching positions at the nation's law schools.[6] Third, recent events at Harvard University called the nation's attention to black women law teachers and to a particularly strong version of the role model argument made on behalf of black women law students. The events at Harvard prompted a number of minority scholars to assess the logic and politics of the role model argument.[7]

In the spring of 1990, protests by Harvard Law School students demanding faculty diversity culminated in a "sit-in" demonstration outside the office of Dean Robert Clark. Professor Derrick Bell, Harvard's first and most senior black law professor, stated publicly that he would take an unpaid leave of absence until the law school tenured a black woman. Two years later, Harvard had tenured no black woman, students again demonstrated at the Dean's office, and Bell made plans to be away from the law school for a third year.

Bell's actions were praised in some quarters, criticized in others. Critics charged that Bell's demand for a woman of color on the faculty was unreasonable, in view of the limited pool of qualified minority candidates. Bell replied that the pool of qualified black women candidates appears prohibitively small only because Harvard is determined to perpetuate narrow, self-serving criteria of qualification. Bell's critics also stressed that Harvard's law faculty of about seventy already included six black men, three of whom were tenured, and five tenured white women. To this, Bell responded that the presence of white women and black men on the teaching staff did not answer the full demand for diversity: black women law students, he said, need black women law teachers.

One man's sacrifice in the name of black female role models for black female students drew the attention of the national media. In the wake of publicity, one organization approvingly named Bell "Feminist of the Year." Belittling Bell's efforts in an editorial praising Harvard for offering tenure to four white men, a journalist quipped that "[o]nly in the curious world of university campuses could anyone argue that professors should be judged by their skin color, gender or sexual practices instead of their merit as teachers."[8] Some members of the general public took umbrage at the idea that a school might be pressured by politics to favor a black woman over outstanding white teachers. For them, Bell's demand symbolized the demise of excellence and the excesses of preferential affirmative action policies. Yet, as affirmative action entered its third decade, black women remain largely absent in most fields as higher education teachers. The population of black women tenured as professors of philosophy, mathematics, economics, and the natural sciences is exceedingly small.

From the point of view of Professor Bell and the law students of all races who have risked arrest in the name of faculty diversity, being and providing role models is a distinct moral imperative for faculty and administrators in American higher education. More precisely, being and providing *same-kind* role models is often a moral imperative: black men for black men, black women for black women. Some who oppose the political tactics employed by Bell and the Harvard law students nevertheless share their perspective on the importance of same-kind role models. Indeed, as elaborated below, I share the perspective that minority students need same-kind faculty role models. The demand for same-kind role models is not illegitimate in principle.

The stance that institutions and appropriate individuals ought to provide same-kind role models does not, however, translate into unqualified endorsement of the role model argument for faculty appointments. On the contrary, one might believe, as I will argue here, that when it is used as the centerpiece of the case for minority faculty appointments, the role model argument is profoundly problematic. Obscuring both the varied talents of minority teachers and the varied tasks their institutions expect them to perform, "centerpiece" uses of the role model argument impede fairness and honesty in the faculty appointments process.

Against the Role Model Argument

Who is a Role Model?

I maintain that, despite the very real value to students of faculty role models, we should abandon the minority role model argument heard today in the context of faculty appointments. However, before turning to the case for outright abandonment, I want to make the case for a weaker claim—that greater care should be taken in the phrasing of the role model argument.

The role model argument tolerates an intolerable degree of ambiguity about what it means to be a "role model." Judith Thomson, George Sher, and other philosophers who have attempted to assess the role model argument for race-based and gender-based preferences, have not grappled with the ambiguity of the concept.[9] Thomson's admirable defense of the role model argument was undercut by ambiguity about precisely what she understood a role model to be.

Not everyone means the same thing when they refer to themselves or others as "role models." For example, one academic dean may describe excellent classroom teachers who rarely counsel students outside of class as role models. Another dean may reserve the term for teachers who also counsel students outside of class about career and personal concerns. Different individuals may define "role model" differently; but also, the same individual may define it differently in different settings. A university provost may on one occasion employ "role model" as a term applicable to all faculty members and administrators, yet on another occasion employ it as a term of special approbation for outstanding faculty and administrators.

The ambiguity of the expression "role model" is not so fundamental that moral claims about the importance of role models cannot be sustained. However, it is incumbent upon those who rely upon the term to get beyond the initial ambiguity of "role model." It is helpful to begin by distinguishing the three most common senses in which educators currently employ the term. When we say that a teacher is a "role model," we generally mean that that individual serves as one or more of these:

(1) an *ethical template* for the exercise of adult responsibilities;
(2) a *symbol* of special achievement;
(3) a *nurturer* providing special educational services.

Philosophers must hope in vain to alter by fiat the ordinary language practices of the general public. However, it would greatly clarify academic debates about the value of role models and the role model argument were the academic community always to specify whether the role models at issue in a given instance are supposed to be templates, symbols, or nurturers.

All teachers are ethical templates, but only some significantly function as symbols and nurturers. When teachers teach, they model the role of teacher. They are ethical templates, men and women whose conduct sets standards for the exercise of responsibilities. Like other teachers, law school teachers are role models in the ethical template sense. The manner in which faculty members exercise their responsibilities as teachers sets standards for how those responsibilities ought to be exercised. How law school teachers speak and behave will suggest something to their students about how law school teachers ought to speak and behave. Because most law professors are also members of the bar or bench, the conduct of law professors also carries general messages about the exercise of responsibility in adult roles other than teaching, especially the roles of attorney and judge.

As ethical templates, teachers can set high standards or low. An alcoholic teacher who routinely teaches classes in a state of intoxication would set an arguably low standard. Even if the content of an inebriated teacher's lectures were otherwise adequate, one could still argue that the lecturer was a poor role model. An arguably praiseworthy role model who set a high standard may not be viewed as such by students. When visiting professor Patricia Williams taught a commercial law course at a prestigious law school several years ago, students quickly devalued her modeling of the commercial law professor role.[10] As a black female professor attempting to advance original scholarly perspectives, Williams represented a new kind of template. Many students admired her teaching and some said they admired her clothes; but a number wanted a traditional professor's perspective and complained about Williams' teaching to the Dean.

All teachers are ethical templates, but only some are symbols of special achievement. The "symbol" is the kind of role model philosophers most commonly acknowledge. As explained by Thomson and Sher, "role models" are individuals who inspire others to believe that they, too, may be capable of high accomplishment.[11] Kent Greenawalt had this same understanding in mind when he described the utilitarian, "role models for those in the minority community" argument for racial preferences:

> If blacks and other members of minority groups are to strive to become doctors and lawyers, it is important that they see members of their own groups in those roles. Otherwise they are likely to accept their consignment to less prestigious, less demanding roles in society. Thus an important aspect of improving the motivations and education of black youths is to help put blacks into positions where blacks are not often now found so that they can serve as effective role models.[12]

125

Like members of racial minority groups and white women, white men can also be symbols of special achievement. A criminally delinquent white juvenile who reformed himself and became a respected professional' could serve as a role model for others of his same background.

If an individual is to serve as a symbol of special achievement for a group, group members must recognize the individual as belonging to their group. A recognizability requirement thus constrains would-be role models. With this in mind, some have occasionally argued that institutions seeking to hire blacks as role models should hire blacks who "look black" rather than blacks who "look white." But such a requirement does not follow from the recognizability imperative. Physical appearance is only one basis for racial recognition. Outward appearance has never been the only basis of racial identification, not under American race law and not under prevailing American custom. For African Americans, Native Americans, and Hispanic Americans who look— or look to some—like Caucasians, recognition by strangers as members of minority groups may require deliberate verbal disclosure.

Disclosure is essential for the identification of members of a number of minority groups. The faculty diversity movement at Harvard included a demand for openly gay and lesbian law teachers. One cannot be a gay or lesbian role model if no one knows one is gay or lesbian. Serving as a symbol of gay achievement depends upon first disclosing that one is gay. The situation is somewhat analogous for blacks, Native Americans, and Hispanics who "look white." The mere fact that a person is not visually recognizable to strangers as a member of a racial minority group does not mean that such a person will not eventually disclose their racial affiliation and become an effective symbol of special minority achievement. A light-skinned person with African ancestors and a black cultural self-understanding can be as effective as a dark-skinned person with African ancestors and a black cultural self-understanding. Throughout American history black communities have embraced high-achieving blacks of whatever hue as symbols of special achievement for the race, where a black racial heritage was discernable either through appearance, family history, or credible self-disclosures. Indeed, a number of historically important black political leaders have been men of mixed race ancestry who "looked white," but opted against "passing."[13]

Teachers who directly engage students through mentoring, tutoring, counselling, and special cultural or scholarly events are role models in a final sense. They are nurturers. Educators sometimes assume nurturing roles as personal, supererogatory commitments to students they believe would not be adequately served by mere templates and symbols.

The roles of template, symbol, and nurturer are typically conflated in the role model argument for including minorities in higher education. Yet, being a minority group member is neither a necessary nor a sufficient condition for being a "role model" for minority students in every sense identified. For example, a black woman's mere presence in an institution can help to reshape conceptions of who can be a law teacher. Her style and perspectives can perhaps reshape conceptions of what it is appropriate for law teachers to do and say.

But only some black women teachers are role models in the sense of "symbols" of special achievement and "nurturers" of students' special needs. Blacks nominally hired as symbols may turn out to be nurturers. In this vein, Robert K. Fullinwider once hinted that implicit in the rationale for placing blacks in "visible and desirable positions" is the possibility that individual blacks will provide "better services to the black community."[14]

However, some black women "symbols" do not give a "nurturer's" priority to the advancement of the interests of black students and wider black communities. These women would understandably resent students and colleagues who assume on the basis of their race and gender that they are willing to add nurturing to a long list of tasks that include teaching, writing for publication, and committee assignments. In arguments for academic role models for black women, a high degree of clarity requires specification of the tasks one expects the role model to perform. Not every black woman will be willing or able to perform every task.

The Cost to Integrity and Well-Being

We can continue to speak ambiguously about role models and breed misunderstanding. Or, we can begin to speak less ambiguously, as I suggest, about templates, symbols, and nurturers. But the ambiguity of the expression "role model" is only a small part of what makes the role model argument problematic. Even after conceptual clarity is achieved about what "role model" denotes, premising minority recruitment centrally on the capacity to serve as role models proves too costly.

One cost is that reliance upon the role model argument helps to sustain the widespread prejudice that African Americans, Hispanics, and members of certain other minority groups are intellectually inferior to whites. Faculties typically use the role model argument for minority appointments in situations in which they would rarely think to cite role modeling capacities as a reason for hiring whites. They hire white men on the expectation that they will excel as teachers, scholars, or administrators. They hire minorities, notwithstanding a presumption of lesser talent, on the expectation that they will serve as minority role models. The role model argument therefore functions as an excuse for employing someone regarded as lacking full merit.

Believing that they are better than prejudiced colleagues assume they are, and knowing that they will in fact serve as templates, symbols, or nurturers, some minority job candidates may be content to secure academic employment on grounds that imply inferiority. This is why conservative efforts to shame minorities out of accepting affirmative action appointments have largely failed. Minorities understand how valuable they are to their institutions, even if conservative opponents to minority recruitment do not. Yet to escape the degradation of fair process that role model–based recruitment represents, higher education has two choices consistent with integrity. It can limit minority recruitment to individuals who satisfy the traditional, narrow conceptions of merit purportedly applied to white men. Or, it can premise recruitment on revised, broader conceptions of merit proposed by progressives who aggressively contest tradition.

A second cost of the role model argument relates to the first. It perpetuates institutional bad faith. The role model argument mires those who rely upon it in self-deception. The role model argument dishonestly understates the actual contributions of minority faculty. Like nonminority colleagues, minority faculty must prepare and teach courses, supervise student projects, write for publication, and serve on committees. The role model argument obscures these typical responsibilities. Blacks retain posts as pilots, not because they are role models, but because they are skilled at keeping their aircraft aloft. By analogy, black college and university professors ultimately receive tenure, not because they are symbols and nurturers, but because they provide essential services. Colleges and universities should not be permitted to pretend that the only valuable service performed by minority faculty is role modeling.

The role model argument has a third cost. Reliance on the role model argument can easily result in the search for someone's stereotype of the best or the most "positive" minority. Those charged with making judgments about who is and is not a positive minority role model can easily run amok. Blacks and other minorities who look, sound, or think like upper middle class whites may be overvalued by decision makers who are not at ease with cultural diversity. Those with the power to appoint faculty may interpret traits of ethnic differences as indicia of lesser competence.

But by the same token, minorities with "white" attributes may be undervalued by decisionmakers who see no point to hiring minorities who are not discernably ethnic in appearance, speech, or perspective. At Harvard Law School, Professor Bell and the student diversity activists expressed a preference for minority faculty with culturally distinct perspectives, significant ties to the minority community, and an express willingness to nurture.

The knowledge that they are hired as minority role models in an atmosphere penetrated by stereotypes of race and gender can impose undue psychological burdens on affected faculty. The burden in question is the burden of measuring up to an unreasonable number of externally imposed standards as a condition for community approval. It can make a black woman feel that she must be perfectly black, not just black; perfectly female, not just female. Even an enthusiastic role model can tire of the extraordinary service she is expected to give her school. She can grow weary under the weight of having to wear her racial commitment and feminism always on her sleeve.

A final cost of the role model argument is that it can signal to white male faculty that they do not have role-modeling obligations toward minority students. The possibility that white faculty may regard minority students as unreachable and thus, to an extent, unteachable, is an alarming one. Even today, white males are the predominant group in most departments in most institutions in the United States. It is from white men that black women, for example, are required to learn most of what they need to know. Race-related faculty indifference is a commonly heard student complaint. Appointing a quota of same-kind role models in response to such complaints may strike some whites as all they need to do to address the special needs of minority students. Minority students can greatly benefit from same-kind minority role models. But it does not follow that black role models on campus leave white faculty with less than equal educational obligations towards minority and nonminority students.

Affirmative Action

I support many of the goals and practices of affirmative action in faculty appointments, especially the practice of relying upon broad criteria of merit that encompass a range of talents and methods. Yet one could easily mistake my criticism of the role model argument for a criticism of affirmative action in faculty appointments. This is because, in the political realm, the role model argument is closely associated with the case for affirmative action. The role model argument ties the case for affirmative action in student admissions to the case for affirmative action in faculty appointments in the following way. Once historically white institutions begin to admit minority group members in large numbers, they create a need for minority teachers to teach, inspire, and mentor. The role model argument acknowledges the needs of affirmative action students for affirmative action to supply appropriate faculty.

However, the logical relationship between the affirmative action and role model argument is less snug than first appearances might suggest. In theory, a staunch opponent of affirmative action could advocate hiring minority role models to improve the educational experiences of "wrongly" admitted, "unqualified" affirmative action students. To put it starkly, even a racist or sexist could advance the role model argument.

The soundness of the role model argument does not entail or presuppose the soundness of all of the liberal egalitarian arguments for affirmative action found in the philosophical literature.[15] In fact, because what I am calling the role model argument defends minority faculty recruitment on utilitarian grounds referring to student and institutional need, rather than on grounds referring to compensatory justice, reparative justice, or moral desert, the role model argument is neutral as among affirmative action's possible forward- and backward-looking rationales. Possibly some of the best reasons for pro- viding minority students with same-kind teachers relate narrowly to educa- tional necessity rather than broadly to the moral necessity of redressing slavery or addressing current economic injustices in the wider society.

In light of the foregoing, the logical linkage between the role model ar- gument and the case for affirmative action is attenuated. Nevertheless, some for whom the end of increasing the number of minority faculty is paramount may object on practical grounds to my call for the abandon- ment of the role model argument. "Sure, the role model argument has the drawbacks you identify; but it works to get minorities onto faculties; it therefore has strategic value for minority inclusion and empowerment."

This strategic defense of the role model argument is ultimately unper- suasive. To counteract myths of minority inferiority, while avoiding stereo- typing and institutional self-deception, minority appointments must be made on grounds that yield to or aggressively contest traditional notions of merit. It is tempting to view the presence of institutionally designated mi- nority role models as necessarily a step toward satisfying the need for bet- ter representation and resources for minority communities. But it is unrealistic to suppose that an isolated black woman law teacher or Latina mathematician represents meaningful gains in minority power. Minority professors are sometimes disaffected by their labors and marginalized by their colleagues. The presence of minority faculty does not guarantee that minorities share power in the simplistic cause-and-effect fashion suggested by defenders of strategic approval of the role model argument.

The Need for Same-Kind Role Models

The claim Professor Bell made for a black female law professor for black female students at Harvard Law School struck many as untenable. I would conjecture that most in higher education greet the claims made for same- kind role models with frank skepticism. Would law students of any race or status be better off if schools provided more same-kind faculty role mod- els? There appears to be evidence to the contrary. Blacks who attend his- torically black colleges, where black faculty role models abound, receive lower scores on average on the law school admissions test than blacks who attend historically white schools.[16]

130

Some critics dismiss the claim for same-kind role models as just so much political rhetoric. Black "role models," they argue, have political, not educational importance. Mere politics should not, the argument continues *reductio ad absurdum,* lead schools to invest in endless searches for black females, handicapped lesbians, and every other minority group that might claim special needs.

To get beyond this skepticism, some insight is needed into the experiences of persons from traditionally excluded minority groups, such as black women. Until recently, little was known about the experiences of black women in legal education. The number of black women law teachers and students was small and their misfortunes were their closely guarded secrets.

First as a student and professor in the field of philosophy, and later as a student and professor in the field of law, I have had numerous experiences that point toward the need for faculty diversity and same-kind role models. My experiences, sketched below in illustrative examples, suggest why so many minority group members and their supporters strongly believe in the need for minority templates, symbols, and nurturers. As the dates of each of my examples suggest, there may be as much old-fashioned prejudice and insensitivity to contend with in the 1990s as there was in the infancy of the civil rights and women's movements, over two decades ago.

Perhaps the most important rationale for same-kind role models is this. White men, who predominate in higher education, have frequently failed to communicate confidence in the possibility of minority achievement. Snap judgments made on the basis of skin color alone are not uncommon; nor are begrudging affirmative action appointments. Black women have been made to feel inferior and out of place in higher education:

(1) In 1971, a white male classics professor to a black female student: "Why don't you forget about college and become an airline stewardess?"

(2) In 1976, a white male undergraduate to his black female teaching fellow in philosophy on the first day of class: "What gives you the right to teach this class?"

(3) In 1978, the white chairman of a philosophy department to a black female candidate for an assistant professorship: "You don't have the kind of power we are looking for, but I am personally committed to affirmative action."

Increasing the number of minority faculty could increase the chances that minority group members will find peers and role models in the ivory tower capable of believing sincerely in their competence. Moreover, a flourishing minority community within an institution could reduce the tendency to stereotype nontraditional students and faculty members as third-rate intellects.

White male professors have often defined agendas that ignore the intellectual needs of minority students. This can happen when "traditional" faculty take narrowly western perspectives or exclude from their courses issues affecting minority communities. It can also happen, however, when "progressive" faculty view their classrooms as opportunities to convert conservative students into radicals:

> (4) In 1982, a white male law professor to a black female law student: "I'm not aiming this class at people like you, I'm aiming it at the conservative white males headed for Wall Street."

In law schools, one problematic side effect of white professors ignoring the intellectual needs of minority students is that students come to believe that whites teach an established "white" version of the law, and blacks teach a different "black" version:

> (5) In 1987, a black male law student to a black female professor: "I'm not taking any courses from blacks; I want to learn the same thing the white boys are learning."

In a different vein, white professors' racial slights can seriously undercut professional relationships based on mutual respect:

> (6) In 1981, a distinguished white male philosophy professor to a black female, now a professional colleague: "You look like the maid my family once had."
> (7) In 1990, a white colleague to a black female colleague with curly hair tied back with a bandanna: "You look like Buckwheat."

Sexual harassment, including unique, race-related forms of sexual harassment can also undercut professional relationships:

> (8) In 1977, a white male professor to a black female former student who dropped him as an advisor after an uninvited kiss: "I thought you were my student; I was surprised to learn you'd completed your dissertation under someone else."
> (9) In 1990, a white male college professor to a black female law professor at a conference panel on discriminatory harassment on

campus: "You shouldn't mind being called a jungle bunny; bunnies are cute and so are you."

Painful, demoralizing experiences such as these lead black women to develop personal skills, social perspectives, and concerns to which their students are beneficially exposed throughout the course of formal education. It can teach a black female student a great deal to have access to black women teachers who have negotiated the gauntlet of racism and sexism that she, too, must negotiate.

It is important for minorities training to be professionals to know how to maintain composure and self-respect in situations like these:

(10) In 1983, a white female undergraduate in a class on the subject of affirmative action taught by a black female: "There are no intelligent black people in Oklahoma."

(11) In 1983, a partner at a prestigious law firm to a black woman law student working as his summer intern: "Write a memo explaining why legislation requiring private eating clubs to admit minorities and women would be unconstitutional."

(12) In 1990, a white female law student to an Hispanic student in the presence of a black woman law professor: "Forget about trying to improve this school's loan forgiveness program for public interest lawyers. If you ever have any problems paying back your student loans you can always contact me, a person of privilege and increasing privilege, for help."

Those who disparage the demands for same-kind role models must try to understand the kinds of life experiences that prompt them. Behind the demands for same-kind black female faculty role models for black female students lies a fundamental sense of abandonment. As undergraduate, graduate, and professional school students, black women often feel that their institutions have abandoned them to racism, prejudice, and indifferent or hostile teachers.

This feeling of abandonment increases the alienation and hostility of minority students. It may correlate with underachievement among black women who attend even the best predominately white schools; and it may help to explain the high rate of minority undergraduate attrition. Quite possibly, good black female students would do even better if "same kind" role models were available to serve as examples (ethical templates), motivators (symbols of special achievements), and attention givers (nurturers).

Although white males, black males, and other categories of teachers could serve black women in these ways, the fact of the matter is they do not, they have not, and, to some extent, they cannot in the current social and political climate. The demand for same-kind role models heard today underscores the diversity of student needs that results from the diversity of Americans' social experiences.

Conclusion

My thesis has the flavor of a paradox. I argue for role models, but against the role model argument. But it is no paradox to say that we should praise faculty role models who take seriously their power and responsibilities as templates, symbols, and nurturers—but condemn uses of the role model argument that treat minorities like inferiors. Nor is it a contradiction to say that we should praise the minority and white female faculty who are willing to accept jobs others believe they are not qualified to hold, but condemn those who offer jobs to minorities and white women whose professional equality they are not prepared to admit.

After twenty years in higher education as a student and teacher, I have come to accept as true empirical claims commonly made by friends of the argument for same-kind role models: minority students have special role modeling needs that minority faculty are uniquely placed to service. The same decades of experience point toward the need for an egalitarian and empowered vision of minority teachers, scholars, and administrators. The "role model" argument for minority appointments simply obstructs such a vision.

Higher education has taken on the education of students from all segments of the community. In doing so, it has assumed an obligation to provide role models for students who need them. To meet this obligation, colleges and universities will have to diversify their faculties to include men and women of varied backgrounds. The goal of faculty diversification is distorted when the search for minority candidates—and not others—is understood principally as a search for role models rather than as a search for talent in its many and diverse forms. Faculties will have to diversify their talent, but diversification is not enough to satisfy the need for role models. Schools will have to encourage their faculties to be more responsive and respectful than ever before.

18

Proportional Representation of Women and Minorities

Celia Wolf-Devine

I begin by asking a question, an affirmative answer to which seems pre-supposed by the current debate on affirmative action[1]: Is there necessarily something wrong if there is a low percentage of African Americans or women or Hispanics, et cetera, in the field of college teaching relative to their proportion in the population at large? Why is this a goal we should aim at? I do not mean to deny that women and racial and ethnic minori-ties have been victims of discrimination in academia (although this is by no means limited to blacks, Asians, Hispanics, and Native Americans—con-sider, for example, Polish, Lebanese, or Portuguese Americans) or that some discrimination still persists. Such discrimination is bad and should be eliminated; in fact, we ought to put more resources into enforcing anti-discrimination laws. My argument here is that there is no reason to believe that proportional representation of minorities and women among the pro-fessoriate is a requirement of justice or that a situation where such pro-portional representation obtained would necessarily be better than one in which it did not.[2]

Arguments that might be advanced in favor of the claim that something is wrong if women and minorities are not proportionally represented fall into two general categories: those that take the existence of such statistical dis-

Reprinted with minor omissions from *Affirmative Action and the University: A Philosophical Inquiry*, ed. Steven M. Cahn (Philadelphia: Temple University Press, 1993), by permission of the pub-lisher and the author.

parities to be evidence of discrimination or injustice, and those based on the value of diversity. These two types of arguments differ in that those based on the need for diversity would not prove that universities are required as a matter of justice to appoint more women and minorities, but merely that it would be educationally desirable were they to do so. But if it could be shown that the lack of proportional representation of minority groups among the professoriate either itself constituted an injustice or provided adequate evidence of the existence of ongoing injustice, then the case for involvement of the federal government to correct this becomes stronger.[3]

Is Proportional Representation a Requirement of Justice?

Does the lack of proportional representation of women and minorities among the professoriate constitute an injustice? Or is it necessarily evidence of discrimination or injustice of any sort? It would be evidence of injustice or discrimination only if it is reasonable to believe that, in the absence of discrimination and injustice, women and all racial and ethnic minorities would be proportionately represented in college teaching (and other professions). But *is* it reasonable to believe this?

The important issue here philosophically is where we place the burden of proof. Should we assume, as Becker does, that the statistics reflect some sort of discrimination or injustice unless we have evidence to the contrary?[4] But why put the burden of proof here? While it is legitimate to put the burden of proof on the employer in cases where the proportion of women and minorities hired is radically lower than their proportion *in the applicant pool*, the case is totally different when we are comparing the proportion of women and minorities in the professoriate with their proportion in the population as a whole.

Looking first at racial and ethnic groups, there is no prima facie reason to suppose that members of different racial and ethnic minorities would be equally likely to want to go into the professoriate and, on the contrary, many reasons to expect that they would not. To the extent that ethnic and racial groups form at least partially self-contained communities (and they do), members of one community will value different sorts of character traits, encourage the acquisition of different skills, and have different ideas about what sorts of jobs carry the most prestige.[5] Most arguments in favor of affirmative action in fact suppose that racial and ethnic groups differ in these sorts of ways; if they did not then bringing in a wider variety of such groups would not contribute to diversity.

In one culture, scientists might be particularly respected, while in another being a media personality might be viewed as the height of success.

Sometimes traditional patterns in a culture predispose members toward certain professions, as the great respect for Torah scholars in Jewish culture fits very naturally with aspirations for careers as scholars or lawyers. Cultures that are highly verbal might be expected to produce more teachers than others. In addition, of course, as some members of a community go into a particular field, others aspire to go into it also since they already know something about it from their friends and relatives and have contacts in the field.[6]

So even if equal percentages of the members of all racial and ethnic groups might desire some sort of prestigious job, there is no reason to suppose that all of them would regard the same jobs as prestigious. Or to put the point more bluntly, not everyone would regard being a professor as prestigious. And there are special reasons why college teaching might be less attractive than other professions to those (for example, blacks and Hispanics) who are trying to struggle out of poverty. Due to its low salaries relative to the amount of training required, college teaching has long tended to attract people brought up in relatively secure financial conditions, plus a few other individuals who feel a strong calling to the intellectual life.

To put the dialogue about affirmative action in academia in the proper perspective, we need to keep in mind some background facts. Certainly there are some prestigious research institutions where professors make excellent salaries, and in business or technical fields professors can often make good money consulting and exercise some power in the larger society. But the salary of the average academic has not kept pace with salaries in other fields; non-academics I meet are universally shocked to learn how little professors are paid. An associate professor I know is forced to teach an extra night course each term, to teach both summer sessions, and on top of that to sell suits at a men's store during the Christmas season in order to be able to support a wife and two children and to meet mortgage payments on a house in an area that is adequate but by no means fancy.

In addition, the social status of professors (particularly in the humanities) has declined significantly from what it was in the 1950s and 1960s. (And if affirmative action is stronger in academia than elsewhere, this might lower the status of professors still more, since they would be perceived as being appointed because of their sex or race.) These problems, together with a widespread loss of a sense of purpose among academics, have led to a lot of demoralization among faculty. Ambitious young members of minority groups may quite reasonably prefer careers in law, politics, industry, or the media. Indeed, the problem of how to attract bright young people of *any* racial or ethnic group into college teaching is becoming increasingly severe. Even students who feel strongly drawn to the intellectual life are often deterred from pursuing academic careers by poor salaries and by what they hear about academic politics.

If I am right, then, one important reason why racial and ethnic minorities are not proportionately represented in the professiorate is because those who are in a position to acquire the credentials are going into other professions. Bright, ambitious members of such groups who have B.A.s often find careers in other areas more attractive than college teaching. This is partly a function of their cultures, which may not accord high prestige to professors relative to other professions, and partly a result of low salaries and demoralization among many (although certainly not all) professors. And in order to attract them into the professoriate, it is essential to begin by improving the situation of those already in the field in a number of ways (and not just salary, although that is important). We should then make it clear to minority members that they are genuinely welcome in academia and will receive fair consideration.

Another reason why racial and ethnic minorities are not proportionally represented in the professoriate is because large numbers of them have been deeply scarred by poverty (and often racism) and do not enter college. They are therefore not even in the running for becoming college teachers or for pursuing most careers with high status and pay. The difficulties involved in remedying this situation are massive, and the universities can play only a limited role. Universities could, for example, set up tutorial programs aimed at helping disadvantaged students (and staffed by faculty and student volunteers). Or they could offer scholarships for college and graduate school to talented disadvantaged students or have need-blind admissions if they can afford to do so. Since such programs are costly, government assistance would probably be necessary.

The big question that arises at this point is to what extent such remedial programs should be directed at racial and ethnic minorities. At this point I believe another background fact becomes relevant—one that is too often overlooked by supporters of affirmative action. During the Reagan years, American society underwent a marked polarization between rich and poor. We have, in fact, the most extreme polarization of any industralized country (measured by the gap between the wealth of the upper fifth of society and that of the lower fifth). And it is arguable that affirmative action has contributed to this polarization (at least it has done nothing to prevent it), since those women and blacks who were in a position to take advantage of it (i.e., those who had suffered less discrimination) did so, leaving the really poor no better off and simply displacing other groups and pushing them down into poverty.[7]

The problem of the widening gap of rich and poor should be confronted directly, rather than gearing remedial programs too closely to race

and ethnic group (as affirmative action does). In addition to making people more rather than less race conscious and generating resentments along
racial and ethnic lines, such programs are not radical enough, because they
lead people to think that by appointing middle-class blacks, Hispanics, or
Asians that they have thereby really helped the poor.

The poor need direct assistance, and it is not only minority members
who are poor. There are enormous numbers of white poor, particularly in
rural areas of the South. Many ethnic groups are impoverished and have
suffered discrimination at least as severe as that against Hispanics and
Asians. The children of single mothers of all races and ethnic groups have
been pushed down into severe poverty, and many blue-collar workers have
been impoverished (e.g., small farmers or residents of the Minnesota Iron
Range). Programs targeted at the economically disadvantaged should perhaps be supplemented by special compensatory programs aimed at blacks
and Native Americans (since most Hispanics and Asians are recent immigrants, compensatory arguments do not carry the same force in their case).
I do not here take a position on this thorny issue, except to say that not all
scholarships and special assistance programs should be earmarked for such
groups, but a significant proportion should be awarded on the basis of
merit and financial need alone.

The more poor people are brought up into the middle class, the more
of them will obtain B.A.s and be in a position to consider college teaching as a career. We will still need to improve the situation of the professoriate if we are to be able to attract good Ph.D. candidates. But at least
more people will have a chance to enter the profession, especially if graduate school scholarships are available to talented students who need them.
The poor who are not upwardly mobile (e.g., the retired, the chronically
ill, the mentally retarded, etc.) will still need direct financial and medical
assistance.

The situation of women in academia is somewhat different from that of
ethnic and racial minorities, in that they are closer to being proportionally
represented, at least in the humanities, although they tend still to be absent
from some scientific and technical fields and from the very most prestigious
positions. Does this prove they are being discriminated against? Certainly
in some cases they have been and still are discriminated against (especially
in promotion and pay), and these abuses should be corrected. But here also
the statistics alone do not establish discrimination. Their own choices to
spend more time with their children may account for their failure to advance as far or as quickly as their male colleagues and for the fact that they
hold part-time positions more frequently. Certainly not all women make
these sorts of choices, but enough do to affect the statistics. (It could, of
course, be argued to be unjust that women take on a larger share of child

care, but we should beware of paternalistically telling people what choices they ought to make.)

In order to establish the presence of injustice or discrimination, we need to know more about the actual preferences of the women in question, and not just adopt a bureaucratic approach of trying to get the numbers to come out right. Suppose an academic couple who wish to combine career and family decide between themselves that he will work full time and she will work part time in order to spend time with the children. Then suppose that due to affirmative action he is unable to get a full-time job and she is forced to take full-time work to support the family. The statistics may look better, but both people are less happy than they would have been without affirmative action.

Proportional representation of women and of blacks, Hispanics, Native Americans, and Asians in the professoriate, then, is not a requirement of justice, and a situation where such proportional representation is present is not necessarily more just than one where it is not—for example, if it was obtained by overriding the preferences of those concerned without some reason other than a desire to get the statistics to come out right.[8] Furthermore, a society where such proportional representation was present along with a vast and unbridgeable gap between rich and poor would be less just than one with a more equitable distribution of wealth and opportunities for advancement but which lacked proportional representation of women and minorities in some professions.

Promoting Diversity

Affirmative action is often defended as a means to greater diversity on college faculties, and a faculty that does not have proportional representation of women and minorities is regarded as not diverse enough. Diversity, unfortunately, has become something of a buzz-word these days, and it is necessary to give thought to what sorts of diversity should be promoted and why. And this requires some reflection about what the purposes of the university are. Diversity of opinion is not enough, but neither is diversity of methodology. Not all methodologies deserve representation. Consider, for example, astrology, or the systematic vilification of one's opponents.

If one agrees that encouraging intelligent dialogue about important issues is one of the purposes of the university (and I do), then this has at least some implications for the sort of diversity we want. If dialogue is of central importance, then it is desirable to have intellectual diversity. But limitless intellectual diversity is not good; the value of diversity must be weighed against the value of community. Certainly, there can be communities that are too ingrown and homogenous. If a psychology department appoints only behaviorists, then students are deprived of exposure to other quite legitimate traditions of thought within their discipline. And the same is true if an economics department appoints only followers of Milton Friedman, or a philosophy department appoints only Thomists or only phenomenologists. But on the other hand, too much diversity leads to the breakdown of communication between groups. If this occurs, faculty become unable to talk with each other and work within totally different conceptual frameworks, making no attempts to respond to positions other than their own. Students, then, tend to become hopelessly confused, give up even trying to develop coherent beliefs of their own, and retreat into just giving each professor what he or she wants. Maintaining community is, thus, just as important for education as introducing intellectual diversity.

Suppose, then, we are agreed that intellectual diversity, per se, is not simply a good to be maximized (and in real life, no one, not even the defenders of affirmative action, believe in the value of limitless diversity); we then must specify what sorts of diversity will contribute to stimulating intelligent dialogue and learning on college campuses. And I see no reason why proportional representation of groups now officially recognized as protected minorities should be expected to produce the right sort of diversity. First of all, diversity of skin color is quite consistent with total ideological conformity and therefore need not conduce to dialogue at all.

Furthermore, as people like Stephen Carter have been pointing out lately, we ought not to suppose that because a person is black or Hispanic that he or she will have some particular set of beliefs or espouse a particular methodology.[9] This expectation is a form of racial stereotyping and as such is demeaning to the person. Pressures toward ideological conformity among members of minority groups are increased by this sort of dishonest attempt to smuggle in one's ideological agendas under the guise of affirmative action. A Hispanic who is a Republican is no less a Hispanic, and a woman who is not a feminist is no less a woman.

There is, then, no good reason to suppose that proportional representation of the minority groups now officially recognized will yield the right sort of intellectual diversity. And the same sorts of arguments developed above could be applied to cultural diversity as well as to intellectual diversity. People from the same cultural background share common prereflective attitudes, patterns of feeling and imagination, ways of talking, and styles of behavior. But although it is educationally valuable for students to be exposed to people from different cultures, limitless cultural diversity is not a good thing (for the same reasons that limitless intellectual diversity is not), and skin color is not a reliable guide to culture. An enormous amount of cultural diversity exists, for example, among blacks and Hispanics. Poor rural Southern blacks, for example, may be culturally more similar to poor rural Southern whites than they are to Northern middle-class urban blacks.

In short, one cannot generate the right sort of diversity (intellectual or cultural) by simply pursuing neatly measurable goals like proportional representation of women, blacks, Hispanics, Asians, and Native Americans. In addition, the sort of diversity needed at a given school will itself be a function of a number of factors, such as the character of the faculty already there, the student body, and the sorts of vocations for which students are preparing. A school preparing students for careers in international business or diplomacy might find that the sort of diversity introduced by appointing foreign nationals to their faculty was particularly valuable, for example. These sorts of judgments involve a great many complex considerations and cannot be made mechanically by trying to get statistics to meet some target percentages (comforting though it would be if things were so simple).[10]

IV. Preference or Impartiality?

19

Reverse Discrimination

Sidney Hook

The phrase *reverse discrimination* has come into recent English usage in consequence of efforts to eliminate the unjust discrimination against human beings on the basis of race, color, sex, religion, or national origin. The conscience of the American community has caught up with the immoral practices of its past history. The Civil Rights Act of 1964 and the presidential executive orders which it inspired have made the absence of open or hidden discrimination of the kind described a required condition of government contracts. An equal opportunity employer is one who pledges himself to a program of affirmative action in order to insure that the invidious discriminations of the past are not perpetuated in masked or subtle form.

An appropriate affirmative action program requires that an intensive and extensive recruitment search be undertaken in good faith, sometimes supplemented by remedial educational measures, in order to equalize opportunities for employment or study. Such programs presuppose that once the recruitment search is over, once the remedial training is completed, the actual selection of the candidates for the post will be determined by one set of equitable standards applied to all. If the standards or tests are not equitable, if they are not related to or relevant to the actual posts that are to be filled, then the standards or tests must be modified until they are deemed

Reprinted from *Philosophy and Public Policy* (Carbondale and Edwardsville: Southern Illinois University Press, 1980), by permission.

satisfactory. In no case must a double standard be employed which enables one group to benefit at the expense of any other. Customarily this adhesion to one set of standards designed to test merit or to determine who of all contending candidates is the best qualified for the post has been known as the civil service principle. It is the only way by which incompetence, corruption, and invidious discrimination can be eliminated. Preferential hiring on the basis of sex, race, color, religion, or national origin clearly violates the civil service principle and the programs of affirmative action that seek to enlarge the areas of equal opportunity.

Why, then, is the demand made for reverse discrimination under various semantic disguises? If all invidious or unfair discrimination is wrong, how can reverse discrimination be justified? The answer sometimes made is that reverse discrimination is not unfair, for it seeks to undo the injustice of the past and the effects of that injustice in the present, by compensating the victims of past injustice at the expense of those responsible for their plight. Were this the case with respect to any particular individual who has suffered from discriminatory practice there would be no moral objection to compensating him or her for the loss and depriving or punishing those responsible for the past act of discrimination. This would be a simple matter of justice, redressing the grievance of the past, and in no sense an act of discrimination—direct or reverse.

It is an altogether different situation, however, when we discriminate against members of any group today in favor of members of another group, not because the individuals of the first group have been guilty of past or present oppression or discrimination against members of the second group, but because the ancestors of the latter have been victimized in previous times. Yet this is precisely what is being done today when preferential hiring practices on the basis of race or sex are followed or when numerical goals or quotas are used as guidelines instead of criteria of merit or qualification.

All such practices which stem from the distortions or misreading of the Civil Rights Act of 1964 and the presidential executive orders are attempts to undo the injustices of the past against members of minority groups and women by perpetrating injustices against members of nonminority groups and men in the present. Can such practices be defended on moral grounds? Let us consider a few historic cases to get our moral bearings:

It is commonly acknowledged that the Chinese laborers who were employed during the last century in building the transcontinental railroad were abominably treated, underpaid, overworked, wretchedly housed, and subjected to all sorts of humiliating discriminations. Is anyone prepared to argue that their descendants today or other Chinese should therefore be paid more than non-Chinese or given preference over non-Chinese with respect to employment regardless of merit or specific qualifications?

Until the Nineteenth Amendment of the U.S. Constitution was adopted in 1920, American women, who were citizens of the country and subject to all its laws, were denied the right to vote. Would it be reasonable to contend that women should have been compensated for past discrimination against their maternal forebears by being given an extra vote or two at the expense of their male fellow citizens? Would it have been just to deprive the male descendants of prejudiced white men of the past of their vote in order to even the score?

Take a more relevant case. For many years blacks were shamelessly and unfairly barred from professional sports until Jackie Robinson broke the color bar. Would it not be manifestly absurd to urge therefore today that in compensation for the long history of deprivation of blacks there should be discrimination against whites in professional athletics? Would any sensible or fair person try to determine what the proportion of whites and blacks should be on our basketball or football or baseball teams in relation to racial availability or utilizability? What could be fairer than the quest for the best players for the open positions regardless of the percentage distribution in relation to the general population or the pool of candidates trying out? What would be the relevance of numerical goals or quotas here? Why should it be any different in any situation in which we are looking for the best qualified person to fill a post? If we oppose, as we should, all invidious discrimination, why not drop all color, sex, religious, and national bars in an honest quest for the best qualified—regardless of what the numerical distribution turns out to be. Of course, the quest must be public and not only be fair but must be seen to be fair.

Whenever we judge a person primarily on the basis of membership in a group, except where membership in a group bears on the task to be performed (soprano voices, wet nurses, clergymen of the same denomination), an injustice is done to individuals. This is the point of my final illustration. When I graduated from the City College of New York in the early twenties, many of my classmates who had taken the premedical course applied to American medical schools. Most of them were rejected because at the time a thinly disguised quota system existed limiting the number of Jewish applicants. This was a great blow to those affected. A few went abroad. Some entered the Post Office system and prepared for other vocations. Now consider the position of their grandchildren who apply to medical schools that have admission practices based on numerical goals or quotas designed to counteract the discriminatory practices of the past against women and minorities. These candidates do not request preferential treatment but only that they be evaluated by equitable standards applicable to all. Is it fair to them to select those who are less qualified under professionally relevant standards? Can they or their forebears be taxed with responsibility for the unjust discriminatory practices of the past which victimized them as well as others? And cannot students of Italian, Polish, Slovak, Armenian, Irish, and Ukrainian origin ask the same questions?

There are certain questionable assumptions in the rationale behind the practices of reverse discrimination. The first is that preferential hiring (or promotion) on the basis of race or sex to correct past bias is like school desegregation rulings to correct the admittedly immoral segregation practices of the past. This overlooks the key difference. In correcting the immorality of past segregation we are not discriminating *against* white students. They are not being injured or deprived of anything by the color of their classmates' skin. All students may profit in virtue of desegregation. But the situation with respect to the allocation of jobs is different. If X and Y are competing for a post, my decision to hire X is in the nature of the case a decision not to hire Y. And if my decision is based on X's sex or race, and not on merit, then it is a case of racial or sexual discrimination *against* Y, which is morally wrong. All invidious discrimination *in favor* of anyone is invidious discrimination *against* someone else.

A second assumption is that one can tell by statistical distribution alone whether objectionable discrimination exists that calls for corrective action. This is absurd on its face. Unless there is specific evidence of individual discrimination, at most only a suspicion of discrimination can be drawn warranting further inquiry. Only when we are dealing with random selection where no criteria of merit are involved, as in jury rolls or in registration procedures or voting behavior, are statistical disproportions at variance with population distribution prima facie evidence of bias in the process of selection. My favorite example of nondiscriminatory statistical disproportion is that in the past the overwhelming majority of the captains of the tug boats in New York Harbor were of Swedish origin but this constituted no evidence of the presence of anti-Semitism or prejudice against blacks. The disproportion of black teachers in black college faculties is certainly not evidence of a policy of discrimination against whites.

A third related assumption is a particularly mischievous one. It holds that where there is no overt or covert discrimination, and equal opportunities are offered, the various minorities within the community will be represented in all disciplines, professions, and areas of work in roughly numerical proportionality to their distribution in the total pool of the population or in the community pool or in the pool of the potentially utilizable. There is not a shred of evidence for this assumption. Human beings do not constitute a homogenized mass in which interests, ambitions, historical and social traditions are equally shared. Potentially all groups may be capable of acquiring or developing any cultural interest just as at birth any normal child is equipped with the capacity to speak any language. But in actual practice family, national, regional traditions, and allegiances as well as the accidents of history incline some groups toward some occupational activities rather than others even where there are no legal obstacles to the pursuit of any. For historical reasons, Polish immigrants and their descendants did not go into sheepherding or fishing while Basques and Portguese did. Whenever any-one maintains, in the absence of discriminatory practices, that minority persons or women are "underrepresented" or "under-utilized," the as-sumption is unconsciously being made that there is a "natural" or "proper" or "correct" norm or level of their representation. Who determines what is the "natural" representation of women among fire fighters, of Irish among policemen and politicans, of Italians among opera singers, of blacks among actors, of Jews among pants pressers, diamond cutters, and mathematical physicists? In time there will undoubtedly be *some* representation from all groups in all fields but only political absolutisms will impose fixed quotas.

A fourth assumption is that with respect to minorities and women, even if all present forms of discrimination against them were completely elimi-nated, this would still not enable them to compete on an equal basis with others because of the continuing debilitating effects of past generations of discrimination against them. It is sometimes said in emphasizing this point, "If you handicap a runner at the outset by burdening him with heavy weights and let him run half the race, you cannot make it a fair race by re-moving the weights when the race has been half run. He will still suffer un-fairly from the effects of that handicap." This is perfectly true for that individual runner in that race and possibly in other races he engages in. He is certainly entitled to special consideration to overcome his handicap on the same principle that any specific individual who has been discriminated against in the past is entitled to compensatory treatment. But surely this does not entitle a descendant of this person who is running against others in a subsequent race to a privilege or handicap over them. Who knows but that the ancestors of the others were also handicapped in past races?

This entire analogy breaks down because it really assumes the inheri-tance of acquired characteristics. Women in Elizabethan times were barred from acting in the theatre and from certain industrial pursuits in the nineteenth century. Did this have a continuing debilitating effect upon their capacities in the twentieth century? If past discrimination has a con-tinuing debilitating effect, how can we explain the tens of thousands of cases of members of minorities who have made good in their professions and vocations without benefit of preferential treatment or reverse discrim-ination?

Another conscience-appeasing justification for the manifestly immoral violations of the principle of equal treatment under just law is the claim that measures adopted to implement reverse discrimination are "merely temporary" or "transitional," until such time as the necessity for it disappears, and race and sex can be disregarded in hiring and promotion practices. This is the position among others of the American Civil Liberties Union. It is obviously question-begging. When will the necessity for reverse discrimination disappear? When all minorities and women are represented in all avenues of work in proportion to their numbers in the populations? The American Civil Liberties Union would be outraged at the proposal "to suspend temporarily" a person's right to a fair trial until the crime wave subsides. Why should any morally principled clear-headed opponent of all forms of discrimination temporarily suspend the protection of equal rights under the law?

We know from other situations that nothing is so permanent as the temporary, especially when vested interest develops in its perpetuation. Once numerical goals or quotas are introduced as "temporary expedients" to overcome the alleged discriminations of the past, psychologically any subsequent effort to abandon or even to modify the goals or quotas is likely to be interpreted as a rebirth of invidious discrimination. On the other hand, the mandatory application of goals or quotas in the hiring and promotion of members of minorities and women is certain to generate resentment among members of non-minorities and men who will regard racial and sexual criteria of appointment as arbitrary, motivated by political considerations for which they pay the costs. They will visit this resentment even on those minority persons and women who have obtained advancement purely on the basis of their own merit. The collegiality among workers will be shattered, and existing racial and sexual antagonisms that may abate in time when fair standards of merit are strictly enforced will instead be intensified.

Another dubious assumption is that once careers are truly opened to talents, members of minorities and women will never make it on their own without the crutch of reverse discrimination in their favor. This either gratuitously takes for granted that the practices of invidious discrimination of the past will continue, despite the laws against them, or it is an expression of racism and sexism. The absence of members of minorities and women in many areas today is not a consequence of their failure to perform satisfactorily in them but to social attitudes, stereotyped expectations of what roles men and women are fit for, which happily are now changing, but which in the past discouraged them from trying out. There is no cogent reason to doubt that just as members of ethnic immigrant groups who suffered from the prejudiced judgments of native Americans have overcome the obstacles thrown up in their path, so the blacks and Chicanos will in time also succeed. The main reason why today larger numbers of these minorities are not found in the professions and specialized academic pursuits is not invidious discrimination against them but rather the absence of qualified applicants in consequence of educational and economic disadvantages. Here is where vigorous remedial action must be undertaken not only by public agencies but by private organizations along the lines of the Reverend Jesse Jackson's "Push Towards Excellence."

Special educational measures must be adopted to improve the quality of schooling on the elementary and secondary school levels and to encourage career choices oriented toward professional and academic life. It cannot be too strongly emphasized that despite the social disadvantages from which minority groups suffer, and which the community as a whole has the responsibility to mitigate and ultimately remove, the minorities themselves are not merely passive recipients of what befalls them, helpless wards of the state whose future is shaped by what others decide for them. They can do, and often have done, much to reshape the educational opportunities, to rekindle the pride and strengthen the drive to succeed in a world that requires more skills and more knowledge, and more schooling to acquire them, than in the past. Studies of the adjustments of immigrant groups to the hardships and environmental deprivation they initially encountered have shown that the family atmosphere, the presence or absence of strong parental guidance, has been more decisive in determining the willingness to avail oneself of educational opportunities than the legislative action itself that prolonged the age of mandatory schooling.

Our educational system must be geared not only to meet the educational needs of the superior students but of ordinary students and even of those who are not scholastically gifted. A vast range of talents is found among all peoples and races. The focus must be on each individual student, regardless of sex or color, in order to determine what his or her educational needs are. Provision must be made therefore for various types of educational institutions, beyond the elementary and secondary level, for students of varying capacities and interests, and for continuing adult education in both the liberal and vocational arts to accommodate both personal development and social change. There is a uniqueness about every student which the spirit and practice of a democratic education must respect. This respect is perfectly compatible with the application of a single and relevant standard of achievement or reward for all in any given institution, according to which some pass and some fail. We may and should guarantee the basic needs of food, shelter, health and education of all citizens but we cannot guarantee anyone against educational failure. Further, everyone in a democratic welfare society such as ours has a right to employment (or to some kind of unemployment insurance) but no one regardless of merit and experience can claim a right to any specific job.

It is apparent that this analysis is based on the belief that it is the individual person who is the carrier of human rights and not the ethnic, national, sexual, or racial group. Once we disregard this universalistic approach which is blind to color, deaf to religious dogma, indifferent to national origin or sex where merit should count, we practically insure the presence of endemic conflicts in which invidious discriminations are rife. This has been the sad story of the past which we are or should be trying to get away from. Some progress has been made and much more is possible. Reverse discrimination, however, threatens that progress. It increases the existing tensions among different groups and converts our pluralistic society into a more polarized society. The evidence that this is already happening is at hand whenever the admirable, original purposes of affirmative action programs have been misconstrued by arbitrary bureaucratic fiat, and guidelines promulgated that mandate numerical goals or quotas.

Successive polls have shown that the overwhelming majority of the population have endorsed equality of opportunity but at the same time have strongly disapproved of numerical goals, quotas, or preferential hiring. A majority may be wrong but with respect to the theory and practice of reverse discrimination, the logic and ethics of the argument support the condemnation. The reasons that lead us morally to disapprove of discrimination in the past are the same as those that justify disapproval of reverse discrimination in the present and future.

20

Preferential Treatment, Color-Blindness, and the Evils of Racism and Racial Discrimination

Richard Wasserstrom

The main subject of my address this evening is programs of preferential treatment based on race. These particular programs, as I shall understand them, are distinctive in that they make the race of applicants a relevant, though not a decisive, consideration in the selections that are made among them for positions within various social institutions.

A full and careful examination of the justifiability of these programs would be worth undertaking today both because such programs do exist and because they are now the object of an intense antipathy emanating from governmental agencies such as the Civil Rights Commission and the Department of Justice, agencies which in the past had a special concern for the disadvantageous social position of the members of the racial groups favored by these programs. Such an examination would, of course, also be appropriate because, since their inception, these programs have been controversial within philosophy. They have generated philosophical interest and disagreement because of the moral issues that are so naturally implicated, issues that concern, for example, the evils of racism and racial discrimination, matters of compensatory and distributive justice, and the justifiability of the departure from an exclusive concern for the qualifications of applicants that these programs require.

Reprinted from *Proceedings and Addresses of the American Philosophical Association* 61 (1987), by permission of the American Philosophical Association.

What I have to say this evening addresses some of these issues, primarily the objection to these programs which is grounded on the claim that they are themselves racially discriminatory and for that reason unjust and wrong. In order to do this, I first sketch the outlines of one kind of defense of these programs, and then turn to this objection and to some others that are connected with it. As will be obvious, even if everything I have to say is right, what I offer is a partial, rather than a comprehensive, defense of these programs. It is one that I hope does succeed in focusing attention upon some of the less obvious issues that criticisms of their justifiability give rise to, as well as upon some of the more prominent ones.[1]

There is one simplifying restriction that I have imposed upon my discussion of these programs; I consider only those programs that give a preference to applicants who are black over applicants who are white. I do this in order to introduce the relevant contextual matters that I take to be crucial. I think, though, that what I have to say about preferential treatment programs for blacks is illustrative of how to approach and assess disputes about the justifiability of similar programs which prefer members of other racial minorities or women, provided, of course, that attention is paid to the difference, if any, in the relevant contextual matters.

I begin, then, with a sketch—and it is only that—of the main steps of the argument supporting the view that these programs are justifiable because of what they do to help make the conditions of social life in our society today more racially just and less racially disadvantageous for blacks than would be the case in their absence.

The first step of the argument consists of the claim that we are still living in a society in which a person's race, his or her blackness rather than whiteness, is a socially significant fact about him or her, that, in other words, a person's race matters. The claim is that to be black rather than white is to be at a disadvantage in terms of the prospects for achieving and enjoying a satisfying life whether understood along economic, vocational, political, or social lines. A crude thought-experiment, suggested in a way by Rawls' idea of a veil of ignorance, can be offered as a rough way to see this. Taking the existing structure and character of our society as given, suppose a person wanted to try to assure the chances of being relatively satisfied rather than dissatisfied with his or her employment or career; relatively politically powerful rather than powerless; relatively secure from the receipt of insensitive, inadequate, or unfair treatment at the hands of the major social institutions such as the police, the courts, the medical establishment, and the housing market, rather than especially likely to be the recipient of such treatment; and able more generally to pursue one's goals and develop one's talents in ways that would be satisfying. Suppose all of this and suppose, finally, a choice of one's race at the moment of birth, a choice whether to be born either white or black. My conjecture is that persons would opt to be born white rather than black.

If it is correct that race does matter in these ways today, then the next claim is that there is in place what can plausibly be described as a *system* of black racial disadvantage or oppression. The regular and pervasive fashion in which this wide array of opportunities is differentially distributed is what makes it plausible to identify it as a system, and the fact that it occurs along racial lines is what makes it plausible to describe it as a *racial system* and a system of *racial* disadvantage. Attention to the full nature of this system, including attention to its ideological features, best explains both why the answer to the thought-experiment is what it is and, as I shall argue later, much of what is distinctively unjust about this system's operation and effects.

Given these two claims, the third premise of the argument is this: even if the aspirations and concerns of those persons who occupy the positions of relative power and advantage within the racial system are those of persons concerned not to further the continuing systemic disadvantage of blacks, the fact that it is a racial system makes it very likely that the system will tend to perpetuate itself unless blacks come to occupy a substantially greater share of the positions within the major social institutions than they have occupied in the past and do now. For this reason, therefore, it seems reasonable to think that *one* way, if not *the* way, by which to help to undermine and destroy that complex, interlocking set of social practices, structures, and ideology which constitutes the existing racial system is to have it occur that blacks do come to occupy more of these positions of power, authority, and the like within the system.

What are the good reasons to believe that changes in the racial composition of the major social institutions, such as the university, are so causally central, if the dismantling of the system of racial disadvantage is to occur with any dispatch? Although I advert to them in all too cursory a fashion, there are at least four, mutually reinforcing, causal relationships of importance that can, I believe, be identified.

The first is that of the significance of actual racial role models which can help to supplant the cultural conception, or picture, of the standard holder of these roles, which is that of the holder as a person who is white.

The second is that of the importance of bringing members of this historically excluded and disadvantaged group into relationships of greater equality of power, authority, and status with members of the dominant white group. When the relationships between blacks and whites are those of significant, pervasive inequality of the kind constitutive of our racial system, then that system's ideology concerning both the nature of racial differences and the appropriateness of the lines of racial dominance and subservience is most comfortably and securely preserved.

The third is that of the reality and significance of the differences between the experiences, conceptions, and understandings of persons who are black and those who are white—differences that are caused by the racial system itself but that then help to shape more than persons' views about the racial system and other matters concerning race.

The fourth, and final, causal proposition relates to how changes in the racial identity of the occupiers of positions within the significant social institutions make directly for changes in the quality and quantity of important social services and benefits available to blacks. The general causal claim here is that blacks will, in general, both be more inclined to care about the provision of these social goods to other blacks, and will also be more able, in a variety of respects and for a variety of reasons, to provide them in forms more appropriately beneficial to their recipients.

In light of all of this, the defense of programs of preferential treatment that I offer is that they are at least presumptively justifiable because of their substantial causal role in weakening the existing system of racial disadvantage whose existence and effects make a person's blackness rather than whiteness have the kind of pervasively different, regularly deleterious social meaning and significance that it does have. The aim of these programs, on my way of defending them, then, is, to help to eliminate this system by having the selections for places turn in part on the race of the applicants—and these programs seem capable of furthering that aim for all of the reasons just indicated. This defense of these programs, it should be noted, is perfectly compatible with the idea that in a fully nonracist society the race of a person would never matter in any way, although, as I shall argue later, the question of how to understand the idea of race in a thoroughly nonracist society is more complicated than appears at first, and the answer to that question has implications of an unexpected sort.

It is possible to object to these programs and to my defense of them on a variety of grounds ranging from the claim that there is no system of black racial disadvantage still in place, to the claim that these programs do not work well enough to effect the anticipated changes in the system, to the claim that these programs are for one or more reasons themselves unjust and wrong.

I have only a little to say about the first objection, even less to say about the second one, and a good deal to say about one version of the third one, which is that these programs are unjust because they are, themselves, committed quite explicitly to the practice of racial discrimination, a practice which is unjust whenever and wherever it occurs.

The first objection, that there is no system of black racial disadvantage still in place today, seems to me, on its face, to be an implausible one. For while persons can, I think, reasonably disagree about how firmly en-

trenched the racial system still is or about how extensive its reach still is, especially when compared to the more overt, legally established one of the
past, it seems to me difficult to deny that race does differentially still matter when it comes to all of the sorts of things I referred to in the thought-
experiment I proposed earlier.

There is, though, a less straightforward version of this objection that can
be found in the philosophical literature as well as elsewhere. Many critics of
programs of preferential treatment claim that preferences based upon
grounds other than those of the qualifications of the applicants are justifiable, but they argue that race is the wrong ground because it is at one and
the same time too overinclusive and too underinclusive a category of preference. Almost invariably, these critics assert that the right category is low
socio-economic class, a category which, they concede, may include a disproportionate number of blacks, but which excludes some blacks and includes any number of whites as well. Their argument, I suppose, although
it is seldom developed very explicitly, is that low socio-economic status is always wrongfully disadvantaging and is, therefore, appropriately taken into
account for that reason when deciding which applicants to select.

The full argument of these critics concerning why it is appropriate to
take socio-economic disadvantage into account is probably a different one
from mine for the appropriateness of taking race into account. Their argument, I suspect, is a more backward-looking one which focuses upon the
circumstances and lessened opportunities of those who were and are poor
and upon the unfairness of ignoring these considerations when assessing
the actual qualifications of applicants for positions. Although this argument is different from mine, I have no quarrel with it; indeed, the argument seems to me to offer plausible, alternative grounds upon which to
justify attention to considerations other than those having to do with the
existing qualifications of applicants. But the point is that this, as an objection to preferential treatment programs based upon race, is quite off the
mark, unless one can establish that there is no system of racial disadvantage comparable to the system of socio-economic disadvantage that is also
in place. I think that reductionist accounts of disadvantage are implausible
here, and certainly the assumption is unwarranted that there must be no
more than one real, or basic, system of disadvantage within any society. I
see no reason whatsoever to believe that the system of racial disadvantage,
which does seem quite real and pervasive, is best explained by reference to
socio-economic realities, or for that matter that the system of gender disadvantage is any more susceptible to such a reductionist explanation. And
if the phenomena which appear to be those of the system of racial disadvantage are not reducible to phenomena of socio-economic circumstance
and position, then race is just the right characteristic of applicants in which

to be interested, whether the reason is to correct for the disadvantages wrongly encountered by black applicants as a result of the racial system's effects upon them or, as I have argued, to help to bring it about that the racial system will be eradicated. Low socio-economic position would be an over- and under-inclusive category by which to hope to do either or both of these things in respect to the racial system, for the same reason that race is an over- and under-inclusive category by which to deal with socio-economic disadvantage. Because there is more than one system of disadvantage in place, the only conclusion which this objection really supports is that persons subjected to more than one of these systems of disadvantage are worse off than persons subject to only one of them.

I do not propose to examine at all the objection founded upon the claim that these programs do not work, or do not work well enough, to effect the changes in the system. I have already suggested the reasons why these causal claims seem to be plausible ones, but because they are largely that, i.e., causal ones, I take the question of their plausibility to be less a philosophical matter than is the case for the other questions I consider. If I am wrong in neglecting the objection, it is, I think, one virtue of my kind of defense of programs of preferential treatment that it does succeed in making clear the distinguishable, though interrelated, theoretical and empirical issues upon which judgments about the plausibility of these causal claims depend.

There is, however, one thing about the forward-looking character of my defense of these programs that is worth noticing. In a moment, I will take up the objection that these programs are unjust because they are racially discriminatory, and it might be thought that if that objection, or any other one founded upon injustice, is a good one, then these programs will have been shown to be unjustifiable because the good consequences they envision must give way when injustices result. I will argue that this objection of injustice is not a good one. However, even if I am wrong about this, the objection is not as decisive as supposed. For while it is true that the kind of presumptive case I have sketched for these programs is a forward-looking one which concentrates upon the causal impact of these programs upon the existing racial system, the effects that are sought all have to do with the eradication of an unjust racial system rather than with consequences of other sorts. The continuation of that system means that its continuing injustices are also in the picture, since they will continue to be borne by persons who should not rightly bear them. These injustices also have to be considered, even if programs of preferential treatment give rise to some of their own. The ensuing assessment of their justifiability might, therefore, have to take account of the comparative injustices, so to speak, rather than being easily or decisively settled by an appeal to overriding considerations of justice when countervailing good consequences of other sorts are all that are taken to be opposed. Nonetheless, any objection that these programs are, themselves, unjust is a serious one, and it is upon just such an objection that I propose to concentrate in what follows.

The general objection, you may recall, is that by their very design these programs are committed to the practice of racial discrimination and are for that reason unjust and wrong. If it was and is wrong to take race into account when blacks are the ones subjected to policies and practices of racial segregation and disadvantage, then, so the objection goes, it must also be wrong to do so when the only thing that is different is that the race of the persons subjected to exclusion or disadvantage has been reversed. The injustice, which remains the same in both cases, is that of the occurrence of racial discrimination—of having things go better or worse for one because of, or in virtue of, one's race. If it is wrong whenever things go better for persons because they are white and worse for others because they are black—if what is wrong is that race makes the difference in that case—then, for reasons of intellectual and moral consistency, it must be wrong for that same reason to have the race of applicants make a difference in the case of preferential treatment programs, too.

The difficulty I have with this as an adequate and convincing objection is not with its appeal to the demands of intellectual and moral consistency, but rather with its lack of specificity as to the nature of the wrongness of the policies and practices of racial discrimination against blacks. What is missing, I believe, is an account of why that paradigmatic example of unjust racial discrimination is wrong and an examination of what that implies about the wrongness of ever having matters of social advantage and disadvantage turn upon race.

One such account can be formulated and developed in terms of certain claims about the irrelevance of race. Despite its initial appeal, I shall argue that there is much about this account that we should reject. It goes like this.

The answer that this account gives to the question of what was fundamentally wrong with, say, the system of racial segregation in the South is that the essential wrongness is to be located in the use of an *irrelevant* characteristic, namely a person's race, to fix the various social and political benefits and burdens. It claims, therefore, that it is the irrelevance of race as a characteristic of persons that makes each and every act or practice of taking a person's race into account unjust and wrong because, given this irrelevance, any interest in, or concern for, race is an irrational one, and because any resulting differential treatment of persons in virtue of their race is, of necessity, arbitrary treatment and for that reason a case, also, of injustice. On this view of things, the primary defect of our own historic system of racial segregation and discrimination is to be located, then, in its necessary capriciousness—in the fundamental arbitrariness that obtains wherever and whenever it is the race of persons upon which matters of any significance turn. And because all persons should be free of the injustice of arbitrary treatment, especially at the hands of governmental and other major social institutions, what is required, in every context, is adherence to the very different, far more defensible principle of color-blindness. Color-blindness is the right principle for persons and institutions; and the primary hallmark of a racially just society would be that in such a society, color-blindness would be both the most accurate description of that society's social life and its fully accepted, fully operative individual and institutional norm. Because preferential treatment programs are color-conscious rather than color-blind, the selections that they make are, on this view, as arbitrary and wrong as are selections made by programs practicing racial discrimination against blacks.

Is this, then, the correct diagnosis of the underlying moral evil of racism and racial discrimination? Is color-blindness the right principle and the right social ideal? I do not think so; not, at least, without some major qualifications.

Consider first the diagnosis of the evil of racism and racial discrimination. One thing to notice is the strangeness of the diagnosis when applied to our country's historic racial practices including the most hideous of them, black slavery. Under the account just sketched, the primary thing wrong with the institution of black slavery is that the particular individuals who were made slaves were relegated to their positions arbitrarily because the assignment was made in accordance with an irrelevant characteristic, namely, their race. That does not seem to me to get at the heart of the evil, for the fundamental thing that was and is wrong with slavery is, I believe, the practice itself—the fact that some human beings were able to *own* other human beings, and all that went with the acceptance of that practice and that conception of permissible interpersonal relationships. The problem with focusing upon the irrelevance of race in this context is the implied assumption that there is another characteristic different from race that might have been relevant. That, too, is what is wrong with a comparable account founded upon irrelevance when it comes to an understanding and appraisal of the practices and institutions which comprised the system of black racial segregation and discrimination well after human black slavery was abolished, or when it comes to an understanding and appraisal of the existing system of black disadvantage.

The fundamental wrongness of the system of historic black racial segregation and discrimination had something to do, I think, with arbitrariness, but it is the special arbitrariness attendant upon the use made of race in the constitution and maintenance of any system of oppression and disadvantage so as to make that system a system of racial oppression and disadvantage. In this sense, the irrationality, arbitrariness, and deep injustice of taking race into account in the manner characteristic of the system of black segregation and the system of racial disadvantage cannot, I think, be contextually isolated or severed from an understanding of the distinct place and role of the racial criterion in the constitution and operation of such systems. There is a special and distinctive kind of injustice when one's blackness or whiteness becomes the basis for fixing persons' unequal positions, opportunities, and status in a systematically pervasive fashion. And it is that which is surely one primary, distinguishing characteristic of our historic system of black oppression and disadvantage. If we are correctly to identify the primary evil of the complex set of practices and ideas constitutive of the system of historic racial segregation, we must attend quite specifically, I believe, to one part of the ideology of that system: that part relating to the assertion and acceptance of the appropriateness of distinct grades of moral, social, and political standing within the society, grades where whiteness and blackness constitute the criteria determinative of the fundamentally different, unequal status of persons. What I think is central to an understanding of the deep immorality of that system has to do, that is, with that part of the system's ideology which gave pride of place, as well as meaning, to the idea that blacks were fundamentally lesser and degraded persons, to be understood by all as such, and to be controlled and regulated by whites so that whites would not be contaminated or otherwise degraded by various forms of interaction with blacks. And it is this ideology which both required and justified preventing blacks from intruding upon, or laying claim to, the more material domains of social importance, since they are where and how such contamination must occur. I think that the primary reason why separate *could* never be equal was that embedded in the very point and meaning of the white-enacted and enforced racial separation was the acceptance and endorsement of these ideas of black racial taint, contamination, and inferiority, and the intimacy of the reinforcing interconnections between this set of ideological commitments and their embodiment in the pervasive set of further, more material inequalities imposed upon the lives of black persons in virtue of their race. Whether it is the phenomena of racially segregated bathrooms, restaurants, swimming pools, golf courses, public transportation, schools, or the housing or the job market, the problem is not one of understanding how the facilities or the material opportunities involved might not have been equal in terms of some crude sense of what was materially provided (although it never was equal), but rather one of understanding how the ideology that informed and gave meaning to these practices and arrangements could ever be thought compatible with any morally defensible position concerning the claims of all persons, as persons, to fundamentally equal membership and standing. I am not at all convinced that the wrongness of these ideas is best captured by identifying them as irrational, but if it is, it is important to see that the irrationality is of a far deeper sort than that identified by the original objection's account of the uniform irrationality of all practices which take an interest in a person's race.

There are, perhaps, other ways to try to preserve the original diagnosis of the nature of the evils of racism and racial discrimination in terms of context-independent arguments about irrationality and arbitrariness. But if they are genuinely context-independent they will, I think, all of necessity fail the test of providing an appropriately enlightening explanation of the nature of the evils of our historic racist practices, which no one doubts were evils and very grievous ones. Yet, if they all must be context-dependent ones of the sort that I have offered, then it is very hard to see how they will be able to establish the wrongness, *per se*, the wrongness as a matter of principle, of all social programs that do make race relevant, just because of their interest in race. Given my way of understanding the nature and the evils of the racism and the racial discrimination of our society, at least, the case I presented for preferential treatment programs is left quite unaffected by this understanding, because the interest that these programs take in the race of persons, and the context in which this interest is taken, are both fundamentally different from those of the racial ideology and the racist practices of the all too familiar kind.

More specifically, preferential treatment programs neither subscribe to nor support an ideology which regards persons who are black rather than white as those who are least problematically and most assuredly to be counted as the paradigmatically full members of the moral and social community. There is no explicit or implicit ideological commitment to a view of whites as the persons whose membership and standing is diminished, or with whom associations can be degrading or contaminating. These programs neither embrace or otherwise sustain the morally corrupt ideological features of a system of racially different social arrangements, practices, and opportunities, features in which ideas of racial superiority and inferiority, ideas of grades of fundamental membership or standing within the community, and ideas of racial taint and contamination are central. As programs designed and introduced to help to dismantle the entrenched racial system of black disadvantage, they do none of this. Nor, in addition, is the setting, in the case of preferential treatment, one in which programs giving preferences to persons who are black thereby add to an otherwise rich supply of material resources and opportunities already available to persons of this racial group. In these and other ways the existing social realities of race, as well as the very point and purpose of programs of preferential treatment, would have to be very different from what they are before these programs could be properly found wanting and criticizable on grounds such as these, grounds that do apply to the historic system of racial segregation and the existing system of racial disadvantage.

Even if I am right about the reasons why the proposed diagnosis of the nature of the evil of racial discrimination is a misdiagnosis when applied to our own society's systems of black oppression and disadvantage, it is also worth examining other parts of the original proposal concerning the irrelevance of race and the attractiveness of color-blindness as a principle and an ideal. Color-blindness, it might be argued, has much to be said for it, especially because it shares none of those ideological commitments to ideas of racial taint and racial inferiority that figured so prominently in any analysis. Why, then, it might be suggested, is it not always the right principle for institutions and individuals, and certainly the right social ideal?

I think there is something plausible about this view, but there are also, I believe, some problems with it—problems, in particular, with the ready acceptance of the claim that color-blindness, as a principle and an ideal, can be understood in a way that reveals a complete independence from all aspects of the entrenched racial ideology.

The natural way to do so and to defend color-blindness is in terms, once again, of an argument about the irrelevance of race, this time an argument about the superficiality of persons' racial identities. On this account, the guiding notion is that there is a wholly narrow, wholly ideologically neutral, understanding of the idea of each person's racial identity which is the appropriate one, and which refers to the subset of surface, naturally occurring characteristics comprising how persons look. On this view, the color-blindness of the forms of individual and institutional life in any thoroughly nonracist society, together with the justness of color-blindness as a principle, are underwritten by the recognition that race is only a matter of appearance and by the further recognition that race is a wholly unchosen set of such superficial characteristics. Because race really is, and properly only would be, a matter of unchosen appearance concerning skin hue, hair texture, and the like, there is and would continue to be an awareness of these natural, superficial differences in appearance among persons, but only in the same way in which there is today an awareness of differences in appearance pertaining to features such as eye color or height. Given this understanding of racial identity, any person's race is and properly should be irrelevant in and for virtually all social contexts for the same reasons that differences in eye-color or height are also so largely irrelevant.

It is evident, I think, that even if everything else about this account were unobjectionable, it would not vindicate the rightness of the principle of color-blindness in a way that undermined the rightness of the use of a

color-conscious criterion of selection by programs of preferential treatment, once they are understood to be efforts to bring about a society in
which race would, in all respects, only be a matter of appearance. Instead,
if it is otherwise persuasive, the general argument offers an additional reason for regarding the system of black disadvantage and white advantage as
an unjustifiable and wrong one, since the advantages and disadvantages of
that racial system turn on just such superficial, unchosen, and irrelevant
features of all the persons reached by it.

So the doubts that I have and that I want to pursue about color-blindness and the irrelevance of race are not at all doubts about whether there
is really more to racial difference and racial identity than surface features
of appearance, no matter what the social realities of race. I see no reason
to doubt any of that at all. But I do think that there are reasons to regard
as suspect the claim that the idea of race as appearance is an ideologically
benign and neutral one, because this same idea of race as appearance is
connected, I think, in certain unobvious ways with the historic ideology of
black racial taint, contamination and inferiority. As a result, the arguments
concerning color-blindness depend quite deeply upon features of that
same ideology when they employ this allegedly minimalist, benign idea of
racial identity as appearance in their understanding of what color-blindness supposes and implies.

That there is something puzzling about this idea of race as appearance
can be seen if we notice that *our* concepts for determining who is black and
who is white are not always capable of being correctly applied simply by re-
course to judgments about the appearance of persons. This is shown by the
fact that we can and do, for example, understand the claim that someone is
passing, that he or she looks white but is nonetheless black, and it is also
shown by how our concepts of racial identity make it possible for us to know
that the race of a newborn infant is black before we inspect any of the newborn's features, provided only that we know that either of its parents is black.
Whether a person is black or white is for us not exclusively or exhaustively a
matter of appearance but is instead, as these cases indicate, also a matter of
geneaology, and sometimes a matter of genealogy despite appearance.

It might be thought, though, that none of this bears in an interesting or
significant way upon the arguments concerning the irrelevance of race as
appearance and the importance of color-blindness. For at the very most, it
might be thought, what has to be made clear is that the arguments for color-
blindness should all be understood to presuppose and to employ new, or reconstructed, concepts of racial identity, concepts which do and would refer
only to appearance. These new, or reconstructed, concepts of race as appearance are, and would be, perfectly serviceable, appropriately neutral
ones, whatever may be the case about the origins and ideologically less be-

nign character of the concepts of racial identity we use today, concepts which may appear to be the same as these new ones but which are really different. These new concepts, so this argument might continue, would certainly be the concepts of racial identity in place and in use in any nonracist society. In such a society not only would there be many more racial intermarriages than there are today, because there would be no racial system of any kind operative within it, but it also would not matter any longer, as a consequence, whether all the children of an interracial marriage were still classified as black. And they would not be, since the race of all children of all marriages would be determined solely by the facts of their appearance.

Despite its appeal, I think the temptation uncritically to accept this way of filling out the account should be resisted. The reason is that there is still something puzzling about how to understand these new, or reconstructed, concepts of racial identity, and there is even more that is puzzling about the anticipated social understanding of practices in such a society that would make use of these new concepts of racial identity.

There is no problem that I can see with the idea that the racial concepts might be wholly descriptive ones, referring to the different skin hues of persons, but in that case it also seems very likely that they would have to be different ones from ours in a way not yet attended to. For if skin hue, for instance, is what the concepts of racial identity are to refer to, then the concepts should surely be expected to mark in some regular way the occurring variations in skin hues. Given the variations in skin hue that exist in our society today, hues which range from very light or pink through darker shades of tan, brown, and black, for example, there is something quite peculiar, I think, about the assumption that any racial categories would be preserved, and there is something even more peculiar about the assumption that anything like our mutually exclusive racial concepts would continue to collect and refer to such a wide variety of different skin hues in establishing persons' racial identities as either black or white. The puzzle is why it is assumed that the society would have and use *these* two categories, no matter how otherwise benign, rather than use the numerous, discriminating color concepts that we already have and regularly use in other contexts to classify for descriptive purposes all sorts of entities according to their differing shades of color. Perhaps, though, if these two, very inclusive, descriptive concepts were otherwise really useful, the claim that they were ideologically benign and only descriptive racial ones might withstand skeptical doubts about the curious degree of correspondence between our racial concepts and categories and these new, wholly descriptive ones of race as appearance. But I am still skeptical, nonetheless.

The more substantial problem, though, occurs once we ask about the persistence or disappearance of social practices and understandings, analogous to ours, which centrally depend upon concepts of racial identity. Here, the practice and social understanding of racial intermarriage exemplifies the problem quite sharply, I think, and in the following way. It is certainly plausible, as the account assumes, to suppose that racial intermarriage, as we are now to understand it, would be a more common occurrence because the race of persons, as we are now to understand *that idea*, would be so largely irrelevant. There would be no more reason for any person to be interested in the race of those he or she might marry than there is now for any person to be interested in whether others they might marry are tall or short, or brown- or blue-eyed. The difficulty, though, is with the supposition that the occurrence of interracial marriages would be identified or noticed at all, and with the supposition that there would continue to be even a benign social understanding of the phenomenon of interracial marriage so that there would be a continuing use for a concept which referred to its occurrence. These suppositions do not seem at all plausible or fully coherent to me.

The idea of race as irrelevant appearance, no matter how benign the concepts of racial identity may be thought to be, cannot, I think, coexist with the expectation of a comparably benign social setting which has a continuing use for a concept of racial intermarriage. For, just as today we have no concepts referring to categories of interheight or intereye-color marriages, I see no obvious way to make sense out of a supposition that there would be a different appropriate, lasting place for a wholly descriptive, ideologically benign concept to be used to mark interracial ones.

If, as the account under consideration seems to assume, a color-blind society is one in which there will continue to be a social understanding of the phenomenon of interracial marriage, that society will also require an ideological context in which persons can make sense out of this conceptually identified social interest. And that ideological context will, I think, prove to be a good deal more connected to our racist ideology of black contamination and taint—a good deal less benign and neutral—than the proposed account assumes.

Thus, the underlying difficulty with the proposal for either new or reconstructed concepts of racial identity of the appropriately benign sort is in part that to be both benign and descriptively useful concepts of racial identity they would have to be different ones from ours in terms of how they designated the race of persons, and in part that the reasons offered to make sense of the resulting designations would have to be ones having nothing in common with those of our racial ideology. These difficulties lead to another, more substantial one, moreover, because it is also supposed that we could anticipate and locate a possible, wholly nonideological, stable place for a continuing social interest in racial intermarriage sufficient to explain the use of a concept of a racial intermarriage once these concepts of racial identity were regularly employed within the wholly racially indifferent forms of social life that are envisioned as the naturally appropriate society for their regular use.

If I am right about all of this, there are, finally, two further things that seem to me worth noticing about color-blindness and about color-conscious programs of preferential treatment. The first is a very general observation which applies to both of them. Because all discussions about race in our society must employ our concepts and our categories of racial identity, they do necessarily to some degree invoke the commitments of the racist ideology which first gave them their meaning and their applicability. In this sense, the problems I have identified are endemic to all arguments concerning the relevance or the irrelevance of race in our society, whether the claims at issue are descriptive or normative ones. It is a false aspiration to believe that we could do otherwise and somehow be thereby assured of our liberation from the reach of the racist ideology that we quite properly seek to disavow and reject. And it is an inadequate conception of a nonracist society which anticipates the preservation of *any* concepts of racial identity and racial difference in and for a social context in which all the realities of our system of racial disadvantage are no more. If and when we have a genuinely nonracist society, even new or reconstituted concepts of racial identity will make little if any sense.

The second observation, however, does provide a reason to distinguish many positions which endorse color-blindness from one such as mine, which defends the attention to race taken by programs of preferential treatment. For the former regularly do accept in a quite uncritical fashion our own concepts of racial identity, which they then employ in their reasoning about the irrelevance of race and the rightness of color-blindness as a principle and an ideal. I am uncertain whether all such positions must do so in order to reach their various conclusions, but it seems to me clear that their nature is such that no occasions are generated for calling these concepts into question or for examining the respects in which the arguments that are developed borrow in unnoticed ways upon the same ideological commitments that are essential parts of our racist ideology. Defenses of programs of preferential treatment, on the other hand, more readily avoid these difficulties, as I think, for example, mine does. For one thing, the justification of the use that is made of our concepts of racial identity by programs of preferential treatment is an overtly contextual and provisional one: given how in fact we have and do determine race, and given the unjust significance and systemic effects of that determination for the lives of persons so classified, there are, as I have argued, reasons to regard race as relevant, since attention to it in processes of selection is one means by which to dismantle this unjust racial system. For another thing, the focus upon the existence of an unjust racial system invites explicit attention to its complexity as a racial system that is constituted of both material and ideological features. This focus encourages the search for the occurrence of entrenched social misunderstandings and social self-deception where matters of race are concerned. And third, because the aim and design of these programs is, on my defense of them, to undermine and eradicate that unjust racial system, there is no theoretical tension whatsoever between the realization of that objective and the anticipation of the full disappearance of the concepts of racial identity which are themselves an important element of that system. Persons can, of course, still disagree about whether programs of preferential treatment can reasonably be thought apt or appropriate ways by which to endeavor to achieve the eradication of that system, but there is a real theoretical consistency which obtains between the justifiability of the provisional use of our concepts of racial identity as one means by which to do so and the claim that the disappearance of the meaning and use of all racial concepts will itself be one important indication of that ideal's genuine realization.

21

The Message of
Affirmative Action

Thomas E. Hill, Jr.

Affirmative action programs remain controversial, I suspect, partly because the familiar arguments for and against them start from significantly different moral perspectives. Thus I want to step back for a while from the details of debate about particular programs and give attention to the moral viewpoints presupposed in different *types* of argument. My aim, more specifically, is to compare the "messages" expressed when affirmative action is defended from different moral perspectives. Exclusively forward-looking (e.g., utilitarian) arguments, I suggest, tend to express the wrong message, but this is also true of entirely backward-looking (e.g., reparation-based) arguments. However, a normal outlook that focuses on cross-temporal narrative values, such as mutually respectful social relations, suggests a more appropriate account of what affirmative action should try to express. Assignment of the message, admittedly, is only one aspect of a complex issue, but a relatively neglected one. My discussion takes for granted some common sense ideas about the communicative function of action, and so I begin with these.

Actions, as the saying goes, often *speak* louder than words. There are times, too, when only actions can effectively communicate the message we want to convey, and times when giving a message is a central part of the purpose of action. What our actions say to others depends largely, though not entirely, upon our avowed reasons for acting; and this is a matter for reflective deci-

Reprinted from *Social Philosophy & Policy* 8 (1991), by permission of Blackwell Publishers.

sion, not something we discover later by looking back at what we did and its effects. The decision is important because "the same act" can have very different consequences, depending upon how we choose to justify it. In a sense, acts done for different reasons are not "the same act" even if otherwise similar, and so not merely the consequences but also the moral nature of our acts depend in part on our decisions about the reasons for doing them.

Unfortunately, the message actually conveyed by our actions does not depend only on our intentions and reasons, for our acts may have a meaning for others quite at odds with what we hoped to express. Others may misunderstand our intentions, doubt our sincerity, or discern a subtext that undermines the primary message. Even if sincere, well-intended, and successfully conveyed, the message of an act or policy does not by itself justify the means by which it is conveyed; it is almost always a relevant factor, however, in the moral assessment of the act or policy.

These remarks may strike you as too obvious to be worth mentioning; for, even if we do not usually express the ideas so absractly, we are all familiar with them in our daily interactions with our friends, families, and colleagues. Who, for example, does not know the importance of the message expressed in offering money to another person, as well as the dangers of misunderstanding? What is superficially "the same act" can be an offer to buy, an admission of guilt, an expression of gratitude, a contribution to a common cause, a condescending display of superiority, or an outrageous insult. Because all this is so familiar, the extent to which these elementary points are ignored in discussions of the *pros* and *cons* of social policies such as affirmative action is suprising. The usual presumption is that social policies can be settled entirely by debating the rights involved or by estimating the consequences, narrowly conceived apart from the messages that we want to give and the messages that are likely to be received.

I shall focus attention for a while on this relatively neglected issue of the message of affirmative action. In particular, I want to consider what message we *should try* to give with affirmative action programs and what messages we should try to avoid. What is the best way to convey the intended message, and indeed whether it is likely to be heard, are empirical questions that I cannot settle; but the question I propose to consider is nonetheless important, and it is a *prior* question. What do we want to say with our affirmative action programs, and why? Since the message that is received, and its consequences, are likely to depend to some extent on what we decide, in all sincerity, to be the rationale for such programs, it would be premature and foolish to try to infer or predict these outcomes without adequate reflection on what the message and rationale should be. Also, for those who accept the historical/narrative perspective described in Section IV, there is additional reason to focus first on the desired message; for that perspective treats the message of affirmative action not merely as a minor side effect to be weighed in, for or against, but rather as an important part of the legitimate purpose of affirmative action.

Much useful discussion has been devoted to the constitutionality of affirmative action programs, to the relative moral rights involved, and to the advantages and disadvantages of specific types of programs.[1] By deemphasizing these matters here, I do not mean to suggest that they are unimportant. Even more, my remarks are not meant to convey the message, "It doesn't matter what we do or achieve, all that matters is what we *say.*" To the contrary, I believe that mere gestures are insufficient and that universities cannot even communicate what they should by affirmative action policies unless these are sincerely designed to result in increased opportunities for those disadvantaged and insulted by racism and sexism.

I divide my discussion as follows: *First*, I describe briefly two affirmative action programs with which I am acquainted, so that we can have in mind some concrete examples before we turn to controversial principles. *Second*, I summarize why I think that affirmative action programs need not be illegitimate forms of "reverse discrimination" that violate the rights of nonminority males. This is a large issue, well discussed by others, but it must be considered at least briefly in order to open the way for more positive considerations. *Third*, I discuss two familiar strategies for justifying affirmative action and give some reasons for thinking that these should not be considered the whole story. The "forward-looking" strategy appeals exclusively to the good results expected from such programs, and the "backward-looking" focuses on past injustice and demands reparation. One of my main points is that this very division leads us to overlook some other important considerations. *Fourth*, in a brief philosophical interlude, I sketch a mode of evaluation that seems to provide a helpful alternative or supplement to the traditional sorts of evaluation that have dominated discussions of affirmative action. This suggestion draws from recent work in ethical theory that stresses the importance of historical context, narrative unity, and interpersonal relations. *Fifth*, combining these ideas with my proposal to consider the message of affirmative action, I present some analogies that point to an alternative perspective on the aims of affirmative action programs. Seen from this perspective, programs that stress outreach, encouragement, and development opportunities appear in a more favorable light than those that simply alter standards to meet quotas.

I

Affirmative action programs take various forms and are used in many different contexts. To focus the discussion, however, I shall concentrate on hiring and admission policies in universities and colleges. Even in this area there are many complexities that must be taken into account in the assessment of particular programs. It may matter, for example, whether the program is voluntary or government-mandated, quota-based or flexible, fixed-term or indefinite, in a formerly segregated institution or not, and so on. Obviously it is impossible to examine all these variations here. It is also unnecessary, for my project is not to defend or criticize specific programs but to raise general questions about how we should approach the issue. Nonetheless, though a full range of cases is not needed for this purpose, it may prove useful to sketch some sample programs that at least illustrate what the more abstract debate is about.

A common feature of affirmative action programs is that they make use of the categories of race and gender (more specifically, blacks and women) in their admission and hiring policies, and they do so in a way that gives positive weight to being in one or the other of these latter categories. Policies use these classifications in different ways, as is evident in the cases described below.

When I taught at Pomona College in 1966-68, for example, the faculty/student Admissions Committee was blessed, or cursed, with applications numbering several times the number of places for new students. After a careful study of the correlation between grade-point averages of graduating seniors and data available in their initial application dossiers, a professor had devised a formula for predicting "success" at the college, where success was measured by the student's academic average at graduation and the predictive factors included high school grades, national test scores, and a ranking of the high school according to the grades its previous graduates received at the college. All applicants were then ranked according to this formula, which was supposed to reflect purely academic promise. The top 10 percent were automatically admitted; and a "cutoff" point was established, below which candidates were deemed incapable of handling the college curriculum. Then committee members made a "subjective" evaluation of the remaining candidates in which the members were supposed to give weight to special talents, high-minded ambition, community service, intriguing personality, and, more generally, the likelihood of contributing to the sort of college community that the evaluators thought desirable. Another cut was made, reflecting both the "pure academic" criteria and the subjective evaluations. Next (as I recall) the football coach, the drama instructor, the orchestra leader, and others were invited to pick a specified number from those above the minimum cutoff, according to whether they needed a quarterback, a lead actor, a tuba player, or whatever. Then those identified as minorities but above the minimum cutoff line were admitted, if they had not been already, by a procedure that started with the most qualified academically, moving down the list until the minority applicants to be admitted made up at least a certain percentage of the final number of students to be admitted (10 percent, as I recall). The rest were admitted by their place on the academic list.

Pomona College is a private institution, but some state colleges and universities have adopted policies that are similar in important respects. At the University of California at Los Angeles in the 1970s, I became familiar with a significantly different kind of affirmative action regarding graduate student admissions and faculty hiring and promotion. The emphasis here was on positive efforts to seek out and encourage qualified minority applicants, for example, through recruitment letters, calls, and campus visits. Special funds were allocated to create new faculty positions for qualified minority candidates, and special fellowships were made available to release minority faculty from some teaching duties prior to tenure. Teaching and research interests in race and gender problems were officially recognized as relevant to hiring and promotion decisions in certain departments, provided the usual academic standards were maintained. Guidelines and watchdog committees were established to require departments to prove that each time they hired a nonminority male they did so only after a thorough search for and examination of minority and female candidates. Since decisions to hire and promote were still determined by the judgments of diverse individuals, I suspect that some deans, department heads, and voting faculty members carried affirmative action beyond the guidelines, some countered this effect by negative bias, and some simply refused to deviate from what they perceived as "color-blind" and "sex-blind" criteria.

II

Is affirmative action *necessarily* a morally illegitimate form of "reverse discrimination" that *violates* the rights of white male applicants?

The question here is not whether some particular affirmative action program is illegitimate, for example, because it uses quotas or causes the deliberate hiring of less qualified teachers; rather, the question is whether making gender and race a relevant category in university policy is *in itself* unjust. If so, we need not go further with our discussion of the message of affirmative action and its advantages and disadvantages: for however important the need is to communicate and promote social benefits, we should not do so by unjust means.

Some think that the injustice of all affirmative action programs is obvious or easily demonstrated. Two facile but confused arguments seem to

173

have an especially popular appeal. The first goes this way: "Affirmative action, by definition, gives preferential treatment to minorities and women. This is discrimination in their favor and against nonminority males. All discrimination by public institutions is unjust, no matter whether it is the old kind or the newer "reverse discrimination.' So all affirmative action programs in public institutions are unjust."

This deceptively simple argument, of course, trades on an ambiguity. In one sense, to "discriminate" means to "make a distinction," to pay attention to a difference. In this evaluatively neutral sense, of course, affirmative action programs do discriminate. But public institutions must, and justifiably do, "discriminate" in this sense, for example, between citizens and noncitizens, freshmen and seniors, the talented and the retarded, and those who pay their bills and those who do not. Whether it is unjust to note and make use of a certain distinction in a given context depends upon many factors: the nature of the institution, the relevant rights of the parties involved, the purposes and effects of making that distinction, and so on.

All this would be obvious except for the fact that the word "discrimination" is also used in a pejorative sense, meaning (roughly) "making use of a distinction in an unjust or illegitimate way." To discriminate in this sense is obviously wrong, but now it remains an open question whether the use of gender and race distinctions in affirmative action programs is really "discrimination" in this sense. The simplistic argument uses the evaluatively neutral sense of "discrimination" to show that affirmative action discriminates; it then shifts to the pejorative sense when it asserts that discrimination is always wrong. Although one may, in the end, *conclude* that all public use of racial and gender distinctions is unjust, to do so requires more of an *argument* than the simple one (just given) that merely exploits an ambiguity of the word "discrimination."

A slightly more sophisticated argument runs as follows: "Affirmative action programs give special benefits to certain individuals "simply because they are women or blacks.' But one's color and gender are morally irrelevant features of a person. It is unjust for public institutions to give special benefits to individuals solely because they happen to have certain morally irrelevant characteristics. Hence affirmative action programs are always unjust."

A special twist is often added to this argument, as follows: "What was wrong with Jim Crow laws, denial of the vote to women and blacks, and segregation in schools and public facilities was just the fact that such practices treated people differently simply because they happened to have certain morally irrelevant characteristics. Affirmative action programs, however well-intentioned, are doing exactly the same thing. So they are wrong for the same reason."

174

Now people who argue in this way may well be trying to express something important, which should not be dismissed; but, as it stands, the argument is confused, unfair, and historically inaccurate. The confusion and unfairness lie in the misleading use of the expression "*simply because* they are women or blacks." It is true that typical affirmative action programs, such as those I described earlier, use the categories of "black" (or "minority") and "female" as an instrumental part of a complex policy. This does not mean, however, that the fundamental reason, purpose, or justification of the policy is nothing more than "this individual is black (or female)." To say that someone favors a person "*simply because* that person is black (or female)" implies that there is no further reason, purpose, or justification, as if one merely had an utterly arbitrary preference for dark skin as opposed to light, or female anatomy over male anatomy. But no serious advocate of affirmative action thinks the program is justified by such personal preferences. On the contrary, advocates argue that, given our historical situation, quite general principles of justice or utility justify the temporary classificatory use of race and gender. That being black or white, male or female, does not in itself make anyone morally better or more deserving is acknowledged on all sides.

Thus even if one should conclude that the attempts to justify affirmative action fail, the fair and clear way to express this conclusion would be to say that the grounds that have been offered for using gender and race categories as affirmative action programs do are unconvincing. Unlike the rhetorical claim that they favor indviduals "merely because they are black (or female)," this does not insinuate unfairly that the programs were instituted for no reason other than personal taste. And, of course, those of us who believe that there are good reasons for affirmative action policies, with their sorting by gender and race, have even more reason to reject the misleading and insulting description that we advocate special treatment for individuals *merely because* they are blacks or women.

The argument we have been considering is objectionable in another way as well. As Richard Wasserstrom points out, the moral wrongs against blacks and women in the past were not wrong just because people were classified and treated differently according to the morally irrelevant features of gender and color.[2] There was this sort of arbitrary treatment, of course, but the main problem was not that women and blacks were treated differently *somehow* but that they were *treated as no human being should be treated*. Segregation, for example, was in practice not merely a pointless sorting of individuals, like separating people according to the number of letters in their names. It was a way of expressing and perpetuating white contempt for blacks and preserving social structures that kept blacks from taking full advantage of their basic human rights. The mistreatment of women was not merely that they were arbitrarily selected for the more burdensome but still legitimate social roles. It was, in large part, that the practices expressed an attitude towards women that subtly undermined their chances of making use of even the limited opportunities they had. The proper conclusion, then, is not that any current program that makes use of race and gender categories is simply committing the same old wrongs in reverse. The worst wrongs of the past went far beyond merely the arbitrary use of these categories; moreover, it has yet to be established that the new use of these categories in affirmative action is in fact arbitrary (like the old use). An arbitrary category is one used without good justification, and the charge that affirmative action programs use race and gender categories unjustifiably is just what is at issue, not something we can assume at the start.

Another argument to show that affirmative action is unjust is that it violates the rights of white males who apply for admission or jobs in the university. This is a complex issue, discussed at length in journals and before the Supreme Court; rather than review that debate, I will just mention a few of the considerations that lead me to think that, though certain *types* of affirmative action may violate the rights of white males, appropriately designed affirmative action programs do not.

First, no individual, white male or otherwise, has an absolute right to a place in a public university, that is, a right independent of complex considerations of the functions of the university, the reasonable expectations of actual and potential taxpayers and other supporters, the number of places available, the relative merits of other candidates, and so on. What rights does an applicant have? Few would dispute that each individual has a right to "formal justice."[3] That is, one should not be arbitrarily denied a place to which one is entitled under the existing and publicly declared rules and regulations. Any university must have rules concerning residency, prior education, submission of application forms, taking of entrance tests, and the like, as well as more substantive standards and policies for selecting among those who satisfy these minimal requirements. Formal justice requires that individual administrators do not deviate from the preestablished rules and standards currently in effect, whether from personal preference or high-minded social ideals. But this is not to say that old policies cannot reasonably be changed. One does not, for example, necessarily have a right to be treated by the rules and standards in force when one was born or when one first thought about going to college.

Formal justice is quite limited, however, for it is compatible with substantively unjust rules and standards. In addition to formal justice, each individual citizen has a right that the rules and standards of the university to which he/she applies be made (and when necessary changed) only for good reasons, consistent with the purposes of the university and the ideals of justice and basic human equality. This is a more stringent standard; and it does establish a *presumption* against using race and gender categories in policies which affect the distribution of opportunities, such as jobs and student status. This is because race and gender, like being tall and muscular, are not *in themselves* morally relevant characteristics. Considered in isolation from their connections with other matters, they do not make anyone more, or less, deserving of anything. As the Supreme Court says, they are classifications that are "suspect."[4] But this does not mean that it is always unjust to use them, but only that their use stands in need of justification. What counts as a justification depends crucially upon our assessment of the legitimate purposes of the institution that uses the categories.

No one denies that the education of citizens and the pursuit of knowledge are central among the purposes of public universities. But, when resources are limited, decisions must be made as to what knowledge is to be pursued and who is to be offered education in each institution. Here we must consider the role of a university as one of a complex network of public institutions in a country committed to democratic ideals and faced with deep social problems. It has never been the practice of universities to disregard their social roles in the name of "purely academic" concerns; given current social problems, few would morally defend such disregard now. The more serious issue is not whether this role should be considered but rather whether the role is better served by affirmative action or by admission and hiring policies that admit only classification by test scores, grades, and past achievements. To decide this, we must look more closely at the purposes that affirmative action is supposed to serve.

III

Some arguments for affirmative action look exclusively to its future benefits. The idea is that what has happened in the past is not in itself relevant to what we should do; at most it provides clues as to what acts and policies are likely to bring about the best future. The philosophical tradition associated with this approach is utilitarianism, which declares that the morally right act is whatever produces the best consequences. Traditionally, utilitarianism evaluated consequences in terms of happiness and unhappiness, but the anticipated consequences of affirmative action are often described more specifically. For example, some argue that affirmative action will ease racial tensions, prevent riots, improve services in minority neighborhoods, reduce unemployment, remove inequities in income distribution, eliminate racial and sexual prejudice, and enhance the self-esteem of blacks and women. Some have called attention to the fact that women and minorities provide alternative perspectives on history, literature, philosophy, and politics, and that this has beneficial effects for both education and research.

These are important considerations, not irrelevant to the larger responsibilities of universities. For several reasons, however, I think it is a mistake for advocates of affirmative action to rest their case exclusively on such forward-looking arguments. First, critics raise reasonable doubts about whether affirmative action is necessary to achieve these admirable results. Thomas Sowell, a noted conservative economist, argues that a free-market economy can achieve the same results more efficiently; even if affirmative action has beneficial results (which he denies), it is not necessary for the purpose.[5] Though Sowell's position can be contested, the controversy itself tends to weaken confidence in the entirely forward-looking defense of affirmative action.

An even more obvious reason why affirmative action advocates should explore other types of defense is that the exclusively forward-looking approach must give equal consideration to possible negative consequences of affirmative action. It may be, for example, that affirmative action will temporarily increase racial tensions, especially if its message is misunderstood. Even legitimate use of race and sex categories may encourage others to abuse the categories for unjust purposes. If applied without sensitive regard to the educational and research purposes of the university, affirmative action might severely undermine its efforts to fulfill these primary responsibilities. *If* affirmative action programs were to lower academic standards for blacks and women, they would run the risk of damaging the respect that highly qualified blacks and women have earned, by leading others to suspect that these highly qualified people lack the merits of white males in the same positions. This could also be damaging to the self-respect of those who accept affirmative action positions. Even programs that disavow "lower standards" unfortunately arouse the suspicion that they don't really do so, and this by itself can cause problems. Although I believe that well-designed affirmative action programs can minimize these negative effects, the fact that they are a risk is a reason for not resting the case for affirmative action on a delicate balance of costs and benefits.

Reflection on the *message* of affirmative action also leads me to move beyond entirely forward-looking arguments. For if the sole purpose is to bring about a brighter future, then we give the wrong message to both the white males who are rejected and to the women and blacks who are benefited. To the latter what we say, in effect, is this: "Never mind how you have been treated. Forget about the fact that your race or sex has in the past been actively excluded and discouraged, and that you yourself may have had handicaps due to prejudice. Our sole concern is to bring about certain good results in the future, and giving you a break happens to be a useful means for doing this. Don't think this is a recognition of your rights as an individual or your disadvantages as a member of a group. Nor does it mean that we have confidence in your abilities. We would do the same for those who are privileged and academically inferior if it would have the same socially beneficial results."

To the white male who would have had a university position but for affirmative action, the exclusively forward-looking approach says: "We deny you the place you otherwise would have had simply as a means to produce certain socially desirable outcomes. We have not judged that others are more deserving, or have a right, to the place we are giving them instead of you. Past racism and sexism are irrelevant. The point is just that the sacrifice of your concerns is a useful means to the larger end of the future welfare of others."

This, I think, is the wrong message to give, and it is unnecessary. The proper alternative, however, is not to ignore the possible future benefits of affirmative action but rather to take them into account as a part of a larger picture.

A radically different strategy for justifying affirmative action is to rely on backward-looking arguments. Such arguments call our attention to certain events in the past and assert that *because* these past events occurred, we have certain duties now. The modern philosopher who most influentially endorsed such arguments was W. D. Ross.[6] He argued that there are duties of fidelity, justice, gratitude, and reparation that have a moral force independent of any tendency these may have to promote good consequences. The fact that you have made a promise, for example, gives you a strong moral reason to do what you promised, whether or not, on balance, doing so will have more beneficial consequences. The Rossian principle that is often invoked in affirmative action debates is a principle of reparation. This says that those who wrongfully injure others have a (prima facie) duty to apologize and make restitution. Those who have wronged others owe reparation.

James Foreman dramatically expressed this idea in New York in 1969 when he presented "The Black Manifesto," which demanded five hundred million dollars in reparation to American blacks from white churches and synagogues.[7] Such organizations, the Manifesto contends, contributed to our history of slavery and racial injustice, and as a result they incurred a debt to the black community that still suffers from its effects. Objections were immediately raised: for example, both slaves and slave-owners are no longer alive, not every American white is guilty of racial oppression; and not every black in America was a victim of slavery and its aftermath.

Bernard Boxill, author of *Blacks and Social Justice*, developed a more sophisticated version of the backward-looking argument with a view to meeting these objections.[8] Let us admit, he says, that both the perpetrators and the primary victims of slavery are gone, and let us not insist that contemporary whites are guilty of perpetrating further injustices. Some do, and some do not, and public administrators cannot be expected to sort out the guilty from the nonguilty. However, reparation, or at least some "compensation,"[9] is still owed because contemporary whites have reaped the profits of past injustice to blacks. He asks us to consider the analogy with a stolen bicycle. Suppose my parent stole your parent's bicycle some time ago, both have since died, and I "inherited" the bike from my parent, the thief. Though I may be innocent of any wrongdoing (so far), I am in possession of stolen goods rightfully belonging to you, the person who would have inherited the bike if it had not been stolen. For me to keep the bike and declare that I owe you nothing would be wrong, even if I was not the cause of your being deprived. By analogy, present-day whites owe reparations to contemporary blacks, not because they are themselves guilty of causing the disadvantages of blacks, but because they are in possession of advantages that fell to them as a result of the gross injustices of their ancestors. Special advantages continue to fall even to innocent whites because of the ongoing prejudice of their white neighbors.

Although it raises many questions, this line of argument acknowledges some important points missing in most exclusively forward-looking arguments: for example, it stresses the (intrinsic) relevance of past injustice and it calls attention to the rights and current disadvantages of blacks (in contrast with future benefits for others). When developed as an argument for affirmative action, it does not accuse all white males of prejudice and wrongdoing but, at the same time, it sees the fundamental value as justice. As a result, it avoids giving the message to both rejected white males and reluctant affirmative action applicants that they are "mere means" to a social goal that is largely independent of their rights and interests as individuals.

There are, however, serious problems in trying to justify affirmative action by this backward-looking argument, especially if it is treated as the exclusive or central argument. Degrees of being advantaged and disadvantaged are notoriously hard to measure. New immigrants have not shared our history of past injustices, and so the argument may not apply to them in any straightforward way. The argument appeals to controversial ideas about property rights, inheritance, and group responsibilities. Some argue that affirmative action tends to benefit the least disadvantaged blacks and women; though this does not mean that they are owed nothing, their claims would seem to have lower priority than the needs of the most disadvantaged. Some highly qualified blacks and women object that affirmative action is damaging to their reputations and self-esteem, whereas the reparation argument seems to assume that it is a welcome benefit to all blacks and women.

If we focus on the message that the backward-looking argument sends, there are also some potential problems. Though rightly acknowledging past injustice, the argument (by itself) seems to convey the message that racial and sexual oppression consisted primarily in the loss of tangible goods, or the deprivation of specific rights and opportunities, that can be "paid back" in kind. The background idea, which goes back at least to Aristotle, is that persons wrongfully deprived of their "due" can justly demand an "equivalent" to what they have lost.[10] But, while specific deprivations were an important part of our racist and sexist past, they are far from the whole story. Among the worst wrongs then, as now, were humiliations and contemptuous treatment of a type that cannot, strictly, be "paid back." The problem was, and is, not just that specific rights and advantages were denied, but that prejudicial attitudes damaged self-esteem, undermined motivations, limited realistic options, and made even "officially open" opportunities seem undesirable. Racism and sexism were (and are) *insults*, not merely tangible *injuries*.[11] These are not the sort of thing that can be adequately measured and repaid with equivalents. The trouble with treating insulting racist and sexist practices on a pure reparation model is not merely the practical difficulty of identifying the offenders, determining the degree of guilt, assessing the amount of payment due, *etc*. It is also that penalty payments and compensation for lost benefits are not the only, or primary, moral responses that are called for. When affirmative action is defended exclusively by analogy with reparation, it tends to express the misleading message that the evils of racism and sexism are all tangible losses that can be "paid off"; by being silent on the insulting nature of racism and sexism, it tends to add insult to insult.

The message suggested by the reparation argument, by itself, also seems objectionable because it conveys the idea that higher education, teaching, and doing research are mainly benefits awarded in response to self-centered demands. The underlying picture too easily suggested is that applicants are a group of self-interested, bickering people, each grasping for limited "goodies" and insisting on a right to them. When a university grants an opportunity through affirmative action, its message would seem to be this: "We concede that you have a valid claim to this benefit, and we yield to your demand, though this is not to suggest that we have confidence in your abilities or any desire to have you here." This invitation seems too concessionary, the atmosphere too adversarial, and the emphasis too much on the benefits rather than the responsibilities of being a part of the university.

181

IV

Here I want to digress from the explicit consideration of affirmative action in order to consider more abstract philosophical questions about the ways we evaluate acts and policies. At the risk of oversimplifying, I want to contrast some assumptions that have, until recently, been dominant in ethical theory with alternatives suggested by contemporary philosophers who emphasize historical context, narrative unity, and community values.[12] Although these alternatives, in my opinion, have not yet been adequately developed, there seem to be at least four distinguishable themes worth considering.

First, when we reflect on what we deeply value, we find that we care not merely about the present moment and each future moment in isolation but also about how our past, present, and future cohere or fit together into a life and a piece of history. Some of our values, we might say, are cross-time wholes, with past, present, and future parts united in certain ways. Thus, for example, the commitments I have made, the projects I have begun, what I have shared with those I love, the injuries I have caused, and the hopes I have encouraged importantly affect both whether I am satisfied with my present and how I want the future to go.

Second, in reflecting on stretches of our lives and histories, we frequently use evaluative concepts drawn more from narrative literature than from accounting. Thus, for example, we think of our lives as having significant beginnings, crises, turning points, dramatic tension, character development, climaxes, resolutions, comic interludes, tragic disruptions, and eventually fitting (or unfitting) endings. The value of any moment often depends on what came before and what we anticipate to follow. And because our lives are intertwined with others in a common history, we also care about how our moments cohere with others' life stories. The past is seen as more than a time of accumulated debts and assets, and the future is valued as more than an opportunity for reinvesting and cashing in assets.

Third, evaluation must take into account one's particular historical context, including one's cultural, national, and ethnic traditions, and the actual individuals in one's life. Sometimes this point is exaggerated, I think, to suggest a dubious cultural relativism or "particularism" in ethics: for example, the thesis that what is valuable for a person is defined by the person's culture or that evaluations imply no general reasons beyond particular judgments, such as "That's our way" and "John is my son."[13] But, construed modestly as a practical or epistemological point, it seems obvious enough, on reflection, that we should take into account the historical context of our acts and that we are often in a better position to judge what is appropriate in particular cases than we are to articulate universally valid premises supporting the judgment. We can sometimes be reasonably confident about what is right in a particular context without being sure about whether or not there are relevant differences blocking the same judgment in seemingly similar but less familiar contexts. We know, as a truism, that the same judgment applies if there are no relevant differences, but in practice the particular judgment may be more evident than the exact scope of the moral generalizations that hold across many cases. Thus, although giving reasons for our judgments in particular contexts commits us to acknowledging their potential relevance in other contexts, moral judgment cannot be aptly represented simply as deducing specific conclusions from clear and evident general principles.

Fourth, when we evaluate particular acts and policies as parts of lives and histories, what is often most important is the value of the whole, which cannot always be determined by "summing up" the values of the parts. Lives, histories, and interpersonal relations over time are what G. E. Moore called "organic unities," i.e., wholes the value of which is not necessarily the sum of the values of the parts.[14] The point is here not merely the obvious practical limitation that we cannot measure and quantify values in this area. More fundamentally, the idea is that it would be a mistake even to try to evaluate certain unities by assessing different parts in isolation from one another, then adding up all their values. Suppose, for example, a woman with terminal cancer considered two quite different ways of spending her last days. One way, perhaps taking a world cruise, might seem best when evaluated in terms of the quality of each future moment, in isolation from her past and her present ties; but another way, perhaps seeking closure in projects and with estranged family members, might seem more valuable when seen as a part of her whole life.

Taken together, these ideas cast doubt on both the exclusively forward-looking method of assessment and the standard backward-looking alternative. Consequentialism, or the exclusively forward-looking method, attempts to determine what ought to be done at present by fixing attention entirely on future results. To be sure, any sensible consequentialist will consult the past for lessons and clues helpful in predicting future outcomes: e.g., recalling that you offended someone yesterday may enable you to predict that the person will be cool to you tomorrow unless you apologize. But beyond this, consequentialists have no concern with the past, for their "bottom line" is always "what happens from now on," evaluated independently of the earlier chapters of our lives and histories. For the consequentialist, assessing a life or history from a narrative perspective becomes impossible, or at least bizarre, as what must be evaluated at each shifting moment is "the story from now on" independently of what has already been written.[15]

The standard Rossian alternative to this exclusively forward-looking perspective is to introduce certain *(prima facie) duties* to respond to certain past events in specified ways, e.g., pay debts, keep promises, pay reparation for injuries. These duties are supposed to be self-evident and universal (though *prima facie*), and they do not hold because they tend to promote anything good or valuable. Apart from aspects of the acts mentioned in the principles (e.g., fulfilling a promise, returning favors, not injuring, etc.), details of historical and personal context are considered irrelevant.

By contrast, the narrative perspective sketched above considers the past as an integral part of the valued unities that we aim to bring about, not merely as a source of duties. If one has negligently wronged another, Ross regards this past event as generating a duty to pay reparations even if doing so will result in nothing good. But from the narrative perspective, the past becomes relevant in a further way. One may say, for example, that the *whole* consisting of your life and your relationship with that person from the time of the injury into the future will be a better thing if you acknowledge the wrong and make efforts to restore what you have damaged. For Ross, the duty is generated by the past and unrelated to bringing about anything good; from the narrative perspective, however, the requirement is just what is required to bring about a valuable connected whole with past, present, and future parts, the best way to complete a chapter, so to speak, in two intersecting life stories.

So far, neither the Rossian nor the narrative account has told us much about the ultimate reasons for their evaluations, but they reveal different ways to consider the matter. The Rossian asks us to judge particular cases in the light of "self-evident" general principles asserting that certain past events tend to generate present (or future) duties. The alternative perspective calls for examining lives and relationships, over time, in context, as organic unities evaluated (partly) in narrative terms.

To illustrate, consider two persons, John and Mary, who value being in a relationship of mutual trust and respect with one another. Each trusts and respects the other, but that is not all. Each also values having the trust and respect of the other; moreover, each values the fact that the other values having his trust and respect.[16] And they value the fact that this all is known and mutually acknowledged.

Now suppose that other people have been abusive and insulting to Mary, and that John is worried that Mary may take things he has said and done as similarly insulting, even though he does not think that he consciously meant them this way. Although he is worried, Mary does not seem to suspect him; and he fears that if he raises the issue he may only make matters worse, creating suspicions she did not have or focusing on doubts that he cannot allay. Perhaps, he thinks, their future relationship would be better served if he just remained silent, hoping that the trouble, if any, will fade in time. If so, consequentialist thinking would recommend silence. Acknowledging this, he might nonethless feel that duties of friendship and fidelity demand that he raise the issue, regardless of whether or not the result will be worse. Then he would be thinking as a Rossian.

But, instead, he might look at the problem from an alternative perspective, asking himself what response best affirms and contributes to the sort of ongoing relationship he has and wants to continue with Mary. Given their history together, it is important to him to do his part towards restoring the relationship if it indeed has been marred by perceived insults or suspicions. To be sure, he wants *future* relations of mutual trust and respect, but not at any price and not by just any means. Their history together is not irrelevant, for what he values is not merely a future of a certain kind but that their relationship over time be of the sort he values. He values an ongoing history of mutual trust and respect that *calls for* an explicit response in this current situation, not merely as a means to a brighter future but as a present affirmation of what they value together. Even if unsure which course will be best for the future, he may be reasonably confident that the act that best expresses his respect and trust (and his valuing hers, etc.) is to confront the problem, express his regrets, reaffirm his respect, ask for her trust, be patient with her doubts, and welcome an open dialogue. If the insults were deep and it is not entirely clear whether or not he really associated himself with them, then mere words may not be enough to convey the message or even to assure himself of his own sincerity. Positive efforts, even at considerable cost, may be needed to express appropriately and convincingly what needs to be said. How the next chapter unfolds is not entirely up to him, and he would not be respectful if he presumed otherwise by trying to manipulate the best future unilaterally.

The example concerns only two persons and their personal values, but it illustrates a perspective that one can also take regarding moral problems involving many persons.

V

Turning back to our main subject, I suggest that some of the values that give affirmative action its point are best seen as cross-time values that fall outside the exclusively forward-looking and backward-looking perspectives. They include having a history of racial and gender relations governed, so far as possible, by the ideals of mutual respect, trust, and fair opportunity for all.

Our national history provides a context of increasing recognition and broader interpretation of the democratic ideal of the equal dignity of all human beings, an ideal that has been flagrantly abused from the outset, partially affirmed in the bloody Civil War, and increasingly extended in the civil rights movement, but is still far from being fully respected. More specifically, blacks and women were systematically treated in an unfair and demeaning way by public institutions, including universities, until quite recently, and few could confidently claim to have rooted out racism and sexism even now.[17] The historical context is not what grounds or legitimates democratic values, but it is the background of the current problem, the sometimes admirable and often ugly way the chapters up until now have been written.

Consider first the social ideal of mutual respect and trust among citizens. The problem of implementing this in the current context is different from the problem in the two-person example previously discussed, for the history of our racial and gender relations is obviously not an idyllic story of mutual respect and trust momentarily interrupted by a crisis. Even so, the question to ask is not merely, "What will promote respectful and trusting racial and gender relations in future generations?" but rather, "Given our checkered past, how can we appropriately express the social value of mutual respect and trust that we want, so far as possible, to characterize our history?" We cannot change our racist and sexist past, but we also cannot express full respect for those present individuals who live in its aftermath if we ignore it. What is called for is not merely repayment of tangible debts incurred by past injuries, but also a message to counter the deep insult inherent in racism and sexism.

Recognizing that problems of this kind are not amenable to easy solutions deduced from self-evident moral generalizations, we may find it helpful instead to reflect on an analogy. Suppose you return to the hometown you left in childhood, remembering with pride its Fourth of July speeches about the values of community, equality, and fairness for all. You discover, however, that the community was never as perfect as you thought. In fact, for year—until quite recently—certain families, who had been disdainfully labeled "the Barefeet," had not only been shunned by most folk but had also been quietly terrorized by a few well-placed citizens. The Barefeet had been arrested on false charges, beaten, raped, and blackmailed into silent submission. The majority, perhaps, would never have done these things, but their contempt for the Barefeet was such that most would have regarded these crimes less important than if they had been done to insiders. Fortunately, the worst offenders have died, and so have the victims of the most outrageous crimes. Majority attitudes have changed somewhat, though often merely from open contempt to passive disregard. Some new citizens have come to town, and a few of the Barefeet (now more politely called "Cross-towners") have managed to become successful. Nonetheless, the older Cross-towners are still fearful and resigned, and the younger generation is openly resentful and distrustful when officials proclaim a new commitment to democratic ideals. It is no surprise, then, that few Cross-towners take full advantage of available opportunities, and that the two groups tend to isolate themselves from each other.

Now suppose you, as one of the majority, could persuade the rest to give a message to the Cross-towners, a message appropriate to the majority's professed value of being a community committed to mutual respect and trust. What would you propose? And, assuming that doing so would violate no one's rights, what means would you think best to convey that message sincerely and effectively? Some would no doubt suggest simply forgetting about the past and hoping that time will heal the wounds. But, whether effective in the future or not, this plan fails to express full respect for the Cross-towners now. Others might suggest a more legalistic approach, trying to determine exactly who has been disadvantaged, the degree of loss, which citizens are most responsible, etc., in order to pay off the debt. But this, taken by itself, faces the sorts of disadvantages we have already considered. If, instead, the value of mutual respect and trust is the governing ideal, the appropriate message would be to acknowledge and deplore the past openly, to affirm a commitment to promote mutual respect and trust in the future, to welcome full interchange and participation with the Cross-towners, and to urge them to undertake the risks of overcoming their understandable suspicions by joining in a common effort to work towards fulfilling the ideal. This would address not merely the injury but also the insult implicit in the town's history.

The more difficult question, however, is how to express such a message effectively and with evident sincerity in an atmosphere already poisoned by the past. Mere words will be taken as mere words, and may in fact turn out to be just that. What is needed is more positive action—concrete steps to prove commitment, to resist backsliding, and to overcome reluctance on both sides. The sort of affirmative action taken in the U.C.L.A. program described in Section I seems especially appropriate for this purpose. Here the emphasis was on outreach, increasing awareness of opportunities, accountability and proof of fairness in procedures, and allocating resources (fellowships, release time, etc.) in a way that showed trust that, if given an adequate chance, those formerly excluded would enrich the university by fully appropriate standards. These seem the most natural way to give force to the message, though arguably other methods may serve the purpose as well.

There is another historical value that is also relevant and seems to favor even more radical steps in affirmative action. The issue is too complex to address adequately here, but it should at least be mentioned. What I have in mind might be called "fair opportunity." That is, implicit in our democratic ideals is the idea that our public institutions should be so arranged that they afford to individuals, over time, more or less equal opportunities to develop and make use of their natural talents and to participate and contribute to those institutions. The idea is hard to make precise, but it clearly does not mean that all should have equal chances to have a desirable position, regardless of effort and natural aptitude. The physically handicapped and the mentally retarded suffer from natural misfortunes, and, though society should not ignore them, they cannot expect standards to be rigged to ensure the former equal odds at making the basketball team or the latter equal odds of being appointed to the faculty. Similarly, those who choose not to make the effort to develop their capacities have no right to expect public institutions to include them in a pool from which candidates are selected by lot. But when persons have been disadvantaged by social injustice, having had their initial chances diminished by the network of public institutions themselves, then positive steps are needed to equalize their opportunities over time.

This ideal calls for something more than efforts to ensure that future generations do not suffer from the same disadvantage, for those efforts fail to respond to the unfairness to the present individuals. But, for obvious practical reasons, legal efforts to remedy precisely identifiable disadvantages incurred by individuals are bound to be quite inadequate to address the many subtle losses of opportunity caused by past institutional racism and sexism. Since no perfect solution is possible, we need to choose between this inadequate response and policies that address the problem in a less fine-grained way. Affirmative action programs that employ a working presumption that women and minorities generally have had their opportunities restricted to some degree by institutional racism and sexism will admittedly risk compensating a few who have actually had, on balance, as much opportunity as white males. But the practical alternatives, it seems, are to accept this risk or to refuse to respond at all to the innumerable ways that institutional racism and sexism have undermined opportunities too subtly for the courts to remedy.

Given these options, what would be the message of choosing to limit redress to precisely identifiable losses? This would say, in effect, to women and minorities, "We cannot find a way to ensure *precisely* that each talented and hard-working person has an equal opportunity over time; and, given our options, we count it more important to see that *none* of you women and minorities are overcompensated than to try to see that the *majority* of you have more nearly equal opportunities over your lifetime. Your grievances are too subtle and difficult to measure, and your group may be harboring some who were not disadvantaged. We would rather let the majority of white males enjoy the advantages of their unfair headstart than to risk compensating one of you who does not deserve it."

Now *if* it had been established on antecedent grounds that the affirmative action measures in question would violate the *rights* of white male applicants, then one could argue that these coarse-grained efforts to honor the ideal of fair opportunity are illegitimate. But that premise, I think, has not been established. Affirmative action programs would violate the rights of white males only if, all things considered, their guidelines temporarily favoring women and minorities were arbitrary, not serving the legitimate social role of universities or fulfilling the ideals of fairness and respect for all. The considerations offered here, however, point to the conclusion that some affirmative action programs, even those involving a degree of preferential treatment, are legitimated by ideals of mutual respect, trust, and fair opportunity.

All this, I know, is too brief, loose, and incomplete, but, I hope, it is worth considering nonetheless. The main suggestion is that, ideally, a central purpose of affirmative action would be to communicate a much needed message sincerely and effectively. The message is called for not just as a means to future good relations or a dutiful payment of a debt incurred by our past. It is called for by the ideal of being related to other human beings, over time, so that our histories and biographies reflect the responses of those who deeply care about fair opportunity, mutual trust, and respect for all.

If so, what should public universities try to say to those offered opportunities through affirmative action? Perhaps something like this: "Whether we individually are among the guilty or not, we acknowledge that you have been wronged—if not by specific injuries which could be named and repaid, at least by the humiliating and debilitating attitudes prevalent in our country and our institutions. We deplore and denounce these attitudes and the wrongs that spring from them. We acknowledge that, so far, most of you have had your opportunities in life diminished by the effects of these attitudes, and we want no one's prospects to be diminished by injustice. We recognize your understandable grounds for suspicion and mistrust when we express these high-minded sentiments, and we want not only to ask respectfully for your trust but also to give concrete evidence of our sincerity. We welcome you respectfully into the university community and ask you to take a full share of the responsibilities as well as the benefits. By creating special opportunities, we recognize the disadvantages you have probably suffered, but we show our respect for your talents and our commitment to ideals of the university by not faking grades and honors for you. Given current attitudes about affirmative action, accepting this position will probably have drawbacks as well as advantages.[18] It is an opportunity and a responsibility offered neither as charity nor as entitlement, but rather as part of a special effort to welcome and encourage minorities and women to participate more fully in the university at all levels. We believe that this program affirms some of the best ideals implicit in our history without violating the rights of any applicants. We hope that you will choose to accept the position in this spirit as well as for your own benefit."

The appropriate message is no doubt harder to communicate to those who stand to lose some traditional advantages under a legitimate affirmative action program. But if we set aside practical difficulties and suppose that the proper message could be sincerely given and accepted as such, what would it say? Ideally, it would convey an understanding of the moral reasoning for the program; perhaps, in summary, it would be something like the following.

"These are the concerns that we felt made necessary the policy under which the university is temporarily giving special attention to women and minorities. We respect your rights to formal justice and to a policy guided by the university's educational and research mission as well as its social responsibilities. Our policy in no way implies the view that your opportunities are less important than others', but we estimate (roughly, as we must) that as a white male you have probably had advantages and encouragement that for a long time have been systematically, unfairly, insultingly unavailable to most women and minorities. We deplore invidious race and gender distinctions; we hope that no misunderstanding of our program will prolong them. Unfortunately, nearly all blacks and women have been disadvantaged to some degree by bias against their groups, and it is impractical for universities to undertake the detailed investigations that would be needed to assess how much particular individuals have suffered or gained from racism and sexism. We appeal to you to share the historical values of fair opportunity and mutual respect that underlie this policy and hope that, even though its effects may be personally disappointing, you can see the policy as an appropriate response to the current situation."

Unfortunately, as interests conflict and tempers rise, it is difficult to convey this idea without giving an unintended message as well. White males unhappy about the immediate effects of affirmative action may read the policy as saying that "justice" is the official word for giving preferential treatment to whatever group one happens to favor. Some may see a subtext insinuating that blacks and women are naturally inferior and "cannot make it on their own." Such cynical readings reveal either misunderstanding or the willful refusal to take the moral reasoning underlying affirmative action seriously. They pose serious obstacles to the success of affirmative action—practical problems that may be more intractable than respectful moral disagreement and counterargument. But some types of affirmative action invite misunderstanding and suspicion more than others. For this reason, anyone who accepts the general case for affirmative action suggested here would do well to reexamine in detail the means by which they hope to communicate its message.[19]

22

The Injustice of Affirmative Action Involving Preferential Treatment

John Kekes

I

The context of affirmative action is the selection of people for prized, scarce, and competitive jobs, opportunities, or honors. It is customary to distinguish between two forms such a policy may take: impartiality and preferential treatment. The aim of impartiality is to assure open access to the initial pool from which people are selected and selection in accordance with procedural rules which apply to everyone equally. The aim of preferential treatment is to alter the procedural rules so as to favor some people in order to increase the likelihood that they rather than others will achieve the desired position. One form of affirmative action, therefore, is committed to impartiality and to the rejection of preferential treatment, while the other form is committed to preferential treatment and to the rejection of impartiality. The claim for preferential treatment is that it is morally justified because those favored by it belong to some group many of whose members have been unjustly excluded from achieving the desired position simply because they were members of the group.

A previous version of this paper, "The Injustice of Strong Affirmative Action," was published in *Affirmative Action and the University: A Philosophical Inquiry*, ed. Steven M. Cahn (Philadelphia: Temple University Press, 1993). Printed with permission of Temple University Press and the author.

The moral justifiability of preferential treatment has been debated since the 1964 Civil Rights Act. Its defenders and opponents somewhat wearily continue to restate their familiar cases, but the controversy appears to have come to a standstill. There are tactical victories and losses on both sides. The resolutions thus reached, however, are unstable, short-lived, and unsatisfactory because they are not the products of principle, but of political in-fighting which is symptomatic of a failure to face the underlying deep moral disagreements.

Given this background, it may seem foolhardy to advance the claim that one side has it right and the other is mistaken, but, for better or worse, that is the claim this paper intends to defend. Its strategy, however, is not to work over yet another time the details of the usual arguments, nor is it to offer original objections to them; the strategy is rather to present an overview that sums up the state of the controversy. What emerges from it is that preferential treatment favored by one form of affirmative action is unjust.

II

Perhaps the most useful way to begin is to impose some restrictions on the scope of the discussion and then proceed to enumerate some assumptions which form part of the common ground among the contending parties. The issue of preferential treatment arises in many areas of life, but the discussion of it will be restricted here to universities and colleges. And within that context, it will be restricted further to consideration of preferential treatment involved in hiring, granting tenure to, and promoting people who belong to certain unjustly treated groups.

Turning now to the assumptions, the first one is that all the people whose proposed preferential treatment gives rise to the controversy are acknowledged by all parties to belong to some group many of whose members have been victims of injustice, such as American blacks, Indians, Hispanics, and women. The fact that injustice has occurred is not doubted; the question is rather whether the injustice warrants preferential treatment.

Second, the controversy centers on the form of affirmative action that involves preferential treatment, and not on the impartial form whose aim is merely to make entry into the initial pool open to members of the unjustly treated groups and to assure the fair application of the procedural rules guiding the selection process. A more precise formulation of the controversy therefore is whether it is morally justifiable to abandon the impartial form of affirmative action and accord preferential treatment to the appropriate people.

Third, it is also agreed by both sides that under normal circumstances preferential treatment is morally wrong. This does not mean that it cannot be justified in unusual circumstances, but it does mean that it must be justified because the initial presumption is against it and that the burden of justification rests on those who advocate it. The procedural rules governing the selection of people in a competitive context normally ought not to be altered in favor of some of the competitors. But what holds normally does not hold necessarily. The required justification must therefore show that the circumstances surrounding affirmative action involving preferential treatment are in some ways sufficiently unusual to warrant doing what normally it would be wrong to do. Defenders of preferential treatment of course do offer justifications of this sort. If the controversy is conducted reasonably, it hinges on the adequacy of these justifications. These three assumptions are generally held explicitly; the next three tend to be implicit, implied rather than articulated by participants in the controversy.

Fourth, one reason why preferential treatment is favored by its defenders is that without it members of the unjustly treated groups would be less likely to gain the desired positions than members of other groups who have not suffered injustice. If access to the initial pool is open and the application of the procedural rules is fair, then the greater likelihood that members of the unjustly treated groups will be at a comparative disadvantage should be attributed to handicaps suffered as a result of injustice. It ought to be noticed that although injustice is one explanation of this disadvantage, it is not the only one. Other explanations may be that there are genetic differences or that it is psychologically impossible to overcome the effects of injustice. But since there are serious empirical and moral questions about these alternative explanations, the common ground between defenders and opponents of preferential treatment may be interpreted as concern with the conditionally formulated question that if the difference in qualifications were due to injustice and it could be overcome, would preferential treatment be then just and justified.

In case it is found to be offensive to expect comparatively lower qualifications merely on the basis of membership in a group, it should be noticed that this expectation is central to the case *for* preferential treatment, the case being opposed in this paper, since if there were no such expectation, there would be no perceived need for preferential treatment.

Fifth, it is acknowledged by both sides that the result of preferential treatment is not merely to favor some people who otherwise would be less likely to gain the desired positions, but also that it makes it more difficult for fully qualified people to gain the positions they would be likely to have if difficulties were not put in their way. Preferential treatment consequently means that part of the cost of benefiting some is harm to others. The justification of preferential treatment, therefore, must not only show that it is reasonable to confer the benefits that follow from it, but also that it is reasonable to inflict the harms that it inevitably produces.

Sixth, as has already been noted, the context in which the issue of preferential treatment arises most acutely is higher education. It is generally assumed that the two chief functions of universities and colleges are teaching and research. That assumption follows from the deeper one that these institutions have the responsibility of being guardians of knowledge. The responsibility is discharged by advancing knowledge (through research) and by handing down knowledge from generation to generation (through teaching). Knowledge should be understood quite generally to include the fields of the natural and social sciences, as well as the humanities, and being both pure and applied, theoretical and practical, descriptive and normative, historical and contemporary, taking as its scope the lasting achievements of humanity.

The kind of higher education a society provides for its young tends to reflect and perpetuate the forms of knowledge valued in that society. It is not surprising, therefore, that the nature of higher education should be as controversial as the question of what forms of knowledge should be valued. After all, how higher education goes has a strong influence on how the society will go when the young come to occupy the positions for which they are supposed to be educated.

The issue of preferential treatment arises against this background. Its defenders claim that since members of some groups have been systematically and unjustly excluded from higher education, they ought to be preferentially treated so that they too might influence the direction in which society will go. By contrast, opponents of preferential treatment, while conceding injustice, deny that it could or should be remedied by preferential treatment.

III

Bearing in mind the assumptions just discussed, the question is: What justification is there for the preferential treatment of prospective or actual academics who belong to some group, many of whose members have suffered injustice merely because of their membership? An alternative way of posing the question is: What justification is there for abandoning the impartial form of affirmative action, which aims to assure open access and procedural fairness, and adopting the form which aims at the preferential treatment of people belonging to the appropriate groups?

The questions are *moral* because they deal with how benefits and harms ought to be distributed. And they arise in a particularly acute form because they concern a proposed policy of distribution that goes against what would normally be regarded as fair. It exacerbates the controversy that what is at stake is not merely how benefits should be distributed but also the unavoidable consequence of the proposed policy that it will cause harm to those who would have received the benefits under the impartial distribution scheme which is to be abandoned.

Defenders of preferential treatment have offered three types of justification based on compensation, redistribution or correction, and diversity. Each begins with the generally acknowledged fact of injustice, but they differ because they offer different justifications for adopting the policy of preferential treatment as a remedy.

The idea of compensation as a justification for preferential treatment is that of doing what is possible to balance the moral scales so as to make them as even as they would have been if past injustice had not occurred. Since injustice has harmed members of some groups and benefited others, a just balance can be achieved by favoring those who were harmed in the past at the expense of those who have benefited. Preferential treatment is the means by which this is accomplished.

Compensation is a backward-looking strategy of justification because it is grounded on past injustice. Redistribution or correction often assumes an atemporal attitude to injustice. The guiding thought motivating it is that it is unjust that members of some groups should receive a greater share of scarce, prized, and competitive benefits than members of some other groups, and this judgment holds true quite independently of whether the injustice is past, present, or future. It is injustice *per se* that is being opposed. By redistributing the benefits evenhandedly, this injustice would be corrected. The reason redistribution or correction requires preferential treatment is that a newly introduced impartial method of distribution is unlikely, by itself, to be effective, since the chances are that its implementation will be obstructed by the same prejudices against members of some groups as motivated the previous method of unjust distribution. The policy of preferential treatment is needed to counteract the force of prejudice which may not be conscious or malicious, but merely an unexamined habit of thought. A legally mandated policy of preferential treatment thus coerces people to act as they would act were they not prevented by prejudices.

The justification of preferential treatment derived from diversity concentrates on the future; its claim is that preferential treatment has generally beneficial consequences, and that these go far beyond the benefits received by those who are favored under the policy. These general benefits are associated with pluralism. Part of the reason why pluralism is regarded as an attractive view by many people is that it enriches human possibilities by being hospitable to a multiplicity of different ideals, values, and conceptions of good life. Analogously, part of the reason why racial or sexual prejudice is unreasonable is that it injures not only its victims but also the society informed by it, since prejudiced people impoverish their own prospects by excluding from their lives possibilities represented by members of the unjustly treated groups. Preferential treatment is generally beneficial because it enriches higher education, and thus the future, by providing an important forum for voices which otherwise would be doomed to remaining unheard.

These arguments, of course, have been developed in far greater detail than what has been presented above. The details, however, are irrelevant to the purpose of this paper, which is not to reconsider these arguments but to show how damaging are the objections against them and to persuade those who support preferential treatment either to stop doing so or to find better arguments for it.

IV

There are two general objections directed against all three types of arguments advanced to justify preferential treatment. The first starts by asking whether the arguments for preferential treatment are intended to benefit unjustly treated individuals as individuals or as members of some group. To put this more concretely: is the preferential treatment of, say, a particular black person or a woman supposed to be justified because of the harm they themselves have personally suffered or the benefits their preferential treatment may produce, or is the proposed justification rather that through their preferential treatment the position of the unjustly treated group to which they belong would be improved? In the first case, the justification of preferential treatment must depend on the circumstances of *individuals* who happen to be members of a group; in the second case, the justification concentrates on what has befallen the relevant *group*, and the individuals in question could then be replaced by other members of the same group. The objection is that neither alternative can be reasonably defended.

According to the individualistic interpretation, the preferential treatment of individuals is justified by the injustice they have personally suffered and/or by the benefits that favoring them over others would produce. In view of this, it is extraordinary that the form of affirmative action that involves preferential treatment does not mandate or even recommend finding out whether the individuals in question have actually suffered any injustice that would warrant compensation or redistribution. Nor is there any attempt to find out whether these individuals would contribute to diversity by holding ideals, values, or conceptions of a good life other than those already represented.

It may be said in reply that conducting the required investigation is formidably difficult. But that, of course, merely strengthens the doubts about the feasibility and justice of preferential treatment. Or, alternatively, the rejoinder may be that the investigation is unnecessary because it can be assumed that individual members of some groups have been unjustly treated and that they would enhance existing diversity, since exceptional circumstances would have to be postulated for this assumption not to hold. But this reply will not do either. The individuals being considered for preferential treatment are likely to be selected from among those members of the unjustly treated groups who are least likely to have suffered and who are most likely to have been acculturated to the views prevalent in their society. They are after all typically prospective or actual young faculty members, both male and female, who have received many years of undergraduate and graduate education and who are normally quite different from impoverished slum-dwellers who live without hope and who are the strongest candidates for being victims of injustice.

The individualistic interpretation, however, does not merely select people for preferential treatment without ascertaining whether the injustice that would supposedly justify it has actually occurred to them. By conferring unjustified benefits on them it also harms other specific individuals. The ones harmed are those who have been deprived of the benefits they would normally have earned so that people less qualified than they could be favored. There is no reason provided, and none sought, for supposing that these excluded individuals have done anything to contribute to the groundlessly assumed injustice preferential treatment intends to remedy. The consequence of this interpretation of preferential treatment, therefore, is to institute a policy that arbitrarily favors some individuals while it deliberately injures innocent ones. Even if good reasons were provided for favoring some individuals, the policy would merely substitute one set of innocent victims for another set of equally innocent ones. As it stands, this interpretation merely assumes that just because a particular individual is, say, black or female he or she has suffered injustice. That assumption, without the evidence to back it, is as much a prejudice as the assumption that a particular individual is inferior just because he is black or she is a woman.

There are, therefore, strong reasons for abandoning the individualistic interpretation and turning to the group interpretation. According to it, the object of preferential treatment is to improve the position of the unjustly treated groups; individuals are favored, as it were, not on their own behalf, but on behalf of the group to which they belong. The reasons for this interpretation, however, are no better than the reasons for the previous one.

For one thing, the selection of the groups for preferential treatment is arbitrary. It is true that American blacks, Indians, Hispanics, and women have suffered injustice as a group. But so have homosexuals, epileptics, the urban and the rural poor, the physically ugly, those whose careers were ruined by McCarthyism, prostitutes, the obese, and so forth. There is no good reason for selecting some of these groups over others for preferential treatment. The arguments given to justify preferential treatment apply equally to all.

There have been some attempts to deny that there is an analogy between these two classes of victims. It has been said that the first were unjustly discriminated against due to racial or sexual prejudice, and that this is not true of the second. This is indeed so. But why should it be supposed that the only form of injustice relevant to preferential treatment is that which is due to racial or sexual prejudice? Injustice occurs in many forms and those who value justice will surely object to all of them.

The same arbitrariness pervades the attempt to justify preferential treatment by appeal to the benefits of diversity. It is nothing but cant to praise diversity when it is taken to consist of the differences in the degrees to which people move to the left of the left wing of the Democratic Party. No effort is made to contribute to diversity by according preferential treatment to religious fundamentalists, anti-feminists, political conservatives, defenders of the desirability of American primacy in international affairs, or to those who advocate research into genetic racial differences. As it now stands, diversity is a code word for individuals or views that find favor with left wing academics.

Moreover, the identification of the groups whose members are supposed to be victims of injustice is intolerably vague. No account is taken of socioeconomic status; thus upper middle class women or blacks may be favored over the sons of impoverished white migratory workers. It is not recognized that there have been waves of immigration, and that many blacks and Hispanics, both male and female, have come and are coming to this country voluntarily. It is most implausible to assimilate eager immigrants to those whose ancestors were transported here as slaves or as migratory workers. Nor is there any systematic attempt to distinguish between those members of the unjustly treated groups whose lower qualifications are due to injustice and those whose personal defects are responsible for them. Also, it is often and fallaciously assumed that since there is a statistically significant correlation between injustice and the lower qualifications of members of a group taken collectively, there will also be a like correlation when members of the group are taken individually.

200

What makes matters much worse, however, is that the preferential treatment of members of these unacceptably identified groups not only subverts the original intention of remedying injustice, but that it actually produces similar injustice by creating a new group of victims. For every benefit provided by preferential treatment, there is a corresponding injury inflicted on those who have been penalized so that some members of the unacceptably identified group could receive the benefits to which, as far as anyone knows, they may not be entitled. And are these new victims also to be entitled to preferential treatment? And the victims of that? And if not, why not?

V

This leads to the second general objection against the arguments attempting to justify preferential treatment. The objection focuses on three morally undesirable consequences of the policy: the situation of academics whose appointment, tenure, or promotion was due to preferential treatment; the situation of prospective or actual academics who would have received the positions that have gone to their preferentially treated colleagues; and the way in which preferential treatment is likely to affect the responsibility of universities and colleges to act as guardians of valued forms of knowledge.

Assume, then, that a policy of preferential treatment is in place and that there is a group of academics at a university or college who have been its beneficiaries. This means, of course, that these people would be unlikely to hold the positions they hold if it had not been for the preferential treatment they have received. That this is so is a straight implication of the assumptions upon which preferential treatment rests; namely, that unjustly treated people can be expected to have lower qualifications than non-victims do. If this were not the case, preferential treatment would lose whatever warrant it has. The fact of lower qualification, on this assumption, would be common knowledge and, as such, known by the people who benefited from the policy, by those who were injured by it, and by those who have been affected by it only because they have colleagues who have been favored or injured as a result of preferential treatment.

What would be the attitude of reasonable and decent individuals to the knowledge that they have received their positions through preferential treatment and would not have received them without it? It seems likely that their attitude would be a mixture composed of resentment, shame, guilt, embarrassment, pride, self-doubt, and a desire to prove themselves. Depending on their character and circumstances, in some cases one, in others a different component would assume a dominant role in this mixture. But whatever happens, their position would not be that of a normal academic, and the obstacles in the way of achieving normalcy would be formidable.

There would always remain nagging questions about how they would have fared without the preferential treatment they have received and whether their colleagues are responding to them as individuals or as victims of injustice who could just as easily be replaced by some other victim of the same type. These questions, naturally enough, will nag not only at them, but also at their colleagues. Everybody will know that if it had not been for preferential treatment, their positions would probably have been occupied by others with better qualifications. This cannot but produce bad feelings. It could be hypocritically disguised, but genuine and reciprocal trust and good will would be unlikely to obtain due to perfectly realistic obstacles existing on both sides. In the light of this, it is legitimate to wonder whether coming to occupy positions through preferential treatment is indeed a benefit that would remedy past injustice. It seems much more likely that it would rather perpetuate its memory by putting its victims in an extremely difficult position through this clumsy attempt at social engineering.

But the consequences of preferential treatment for those who have been injured by it must also be remembered. These people will feel unjustly harmed, and they would be right in so feeling. They have not been responsible for the past injustice, or, at the very least, no more so than other people in their society, and yet the effect of the policy is to force them to bear an unfair share of the burden of it. The victims in this group will typically be actual or prospective academics who have invested many years of their lives and considerable financial resources in order to have an academic career, and they have foregone prospects of a different career. And, by hypothesis, the likelihood of their doing well at an academic career is higher than the likelihood of those who ended up getting the appointment, tenure, or promotion, which they sought and which they would have received if it had not been for the preferential treatment of others. It is natural, therefore, for this new class of victims to be as indignant and resentful as were the old class of victims who are now being favored at their expense. This class of new victims will of course increase at exactly the same rate as that with which the supposed benefits are bestowed through preferential treatment on the old class of victims.

Consider finally an indirect consequence of preferential treatment: its effect on the capacity of universities and colleges to discharge their responsibility as guardians of valued forms of knowledge. This responsibility involves teaching and research. It is essential to the welfare of a society that both activities should be done as well as possible. For the welfare of a society is essentially connected with the information, skills, understanding, and values its citizens possess. Through these forms of knowledge, people endeavor to make good lives for themselves, and a good society is one that is hospitable to their endeavors and so the endeavors have a reasonable chance of succeeding. In a good society, therefore, the interests of individuals and the interest of the society are inseparably intertwined.

It is against this background that the unavoidable consequence of preferential treatment should be evaluated: the people favored by it are less qualified for the positions they receive than the people whom they displace. No one would voluntarily choose the services of a physician, a lawyer, an architect, or a dentist if a better one were available on comparable terms. What preferential treatment does is to make it a policy to do what no one would consider doing when acting individually on his or her own behalf. Moreover, by focusing on higher education, preferential treatment imposes this policy not on any particular area of life, but on all areas within which the acquisition of the relevant forms of knowledge depends on higher education. For preferential treatment is the policy of favoring the appointment, tenure, and promotion of less qualified victims of injustice over those of better qualified non-victims. The inevitable result is that as the policy is implemented so the vital functions of teaching and research already compromised by other causes are further weakened.

It will be objected that this way of putting the matter misses the salient point that preferential treatment is not a perverse attempt to weaken society upon whose welfare the welfare of all citizens depends. Preferential treatment, rather, is a policy of remedying injustice, and it is not the aim, but one of the incidental outcomes, of the policy that less qualified victims are favored over better qualified non-victims. It will be said that injustice ought to be remedied, and preferential treatment is the policy that attempts to do so. As all policies, it too has its acknowledged costs. The benefits, however, are said to outweigh the costs because the removal of injustice is more important than the occasional violation of the impartial procedures which normally ought to govern academic appointments, tenures, and promotions.

But this rejoinder is unconvincing. It fails to recognize that protecting impartial procedures is far more important than remedying past injustice. One indication of their differing importance is that if the already existing injustice were permitted to continue to exist without remedy, society would not be harmed more than it has already been. It is true that there would remain one or two generations of victims, but if open access and impartial procedures were guaranteed, no new victims would be added. Injustice is bad, of course, and it ought to be remedied, but, the point is, the welfare of the large majority of non-victims would not be appreciably affected if no feasible remedy were available.

By contrast, if impartial procedures were not protected, the consequences would be much more far-reaching. These consequences are, first, that a new class of unjustly treated people would replace the old class, so the amount of injustice in society would not decrease. Second, the policy contains no feasible way of identifying victims of injustice. It unjustifiably assumes that all members of some groups have been victims of injustice and its selection of the groups themselves is arbitrary. The policy thus offers no procedures that would present a feasible alternative to the ones that it is designed to replace. Third, the essential process of expanding and transmitting valued forms of knowledge would be weakened by favoring less qualified people over better qualified ones. This would not only shortchange the next generation who would not receive what it could and should have, it would also injure generations thereafter by transmitting to them less knowledge, less well taught, by less qualified people as their inheritance. The policy intended to strengthen society by remedying injustice would consequently end up weakening it by undermining its system of higher education. Fourth, preferential treatment is intended to remove the causes of injustice, namely, lack of open access and impartial procedures. But if impartial procedures were suspended, the same causes of injustice would be perpetuated, and thus the policy would be inconsistent with the intention behind it.

VI

To sum up, the logic of the argument is as follows. The form of affirmative action that is committed to impartiality is intended to guarantee that open access and fair procedures guide the competition for academic positions. It has been assumed throughout that this policy is morally justified. The key question that has been considered is whether it is also morally justified to violate impartial procedures in order to overcome the disadvantage past injustice has caused to members of some groups. Three well-known arguments intended to support the affirmative answer have been considered: compensation, redistribution or correction, and diversity. In the previous paragraph the reasons for the claim that none of these arguments succeeds have been summarized. It is reasonable to conclude therefore that the form of affirmative action that calls for preferential treatment is an unjust and unjustified violation of impartial procedures.

Notes

Notes to Chapter 1

1. I do not mean to imply that we are in this situation, where discrimination against blacks is a thing of the past. We are not.

Notes to Chapter 5

1. The idea that there are *a priori* connections between moral and non-moral features is not a new one, though it is still regarded by many as heretical. I have said some of the things I would want to say by way of defense of this notion, as far as concerns connections of the general form "P is a reason for Q," in *Dialogue* 10 (1971):759–67.

Notes to Chapter 7

1. This distinction is elaborated in my essay "Classification by Race in Compensatory Programs," forthcoming in *Ethics*.
2. "The Idea of Equality," in Laslett and Runciman, eds., *Philosophy, Politics and Society*, Series II, p. 113.
3. This example was suggested by Kent Greenawalt.

Notes to Chapter 8

1. "The Justification of Reverse Discrimination," presented at the Eastern Division meeting of the American Philosophical Association, December 27, 1974.
2. Philip Silvestri has used an argument (*Analysis* 34[1]: 31) similar to Nickel's to justify only voluntary reparations. But since preferential hiring is never voluntary for those white males who apply for and do not get the jobs, his position is irrelevant to that crucial issue.
3. I suggest that for the past generation of blacks this might be found to be the case, but not for the generation currently in school, and certainly not for women, who are benefiting most from the current practice in universities.

Notes on Chapter 10

1. This essay is an expanded version of a talk given at the Conference on the Liberation of Female Persons, held at North Carolina State University at Raleigh, on March 26–28, 1973, under a grant from the S & H Foundation. I am indebted to James Thomson and the members of the Society for Ethical and Legal Philosophy for criticism of an earlier draft.
2. To the best of my knowledge, the analogy between veterans' preference and the preferential hiring of blacks has been mentioned in print only by Edward T. Chase, in a Letter to the Editor, *Commentary*, February 1973.
3. Many people would reject this assumption, or perhaps accept it only selectively, for veterans of this or that particular war. I ignore this. What interests me is what follows if we make the assumption—as, of course, many other people do, more, it seems, than do not.

Notes to Chapter 11

I am grateful to the American Council of Learned Societies and to Hamilton College for their support during the period the arguments set forth here were first formulated.
1. Judith Jarvis Thomson, "Preferential Hiring" (pp. 45–61, this volume). All page references to this article will be made within the text.
2. This point also has been argued for recently by J. L. Cowan, "Inverse Discrimination and Compensatory Justice," *Analysis* 33[1] (1972): 10–12.
3. Such a position has been defended by Paul Taylor, in his "Reverse Discrimination and Compensatory Justice," *Analysis* 33[4] (1973): 177–82.
4. Taylor would apparently agree, *ibid.*, 180.
5. *Ibid.*, 180. Parentheses are my own.

6. At the time these arguments were first formulated, I unfortunately did not have access to Charles King's article "A Problem Concerning Discrimination" (presented to a symposium on reverse discrimination at the Eastern Division Meetings of the American Philosophical Association in 1972) in which a similar point is made. King also argues, although along lines somewhat different from my own, that preferential hiring policies distribute compensatory benefits arbitrarily.

7. This will not apply as frequently as might be thought, however, if it is true that membership in a preferred group is itself an *educational* qualification. That this is so is sometimes argued on the grounds, for example, that women and black professors are necessary as "role models" for women and black students. Thomson, however, expresses doubts about arguments of this sort (pp. 365–69). More important, if such arguments were strong, it would seem that a case could be made for hiring black and women professors on grounds of merit. That is, they should be hired because they can do the job better than others, not (only) because they are owed compensation. In any case, however, my argument in the text would still apply to those instances in which the candidate from the preferred group was not as qualified (in the broad sense of "qualified," in which membership in the preferred group is one qualification) as the candidates from nonpreferred groups.

8. For a defense of the provision of monetary compensation or reparations, see Hugo Bedau, "Compensatory Justice and the Black Manifesto," *The Monist* 56[1] (1972): 20–42.

Notes to Chapter 12

I am grateful to Michael Levin, Edward Erwin, and my wife Emily Gordon Sher for helpful discussion of this topic.

1. In what follows I will have nothing to say about utilitarian justifications of reverse discrimination. There are two reasons for this. First, the winds of utilitarian argumentation blow in too many directions. It is certainly socially beneficial to avoid the desperate actions to which festering resentments may lead—but so too is it socially useful to confirm the validity of qualifications of the traditional sort, to assure those who have amassed such qualifications that "the rules of the game have not been changed in the middle," that accomplishment has not been downgraded in society's eyes. How could these conflicting utilities possibly be measured against one another?

   Second and even more important, to rest a defense of reverse discrimination upon utilitarian considerations would be to ignore what is surely the guiding intuition of its proponents, that this treatment is *deserved* where discrimination has been practiced in the past. It is the intention that reverse discrimination is a matter not (only) of social good but of right which I want to try to elucidate.

2.   This argument, as well as the others I shall consider, presupposes that jobs are (among other things) *goods*, and so ought to be distributed as fairly as possible. This presupposition seems to be amply supported by the sheer economic necessity of earning a living, as well as by the fact that some jobs carry more prestige and are more interesting and pay better than others.

3.   As Robert Simon has pointed out in "Preferential Hiring: A Reply to Judith Jarvis Thomson," *Philosophy & Public Affairs* 3[3] (Spring 1974): 312–20, it is far from clear that the preferential hiring of its individual members could be a proper form of compensation for any wronged group that did exist.

4.   A version of this argument is advanced by Judith Jarvis Thomson in "Preferential Hiring," *Philosophy & Public Affairs* 2[4] (Summer 1973): 364–84.

5.   Cf. Simon, "Preferential Hiring," sec. III.

6.   A similar justification of reverse discrimination is suggested, but not ultimately endorsed, by Thomas Nagel in "Equal Treatment and Compensatory Discrimination," *Philosophy & Public Affairs* 2[4] (Summer 1973): 348–63. Nagel rejects this justification on the grounds that a system distributing goods solely on the basis of performance determined by native ability would itself be unjust, even if not as unjust as one distributing goods on a racial or sexual basis. I shall not comment on this, except to remark that our moral intuitions surely run the other way: the average person would certainly find the latter system of distribution *far* more unjust than the former, if, indeed, he found the former unjust at all. Because of this, the burden is on Nagel to show exactly why a purely meritocratic system of distribution would be unjust.

7.   It is tempting, but I think largely irrelevant, to object here that many who are now entrenched in their jobs (tenured professors, for example) have already benefited from the effects of past discrimination at least as much as the currently best qualified applicant will if reverse discrimination is not practiced. While many such individuals have undoubtedly benefited from the effects of discrimination upon their *original* competitors, few if any are likely to have benefited from a reduction in the abilities of the *currently best qualified applicant's* competitor. As long as none of them have so benefited, the best qualified applicant in question will still stand to gain the most from that *particular* effect of past discrimination, and so reverse discrimination against him will remain fair. Of course, there will also be cases in which an entrenched person *has* previously benefited from the reduced abilities of the currently best qualified applicant's competitor. In these cases, the best qualified applicant will *not* be the single main beneficiary of his rival's handicap, and so reverse discrimination against him will *not* be entirely fair. I am inclined to think there may be a case for reverse discrimination even here, however, for if it is truly impossible to dislodge the entrenched previous ben-

eficiary of his rival's handicap, reverse discrimination against the best qualified applicant may at least be the fairest (or least unfair) of the practical alternatives.

8. A somewhat similar difference might seem to obtain between cases (1) and (2). One's ability to learn is more intimately a part of him than his actual degree of education; hence, someone whose ability to learn is lowered by his environment (case 2) is a changed person in a way in which a person who is merely denied education (case 1) is not. However, one's ability to learn is not a feature of *moral* character in the way ability to exert effort is, and so this difference between (1) and (2) will have little bearing on the degree to which reverse discrimination is called for in these cases.

9. The feminist movement has convincingly documented the ways in which sexual bias is built into the information received by the young; but it is one thing to show that such information is received, and quite another to show how, and to what extent, its reception is causally efficacious.

Notes to Chapter 13

1. Judith Thomson, "Preferential Hiring," *Philosophy and Public Affairs* 2 (Summer 1973): 364–84.

2. Thomson asks us to imagine two such applicants *tied* in their qualifications. Presumably, preferring a less qualified teacher would violate students' rights to the best available instruction. If the applicants are equally qualified, then the students' rights are satisfied whichever one is picked. In cases where third party rights are not involved, there would seem to be no need to include the tie stipulation, for if the principle of compensation is strong enough to justify preferring a woman over a man, it is strong enough whether the woman is equally qualified or not, so long as she is minimally qualified. (Imagine hiring a librarian instead of a teacher.) Thus, I leave out the requirement that the applicants be tied in their qualifications. Nothing in my argument turns on whether the applicants are equally qualified. The reader may, if he wishes, mentally reinstate this feature of Thomson's example.

3. Thomson, 380.

4. The comments from which propositions 1–3 are distilled occur on pages 381–82.

5. For a discussion of these issues, see Robert Simon, "Preferential Hiring: A Reply to Judith Jarvis Thomson," *Philosophy and Public Affairs* 3 (Spring 1974): 312–20.

6. There are broader notions of compensation, where it means making up for any deficiency or distortion, and where it means recompense for work. Neither of these notions plays a role in Thomson's argument.

7. On page 378, Thomson says: "Now it is, I think, widely believed that we may, without injustice, refuse to grant a man what he has a right to only if *either* someone else has a conflicting and more stringent right, or there is some very great benefit to be obtained by doing so—perhaps that a disaster of some kind is thereby averted.... But in fact there are other ways in which a right may be overridden." The "other way" which Thomson mentions derives from the force of debts. A debt consists of rights and obligations, and the force of debts can perhaps be accounted for in terms of superior rights. Then, debts would not be a third ground, independent of the first listed by Thomson, for overriding a right.

8. Thomson, 380–81.

9. The U.S. Government owes Japanese companies compensation for losses they incurred when the President imposed an illegal import surtax. May the Government justly discharge its debt by taxing only Japanese-Americans in order to pay the Japanese companies?

10. See Joel Feinberg, "Collective Responsibility," *Journal of Philosophy* 65 (7 November 1968); and Virginia Held, "Can a Random Collection of Individuals Be Morally Responsible?" *Journal of Philosophy* 67 (13 July 1970).

11. George Sher, in "Justifying Reverse Discrimination in Employment," *Philosophy and Public Affairs* 4 (Winter 1975), defends reverse discriminations to "neutralize competitive disadvantages caused by past privations" (165). He seems to view the matter along the lines of my golfing example. Thus, my comments here against the sufficiency of that model apply to Sher's argument. Also, see below, section 6, for arguments that bear on Sher's contention that the justification for discriminating against white male applicants is not that they are most responsible for injustice, but benefit the most from it.

12. Thomson, 383.

13. In the passage quoted, Thomson is attempting to morally justify the community's imposing a sacrifice on WMA. Thus, her reference to "best" compensation cannot be construed to mean "morally best," since morally best means morally justified. By best compensation Thomson means that compensation which will best make up the loss suffered by the victim. This is how I understand the idea of best compensation in the succeeding example and argument.

14. And there are many possible modes of compensation open to the community which are free from any moral taint. At the worst, monetary compensation is always an alternative. This may be second- or third-best compensation for the wrongs done, but when the best is not available, second-best has to do. For the loss of my gun, I am going to have to accept cash from you (assuming you have it), and use it to buy a less satisfactory substitute.

15. Thomson, 383–84.

16. But, if FA is *not* given preferential treatment in hiring (the best compensation), are *her* rights violated? In having a right to compensation, FA does not have a right to anything at all that will compensate her. She has a right to the best

of the morally available options open to her debtor. Only if the community refuses to pay her this is her right violated. We have seen no reason to believe that setting aside the right of white male applicants to equal consideration is an option morally available to the community.

Notes to Chapter 14

1. Robert E. Litan, "On Rectification in Nozick's Minimal State." *Political Theory* 5 (1977): 243.

2. See especially Joel Feinberg, *Doing and Deserving: Essays in the Theory of Responsibility* (Princeton: Princeton University Press, 1970); and the essays in *Individual and Collective Responsibility*, ed. Peter A. French (Cambridge, MA: Schenkman, 1972).

3. Alison Jaggar, "Relaxing the Limits on Preferential Treatment," *Social Theory and Practice* 4 (1977): 231.

4. These may include practices and policies which (as in the case of antinepotism rules or the policy of "last hired–first fired") are not inherently discriminatory and which operate to the detriment of blacks and women "only because of certain contingent features of this society." See Mary Anne Warren, "Secondary Sexism and Quota Hiring," *Philosophy and Public Affairs* 6 (1977): 240–61.

5. Robert K. Fullinwider, "Preferential Hiring and Compensation," *Social Theory and Practice* 3 (1975): 317.

6. For an excellent discussion of these complexities, see Litan, 237–40.

7. For a contrary view, see Hardy Jones, "Fairness, Meritocracy, and Preferential Treatment," *Social Theory and Practice* 4 (1977): 211–26.

8. Under the principle of equal sacrifice, every individual need not contribute the same amount. When money payments are at issue, equality of sacrifice is likely to require progressive taxation. For a discussion of the differing interpretations of equal sacrifice, see Walter J. Blum and Harry Kalven, Jr., *The Uneasy Case for Progressive Taxation* (Chicago: University of Chicago Press, 1953): 39–45.

9. Paul W. Taylor, "Reverse Discrimination and Compensatory Justice," *Analysis* 33 (1973): 177–82.

10. I believe this is implied by Taylor.

11. The assumptions underlying this view are summarized in Blum and Kalven.

12. John Rawls, *A Theory of Justice* (Cambridge, MA: Harvard University Press, 1971), p. 153. See also Rawls, "Reflections on the Maximin Criterion," *American Economic Review* 64 (1974): 143.

13. George Sher, "Justifying Reverse Discrimination in Employment," *Philosophy and Public Affairs* 4 (1975): 162.

14. Sher, 164–65.

15. Sher, 164.

16. This argument has been made most persuasively by Alan H. Goldman. See especially "Affirmative Action," *Philosophy and Public Affairs* 5 (1976): 191–92.

17. The most comprehensive treatment of German reparations is Nicholas Balabkins, *West German Reparations to Israel* (New Brunswick, NJ: Rutgers University Press, 1971). For an excellent summary see Raul Hilberg, *The Destruction of the European Jews* (Chicago: Quadrangle Books, 1961), pp. 746–59. Many important documents are found in *The German Path to Israel*, ed. Rolf Vogel (London: Oswald Wolff, 1969).

18. For excerpts from the parliamentary debates, see Vogel, pp. 32–35, 69–87.

19. Boris Bittker, *The Case for Black Reparations* (New York: Random House, 1973), p. 89.

20. Bittker, 131–32. Bittker estimates the minimum annual cost of a serious reparations program at $34 billion. He also suggests that such a program would have to be carried out "for at least a decade or two."

21. Judith Jarvis Thomson, "Preferential Hiring," *Philosophy and Public Affairs* 2 (1973): 383.

22. See Goldman, 190–91.

23. Edward C. Banfield, *The Unheavenly City: The Nature and Future of Our Urban Crisis* (Boston: Little, Brown, 1970), pp. 126–27.

24. See, for example, Chandler Davidson, "On the Culture of Shiftlessness," *Dissent* 23 (1976): 349–56.

Notes to Chapter 15

I am deeply indebted to Professor Thomas Hill, Jr., for helpful criticisms of earlier drafts of this paper.

1. Michael Harrington and Arnold Kaufman, "Black Reparations—Two Views," *Dissent* 16 (July-Aug. 1969): 317–20.

2. John Locke, *Treatise of Civil Government* and A *Letter Concerning Toleration*, ed. Charles L. Sherman (New York: Appleton-Century Company, Inc., 1937), 9.

Notes to Chapter 17

1. Portions of this paper are adapted from a longer essay. See Anita L. Allen, "On Being a Role Model," *Berkeley Women's Law Journal* 6 (1990–91): 22.

2. Bernard Boxill has suggested that even if affirmative action "sins against a present equality of opportunity, [it may be acceptable because it] promotes a future equality of opportunity by providing blacks with their own successful

"role models." See Bernard Boxill, *Blacks and Social Justice* (Totowa, NJ: Rowman and Allenheld, 1984), p. 171.

3. See Robert Fullinwider, *The Reverse Discrimination Controversy: A Moral and Legal Analysis* (Totowa, NJ: Rowman and Littlefield, 1980); M. Cohen, T. Nagel, T. Scanlon, eds. *Equality and Preferential Treatment* (Princeton, NJ: Princeton University Press, 1977); Kent Greenawalt, *Discrimination and Reverse Discrimination* (New York: Alfred Knopf, 1983); Boxill, *Blacks and Social Justice*, pp. 147–72.

4. See Boxill, *Blacks and Social Justice*, p. 171.

5. See Gertrude Ezorsky, *Racism and Justice: The Case for Affirmative Action* (Ithaca, NY: Cornell University Press, 1991). Ezorsky does not name the need for role models as an argument for affirmative action. Ibid. at pp. 73–94.

6. "Minority Women at the Bottom of Law Faculty," *New York Times*, April 3, 1992.

7. See, for example, Linda Greene, "Tokens, Role Models, and Pedagogical Politics: Lamentations of an African American Female Law Professor," *Berkeley Women's Law Journal* 6 (1990–1991): 81. Professor Greene's essay was part of a symposium issue of the *Berkeley Women's Law Journal* entitled "Black Women Law Professors: Building a Community at the Intersection of Race and Gender," consisting of 15 essays by black women law teachers.

8. L. Gordon Crovitz, "Harvard Law School Finds Its Counterrevolutionary," *Wall Street Journal*, March 25, 1992.

9. I refer to essays by Thomson and Sher reprinted in Cohen, Nagel, and Scanlon, eds., *Equality and Preferential Treatment*.

10. Cf. Patricia Williams, *The Alchemy of Race and Rights* (Cambridge, MA: Harvard University Press, 1991), p. 95.

11. According to Thomson,

    > What is wanted is *role models*. The proportion of black and women faculty members in the larger universities (particularly as one moves up the ladder of rank) is very much smaller than the proportion of them amongst recipients of Ph.D. degrees from those very same universities. Black and women students suffer a constricting of ambition because of this. They need to see members of their own race or sex who are accepted, successful professionals. They need concrete evidence that those of their race or sex *can* become accepted, successful professionals. (Emphasis in original)

    Thomson, "Preferential Hiring," in Cohen, Nagel, and Scanlon, eds., *Equality and Preferential Treatment*, p. 22. Sher considered the argument that

    > Past discrimination in hiring has led to a scarcity of female "role models" of suitably high achievement. This lack, together with a culture which...inculcates the idea that women should not or cannot do the jobs that men do, has in turn made women psychologically less able to do these jobs... [T]here is surely the same dearth of role-models...for blacks as for women.

Sher, "Justifying Reverse Discrimination in Employment," in Cohen, Nagel, and Scanlon, eds., *Equality and Preferential Treatment*, p. 58.

12. Greenawalt, *Discrimination and Reverse Discrimination*, p. 64.

13. Their stories are told in F. James Davis, *Who Is Black? One Nation's Definition* (State College: Pennsylvania State University Press, 1991).

14. Fullinwider, *The Reverse Discrimination Controversy*, p. 18.

15. For a recent survey of the arguments generally, see Ezorsky, *Racism and Justice*.

16. Of course, the racial composition of their faculties is not the only respect in which white and black colleges differ.

Notes to Chapter 18

1. By affirmative action, I mean preferential treatment and not just things like announcing openings and encouraging women and minorities to apply. And tie-breaking affirmative action might, I believe, be justified in some cases on the basis of the role model argument. The reason the role model argument does not support preferential appointments in order to attain proportional representation is that a minority member can only function as a model for excellence if he or she is perceived as having been appointed because of qualifications rather than race or sex. One really good minority faculty member is a more effective and inspiring role model than ten mediocre ones.

2. Note, again, that I am speaking of proportional representation relative to their percentage in the population at large.

3. I do not consider here compensatory arguments. That institutions should make compensation to individuals they have discriminated against is self-evident, but problems arise when those receiving compensation are not the persons who were wronged. For example, how are older women who have suffered discrimination in any way made whole from their injury by the appointment of younger women unrelated to them? In any case, there is no clear way compensatory arguments could tell us what proportion of minority groups should be on university faculties. How can we tell what proportion of Hispanics would have become professors in the absence of discrimination? Or, in the absence of slavery, that the number of blacks teaching in American universities would be no higher than it is now. An additional problem with compensatory arguments is that, like redistributive arguments, they treat teaching appointments as plums to be distributed instead of as focusing on the responsibilities that such positions involve.

4. He holds that we should assume that members of all racial, ethnic, and gender groups are equally interested in the professoriate until we have evidence to the contrary—evidence he could only obtain by putting his plan into effect and seeing how many members of these groups choose to go into college

teaching. But how can we tell when equal opportunity has been attained (i.e., the levers are within the reach of all)? Only, he says, when proportionate representation has been attained.

5.   Perhaps instead of conceptualizing society as a pyramid with one top, we should think of it as a group of hills with many different peaks; people may choose different paths to wealth, power, and prestige.

6.   This is called the "cousinhood advantage." While in academia it operates in favor of WASPs and Jews, this is not the case everywhere. Although building contractors frequently make very good money, a WASP would be at a great disadvantage in this field in many parts of the country where the building trades are heavily dominated by certain ethnic groups.

7.   See Kevin Phillips, *The Politics of Rich and Poor* (New York: Random House, 1990), pp. 18, 203, 207.

8.   People should, I believe, be free to enter the occupation of their choice (subject, of course, to certain broad constraints based on the common good—such as that if everyone wanted to be lawyers and no one wanted to grow crops, some adjustments would be necessary) and make other career decisions as they see fit, even though we might think (rightly even) that it would be better for them to choose otherwise.

9.   Stephen Carter, *Reflections of an Affirmative Action Baby* (New York: Basic Books, 1991).

10. I am indebted to my husband, Phil Devine, for many valuable discussions of the ideas in this article and for reading and commenting on the manuscript. I have also profited from discussions with Beth Soll, John McGrath, Joseph Ryshpan, and my colleagues Richard Capobianco, Soo Tan, and Richard Velkley.

Notes to Chapter 20

Presidential Address delivered before the Sixty-first Annual Pacific Division Meeting of the American Philosophical Association in San Francisco, California, March 27, 1987.

1.   Much of the language on pages 28–29 and 34 of this address is drawn from pages 47–48 and 51 of my piece "One Way to Understand and Defend Programs of Preferential Treatment," in *The Moral Foundations of Civil Rights*, eds. Robert K. Fullinwider and Claudia Mills (Totowa, NJ: Rowman and Littlefield, 1986). And some of the other ideas and arguments discussed in this address borrow upon those I presented in that piece, as well as in others, although I hope my presentation and development here is clearer and more sharply focused. The most substantial change is, I think, in the differences between the discussion of color-blindness on pages 36–41 of this address and the

less adequate discussions of that subject in two earlier pieces: "Racism, Sexism and Preferential Treatment: An Approach to the Topics," *UCLA Law Review* 24 (1977): 581; and "Racism and Sexism," in *Philosophy and Social Issues: Five Studies* (South Bend, IN: University of Notre Dame Press, 1980), pp. 11–50.

Notes to Chapter 21

1. See, for example, the following. John Arthur, ed., *Morality and Moral Controversies*, 2d ed. (Englewood Cliffs, NJ: Prentice-Hall, Inc., 1986), pp. 305–347. William T. Blackstone and Robert D. Heslep, eds., *Social Justice and Preferential Treatment* (Athens, GA: University of Georgia Press, 1977). Bernard Boxill, *Blacks and Social Justice* (Totowa, NJ: Rowman and Allenheld, 1984). Marshall Cohen, Thomas Nagel, and Thomas Scanlon, eds. *Equality and Preferential Treatment* (Princeton, NJ: Princeton University Press, 1979). Kent Greenawalt, *Discrimination and Reverse Discrimination* (New York: Alfred A. Knopf, 1983). Barry R. Gross, ed., *Reverse Discrimination* (Buffalo, NY: Prometheus Books, 1977). Thomas A. Mappes and Jane Z. Zembaty, eds., *Social Ethics*, 2d ed. (New York: McGraw-Hill, 1982), pp. 159–98.

2. See Richard Wasserstrom, "Racism and Sexism" and "Preferential Treatment," in his *Philosophy and Social Issues* (Notre Dame, IN: University of Notre Dame Press, 1980), pp. 11–21, 51–82.

3. William K. Frankena, "The Concept of Social Justice," in *Social Justice*, ed. Richard B. Brandt (Englewood Cliffs, NJ: Prentice-Hall, 1962), pp. 8–9. Henry Sidgwick, *Methods of Ethics*, 7th ed. (London: The Macmillan Company Ltd., 1907), pp. 379, 386f. John Rawls, *A Theory of Justice* (Cambridge, MA: Harvard University Press, 1971), pp. 56–60, 180, 235–39, 504f.

4. *Regents of the University of California v. Allan Bakke*, 98 S.Ct. 2733, 46 L.W. 4896 (1978). Reprinted in 2d ed. *Today's Moral Issues*, ed. R. Wasserstrom (New York: Macmillan Publishing Co., 1975), pp. 149–207. (See especially pp. 156–57.)

5. Thomas Sowell, *Race and Economics* (New York: David McKay Co., 1975), chapter 6; *Markets and Minorities* (New York: Basic Books, Inc., 1981), pp. 114–15.

6. W. D. Ross, *The Right and The Good* (Oxford: The Clarendon Press, 1930).

7. James Foreman was at the time director of international affairs for S.N.C.C. (Student Nonviolent Coordinating Committee). The "Black Manifesto" stems from an economic development conference sponsored by the Interreligious Foundation for Community Organizations, April 26, 1969, and was presented by Foreman at the New York Interdenominational Riverside Church on May 4, 1969. Later the demand was raised to three billion dollars. See Robert S. Lecky and H. Elliot Wright, *Black Manifesto* (New York: Sheed and Ward Publishers, 1969), pp. vii and 114–26.

8. Bernard Boxill, "The Morality of Reparation," *Social Theory and Practice* 1 (1972): 113–22; and *Blacks and Social Justice*, chapter 7.

9. In the article cited in footnote 8 Boxill calls what is owed "reparation," but in the book he calls it "compensation." The latter term, preferred by many, is used more broadly to cover not only restitution for wrongdoing but also "making up" for deficiencies and losses that are not anyone's fault (e.g., naturally caused physical handicaps, damages unavoidably resulting from legitimate and necessary activities). We could describe the backward-looking arguments presented here as demands for "compensation" rather than "reparation," so long as we keep in mind that the compensation is supposed to be due as the morally appropriate response to past wrongdoing.

10. Aristotle, *Nicomachean Ethics*, translated by J. A. K. Thomson (Baltimore, MD: Penguin Books, Inc., 1955), Book 5, especially pp. 143–55.

11. See Boxill, *Blacks and Social Justice*, pp. 132ff; and Ronald Dworkin, "Reverse Discrimination," in *Taking Rights Seriously* (Cambridge, MA: Harvard University Press, 1978), pp. 231ff.

12. See, for example, Alasdair MacIntyre, *After Virtue* (Notre Dame, IN: Notre Dame University Press, 1981). Similar themes are found in Carol Gilligan's *In a Different Voice* (Cambridge: Harvard University Press, 1982); and in Lawrence Blum, *Friendship, Altruism, and Morality* (Boston: Routledge and Kegan Paul, 1980).

13. Regarding cultural and moral relativism see, for example, David B. Wong, *Moral Relativity* (Berkeley and Los Angeles: University of California Press, 1984), with an excellent bibliography; and Richard B. Brandt, *Ethical Theory* (Englewood Cliffs, NJ: Prentice-Hall, Inc., 1959), pp. 271–94. Versions of particularism are presented in Andrew Oldenquist, "Loyalties," *The Journal of Philosophy* 79 (1982): 173–93; Lawrence Blum, *Friendship, Altruism and Morality* (Boston: Routledge and Kegan Paul, 1980); and Bernard Williams, "Persons, Character and Morality" in *Moral Luck* (New York: Cambridge University Press, 1981), pp. 1–9.

14. G. E. Moore, *Principia Ethica* (Cambridge: Cambridge University Press, 1912), pp. 27f.

15. That is, the evaluation is independent of the past in the sense that the past makes no intrinsic difference to the final judgment and the future is not evaluated as a part of a temporal whole including the past. As noted, however, consequentialists will still look to the past for lessons and clues about how to bring about the best future.

16. For an interesting illustration of reciprocal desires (e.g., A wanting B, B wanting A, A wanting B to want A, B wanting A to want B, A wanting B to want A to want B, etc.), see Thomas Nagel, "Sexual Perversion," *The Journal of Philosophy*, 66 (1969): 5–17.

17. Racism and sexism present significantly different problems, but I shall not try to analyze the differences here. For the most part, and especially in the anal-

ogy to follow, my primary focus is on racism, but the relevance of the general type of moral thinking considered here to the problems of sexism should nonetheless be evident.

18. How severe these drawbacks are will, of course, depend upon the particular means of affirmative action that is selected and how appropriate these are for the situation. For example, if, to meet mandated quotas, high-ranked colleges and universities offer special admission to students not expected to succeed, then they may well be misleading those students into a wasteful and humiliating experience when those students could have succeeded and thrived at lower-ranked educational institutions. This practice was explicitly rejected in the policies at Pomona College and at U.C.L.A. described in section I, but William Allen suggested to me in discussion that in his opinion the practice is quite common. The practice, I think, is unconscionable, and my argument in no way supports it.

Geoffrey Miller described in discussion another possible affirmative action program that would be quite inappropriate to the circumstances but again is not supported by the line of argument I have suggested. He asks us to imagine a "permanent underclass" of immigrants who are "genetically or culturally deficient" and as a result fail to succeed. Because we do not share a common social/cultural history of injustice resulting in their condition, the historical dimension of my case for affirmative action is missing. And because they are a "permanent" underclass, and thus the "genetic or cultural deficiencies" that result in their failure cannot be altered, one cannot argue that universities can help them or can even sincerely give them an encouraging "message" by affirmative action. This does not mean, however, that there are not other reasons for society to extend appropriate help. Also any suggestion that certain urban populations now *called* "permanent underclass" are accurately and fairly described by the "fictional" example is politically charged and needs careful examination.

19. Although my aim in this paper has been to survey general types of argument for thinking that some sort of affirmative action is needed, rather than to argue for any particular program, one cannot reasonably implement the general idea without considering many contextual factors that I have set aside here. Thus, although the moral perspective suggested here seems to favor the second method described in section I (recruitment, special funds, accountability) over the first method (proportionality given a fixed lower standard), the need for more detailed discussion is obvious.

About the Authors

STEVEN M. CAHN is Professor of Philosophy at The Graduate School of The City University of New York.

JAMES W. NICKEL is Professor of Philosophy at the University of Colorado.

J. L. COWAN is Professor of Philosophy at the University of Arizona.

PAUL W. TAYLOR is Emeritus Professor of Philosophy at Brooklyn College of The City University of New York.

MICHAEL D. BAYLES (1941–1990) was Professor of Philosophy at Florida State University.

ROGER A. SHINER is Professor of Philosophy at the University of Alberta.

WILLIAM A. NUNN III practices law in Virginia.

ALAN H. GOLDMAN is Professor of Philosophy at the University of Miami.

PAUL WOODRUFF is Professor of Philosophy at the University of Texas at Austin.

JUDITH JARVIS THOMSON is Professor of Philosophy at the Massachusetts Institute of Technology.

ROBERT SIMON is Professor of Philosophy at Hamilton College.

GEORGE SHER is Professor of Philosophy at Rice University.

ROBERT K. FULLINWIDER is Senior Research Scholar at the Institute for Philosophy and Public Policy of the University of Maryland, College Park.

ROBERT AMDUR is Adjunct Assistant Professor of Political Science at Columbia University.

BERNARD R. BOXILL is Professor of Philosophy at the University of North Carolina at Chapel Hill.

LISA H. NEWTON is Professor of Philosophy at Fairfield University.

ANITA L. ALLEN is Professor of Law at Georgetown University.

CELIA WOLF-DEVINE is Assistant Professor of Philosophy at Stonehill College.

SIDNEY HOOK (1902–1989) was Professor of Philosophy at New York University.

RICHARD WASSERSTROM is Professor of Philosophy at the University of California at Santa Cruz.

THOMAS E. HILL, JR., is Professor of Philosophy at the University of North Carolina at Chapel Hill.

JOHN KEKES is Professor of Philosophy at the State University of New York at Albany.

Bibliographical Note

In several cases, authors whose essays are reprinted in this volume subsequently published more fully developed statements of their positions. For James W. Nickel, see "Preferential Policies in Hiring and Admissions: A Jurisprudential Approach," *Columbia Law Review* 75[3] (1975). For Alan H. Goldman, see *Justice and Reverse Discrimination* (Princeton, NJ: Princeton University Press, 1979). For George Sher, see "Preferential Hiring" in *Just Business: Essays in Business Ethics*, ed. Tom Regan (New York: Random House, 1984). For Robert K. Fullinwider, see *The Reverse Discrimination Controversy: A Moral and Legal Analysis* (Totowa, NJ: Rowman and Allenheld, 1980). For Bernard R. Boxill, see *Blacks and Social Justice*, rev. ed. (Lanham, MD: Rowman and Littlefield Publishers, 1992), chapter 7.